Pelican Books

Sex Psyche Etcetera in the Fi

Parker Tyler, born in 1907, has been for about forty
years a resident of New York City, where he became a
poet and a critic of films, painting and literature. His six
books of film criticism have come to identify him
best, since he is a long-acknowledged pioneer in that
field. In creating the now proliferant depth-criticism of
popular films, he crystallized the formula of the film
charade, especially as to sex and its masquerades. He
was also one of the very first advocates of the
underground film movement. Parker Tyler's other
books include three volumes of poetry, a novel,
monographs on painters and a monumental biography
of Pavel Tchelitchew.

Independent of all schools or movements, Parker Tyler
has consistently carved out his own line as a frequent
contributor to major art, film and literary magazines
and anthologies. For four years, he was lecturer and
panellist in the Special Events programmes of the New
York Film Festival, and has given talks and seminars
in many institutions. He has received several
Foundation grants and a Longview Award. Currently,
he is working on two books: *A World Theory of Film*
and *Homosexuality in the Movies*. His *Underground
Film: a Critical History* appeared in 1970.

Sex Psyche Etcetera in the Film

Parker Tyler

Penguin Books

Penguin Books Ltd, Harmondsworth,
Middlesex, England
Penguin Books Inc., 7110 Ambassador Road,
Baltimore, Maryland 21207, U.S.A.
Penguin Books Australia Ltd, Ringwood,
Victoria, Australia

First published in the U.S.A. by Horizon Press 1969
Published in Pelican Books 1971
Copyright © Parker Tyler, 1969

Printed in the United States of America
Set in Linotype Times

to Amos Vogel
strategist of the good fight

Contents

Acknowledgements

Grateful acknowledgement is made to these
periodicals for permission to reprint material
originally appearing in their pages: *American
Quarterly, Art Education, Art News, Cesare
Barbieri Courier, Dance Perspectives, Film Culture,
Film Quarterly, Kenyon Review, Kulchur* and
Sight and Sound.

The following articles appeared in periodicals
which are no longer in existence: 'Revival of the
Matriarchic Spirit' in *Accent* and 'Mass Film
Criticism' in *The New Politics.*

Part 1
Sex Ritual

1. Warhol's New Sex Film

(Note: *In February 1969, a festival of pornographic films was scheduled at Notre Dame University. On the first night, the local police arrived and 'busted' the show. It was suspected, of course, that faculty members of the University had requested the action. Faculty members denied their complicity. The police stated, according to rumor, that on the contrary they had been alerted by the University's faculty. In any case, Andy Warhol's new film, titled* Fuck, *discussed in the following article, was to have been a prominent item on the festival program.*)

The one mistake most dangerous to make about Andy Warhol's films is to assume that their basilisk stare is directed at *reality* in any widely or historically accepted sense of that word. Warhol's inspiration was to decide to be literal toward attitudes *about reality*, or more specifically, attitudes inventing reality before our eyes. First of all, reality (today anyway) is largely the invention of journalism and is based on the formula of the neat, transmissible word-summary of action past. Visual media simply convert this formula into sight terms. In both fiction and so-called fact media, or a fusion of them, the same banal process always takes place: the technicians invent a plausible simulacrum of what is supposed to happen or have happened in life. A newsreel or documentary film is supposed (a) to represent accomplished fact or (b) typical and/or current and continuous fact. Each is an item, more or less edited, detached from the whole continuum of reality yet presumed to stand for reality – reality in an ontological sense, the 'world,' and so on.

Sex happens to be the 'real' subject of Warhol's new film titled by the four-letter word that still tends to burn a hole in the paper it's printed on. But the important thing about *Fuck* – indeed, the *only* important thing about it – is that it does not deal in any familiar reality-formulas. It is neo-Kinsey, one might say, or better, neo-'human sexual response,' and yet it has all scientific interest and scientific preparation pressed out of it beforehand. Even those couples who went to bed in order to be observed by sociologists with ideas of scientific investigation were attempting to achieve a one-shot summary of their regular sexual relations. One might term the whole reality-myth of film (and journalism for that matter) a rational effort to formally summarize 'normal' behavior.

If we take, for example, any of the fiction films nowadays exploiting sex by showing erotically occupied nudes, we see professional actors (more or less skilled as the case may be) providing a simulacrum of something deemed plausible and typical of the human race. Sometimes the photography and the direction make the action look arty, sometimes the photography and direction make it look deliberately coarse, shocking. In any case there is an avowed plan, a script of some sort, which the actors learn by heart and then proceed to demonstrate in person. On the other hand, the peculiar interest of Warhol's blatantly artless films – any aesthetic interest in them is purely coincidental and does not refer to any individual living or dead – lies in the fact that they are direct, technically primitive records of improvised human behavior, quite unconcerned with 'reality.'

True, some of these films have had scripts of a sort. For commercial reasons (as in the Broadway run of *My Hustler*) some have also been edited, given an altered or augmented shape after being made. Yet, by and large, they are unarranged reports on what certain people who desire camera publicity, or consent to it, are willing to do while enjoying that publicity. In one case, the film was simply an anthology of couples doing nothing but kissing. This is not to say that the usually offbeat characters who work for Warhol's cameras (by now their names are fairly well-known) are either innerly depraved, morbid exhibitionists or simple frauds. What we see in *Fuck* is not what might happen (certainly not yet) in broad daylight on Times Square. No! This episode in sexual conjugation is something the couple here 'did for Andy.' Such obligingness gets one automatic prestige in the underground set.

Inevitably, to think à la 'human sexual response,' what we see must resemble, to some extent, this man's and this woman's ordinary behavior in bed. But this information is not at all (here I think all sensitive spectators will agree) the true point of interest in *Fuck*. Rather, starting from scratch, i.e., the first physical point of contact, this couple invent bed-reality bit by bit, rub by rub, word by word, toss by toss, posture by posture. During the tiresome action – boredom is an essential ingredient of warholism: by design left *out* of entertainment, by design left *in* Warhol films – it may occur to some to wonder what the sexual partners are thinking or feeling, how much they are enjoying themselves, how quickly, and so on; for example: do they stall during preliminaries in order to expand the camera time? This, all the same, does not affect the impression that in exploring each other's body, reacting to different parts and getting down to the business of copulating, the two actors are witnessing that perfectly true kind of lazy leisure which is born of the freedom to act as one pleases. We are watching 'reality' in the instance of two organic human bodies on a bed, and elsewhere, intent on doing something, but doing it only as they are prompted by some inner impulse to do it; part of which, as I say, is doing it for Andy.

I daresay that when the couple, the man's entry finally achieved, shift their position to show us their profile (we have been seeing them at rather oblique eye-level from the back), Warhol may have directed the shift either by plan or some spontanous sign of which we are unaware; on the other hand, it may merely have been the impulse of the man to give the camera a more articulated view. Here is, anyway, *Fuck*'s most dramatic moment: one of those crucial shifts of action that are all-important but manage, like great art, to come as a surprise because they utterly conceal their nature as 'devices.' In other words, there is no difference here between 'reality' and 'device' whereas in both fiction and fact representation, including journalism, the device can never quite conceal its mediation between us and reality.

Or take an early Warhol film such as *Empire* or *Eat*. True, we know the Empire State Building is always there (we also know that during a day and night, it wears an everchanging chiaroscuro) but it would not occur to us to watch it for eight or even six hours, not to mention one hour. Time is of immense importance in Warhol's mesmerically boring films simply because the watcher, submissively or rebelliously, is being forced to participate in the actual *durée* of an object – and not, note well, because that is what 'reality' is, but rather because this is what reality (as human consciousness) is *not*. The literalism of Warhol is, first and last, supremely artificial – a calculated impertinence, even an insult. In *Eat*, the modern painter, Robert Indiana, eats a large mushroom in unchanging and unchanged position for a time which begins to make the spectator wonder if really some of the previous mastication is not cleverly being re-run. How could anyone in the world, even purposely, take so long to eat a single mushroom? There is no 'normal' reason for it unless we wish to admit Warhol's kind of film-making into the realm of normality.

It is not normal to *re*live the life which we – that is, all people – live from minute to minute of absolutely continuous time. Even our own subjective consciousness *qua* consciousness is quite incapable of registering everything that passes or rests before our eyes, passes or stays in our minds, because in the twinkle of a clock's second, some distinct train of thought may be utterly obliterated, probably never to return in precisely the same form. Time, as it is lived in consciousness, is of the essence of changefulness. Take the commonplace view of indifferent landscape gazed at from the window of a moving train. Do we not become hypnotized by the way nearer things seem to pass more quickly, farther things more slowly – regardless of what things they may be? Inversely, Warhol attains the same hypnotic abstract effect by the moveless camera eye directed at a relatively moveless point in space. Only actors within the moveless or almost moveless space change and usually they change only at an exasperatingly slow rate. The logical result is for us to be hypnotized by the slow rate of movement and its extremely narrow scope, which (like the eating of the mushroom) is basically repetitious.

What we know as narrative time in fiction (film or otherwise) is strictly formal, selective and summative; it is representation by the memoranda of signs. Nor does it have to be fiction, i.e., imaginary action, for the identical process takes place in reporting a riot or a diplomatic conference on the front page of the New York *Times*. The media regularly give us the gist of a past event in the world, the gist of its human consciousness, without regard to the physical quantity of experience that is literally measured by the clock, and no matter what aspects or aspects of it are handled or for what purpose (documentary or imaginative). This technique results from the *device* of compressing actions of diverse kinds, spread through lengthy clock time perhaps, into a conveniently communicative form (narrative, expository, etc.). Life in Warhol films (as he likes them to remain, unedited, with nothing whatever on the cutting-room floor) is a sort of dead-eye dick when it comes to such accepted formal transmutation. Values, take note, are *not* involved; that is, even here in *Fuck*, the process of fucking is not calculated to depict sexual sensations in a way to illustrate what supposedly is their chief charm: a real excitement, mounting steadily to orgasmic climax. What we know as 'blue films,' however much faked or however real the feelings of those sexually involved, would normally seek to represent a certain palpable excitement, to grow 'hot,' to mount tantalizingly to the climax. If the result be hollow or obviously phony, it is the fault of carelessness or ineptitude or some 'plausible' sort of faking. But all this is not at all the point in Warhol's (actually cool) *Fuck*.

This film is not meant *to represent*; it is meant *to be*. And therein, like it or leave it, lies its great, really cool distinction. Are the performers here self-conscious; do they look at the camera – or the camera man? They certainly do the latter, and if they are also self-conscious at times, it is because they wish to give no version, however artificial, of 'reality.' Actually, the woman seems listless, perhaps narcissistic, not especially man-prone ('. . . disgusting!' she says archly, perhaps not insincerely, of his suddenly exposed genitals); the man seems overcasual, moodily exhibitionistic and routine. When the sex-act is being accomplished, it is he who provides all or nearly all the copulative movement, the woman doing very little to help promote orgasm. They do not kiss passionately meanwhile; they hardly kiss at all. What could be more 'unnatural' than neglecting to kiss so as to 'represent' sexual passion? Yet the negligence has a certain artificial necessity, or 'natural-ness,' precisely because it feels no obligation to represent 'reality.' Even passion, here, is left to take care of itself.

Thus, no matter how much this pair show signs of being watched, everything they do is eminently natural in the sense of being self-initiated. They may not, either of them, have particularly wanted to go to bed together. But they did so – for the camera, for Andy. And doing so, being fairly cool types, they do not trouble to pretend they feel something when they don't. Or if, for some invisible reason, they force their words, their expressions, their postures, there is no canon presupposed by which we can blame them, or even measure, plausibly, how much of what they do is a good-natured put-on. A Warhol film promises or presupposes nothing and achieves, therefore, everything. The everything is 'all too much' according to your taste.

Fuck (especially when peripheral doings are performed) is an action where, strictly speaking, feelings do not matter, so that any feeling which does appear (the man becomes mildly excited and wilfully seeks orgasm) is bound to be perfectly genuine, whatever its degree. Above all, *Fuck* is not a sexploita-tional film of the kind being profusely shown on 42nd Street in New York. In those, everything is calculated, however gauchely, to provide an illusion of erotic pleasure or lust, whether by innuendo or supposed actual copulation. All *blue films* thus begin by wishing to present that domain of reality we know as sexual excitement, which according to its destiny as a pleasure-giving spectacle must be as exciting as possible to the emotions. *Fuck* is definitely not as exciting as possible to the emotions. Which is the sole reason why it is so exciting to the intelligence. . . . It just won't pretend that fucking is Heaven – or Hell. It *may* involve a trip – who knows if the couple are on one? – but if so, it means the dish has an invisible source, and this makes *Fuck* all the more artificial: unreal as a reality-formula. Fucking, it says, *is*. And this is it. *Is it?*

2. The Awful Fate of the Sex Goddess

What, by virtue of the movies, is a sex goddess? It is easy to point, say, to Sophia Loren, imagine her quite naked (as may be done without the camera's assistance) and have the right answer. But Miss Loren's case is relatively simple and unaffected. The matter, with regard to the movies' history of sex, is too complex for mere pointing. The sex goddess's mutation, starting with the celebrated Vampire, is something to arrest and fascinate movie buffs and other susceptible scholars. Its ups and downs, turnabouts and triumphs, take on cosmic dimensions. Going in as straight a line as possible from Theda Bara to Greta Garbo, one's wits are staggered by so vast a change visible in one stroke of the imagination – and that stroke takes us only to 1941. . . . Technically, Garbo is a direct descendant of her distant Hollywood predecessor: the fatal Queen of Love and Ruler of Man which a sex goddess is – or was – supposed to be.

I change the tense and *there's* the rub. For whatever reasons, a sharp decline of divine dimensions in nominal sex goddesses has come about; it is as if 'sex' and 'goddess' were terms that, idiomatically, no longer agreed. Take the case of one who bore a notable physical resemblance to Sophia Loren, Jane Russell, a goddess ephemeral and now long extinct. Miss Russell was two great breasts mounted upon a human pedestal with a doll's head to top it off. Besides being no actress at all (which Loren, after all, *is*), Russell was hardly a sound recipe for a sex goddess. Her peculiar weakness may have lain in the very fact that a California judge, passing on the claim that her film, *The Outlaw,* was obscene owing largely to her salient and partly exposed mammary equipment, decided that anything God-given, such as breasts, could not be 'obscene.' Goddesses, by definition, *are* beyond the law. But voluptuous breasts are but the window-dressing of sex divinity. Jane represented one of the last historic efforts to invent a great personality on the basis of sex-appeal alone.

Plausibly, the physical dimensions of sex goddesses first tended to be ample. Theda Bara had a maternal figure. She was, in fact, remarkably like a suburban housewife circa World War I, bitten by the glamor bug into imagining herself supreme seductress of men, and by some weird turn of fate succeeding at it. Today, an Elizabeth Taylor also succeeds though *her* proportions and personality start by being those of the reigning office minx, from whom neither president of the company nor errand boy is safe. By another weird turn of fate we get instead, in this actress, a universal Miss Sexpot – for a sex goddess, one is obliged to call that a comedown. Nowadays sex-goddessing is more a trade than something, as it were, acquired by divine privilege. Another Italian star, Gina Lollobrigida, oddly resembles Miss Taylor although she is better-looking. Lollobrigida is simply Sophia Loren seen a few paces further off: a sort of reproduction in minor scale. But big and beautiful as La Loren is, we must face the fact that sheer majesty in the female body has become, historically, badly compromised as a glamor asset. Being a sex goddess has nothing whatever to do with the sexual act as such. Getting laid is a strictly human, quite unglamorous occupation.

Mediating between Bara and Garbo, Mae West turned up as an eccentric, utterly unexpected manifestation of sex divinity. Like the old gods of the Greek plays, she appeared with the primal authority of 'Here I am!' Part of the majesty of Mae's corseted figure, hefty of hip and bosom, was its anachronism: she duplicated the physical image of the late nineteenth-century stage, where even chorus girls were girthy. The very pathos of distance helped make West a goddess, and historic. I confess to having been, in 1944, the first to describe what her style owed to the female impersonator: just about everything basic. A true parody of sex divinity, Mae was the opposite of the classic Vampire because she aimed at being both funny and good-natured: qualities more plebeian than royal or divine.

The movie canon of the teens and twenties had it that personified sex-appeal was a destroyer of men. Hence the Vampire embodied irresistible sexual evil. She was no laughing matter till time gave us the modern perspective, in which she's little *but* that. Vintage eroticism, regally portrayed by beautiful ladies throughout the twenties, automatically evokes titters when seen today. Mae West's sudden greatness was to have introduced a *deliberately* comic parody of the sex goddess. Her unique blend of sexiness and vulgar comedy, in other words, was the screen's first sterling brand of conscious sex camp. Other brands developed but these were the cynical farcing of tired-out actresses who had never quite believed in their own eroticism. Mae *did* believe in hers. That was the wonder of the spectacle she made. Few others actually did – probably not even her leading men! What her public believed in was the raw, happy camp of it. That incredible nasality, that incredible accent!

Garbo is virtually unique among the remoter goddesses because, even in some of her earlier roles (such as that in *Romance*), she can still be taken seriously. And yet even Garbo is not foolproof against the sensibility of what once a very few called, and now the world calls, camp. (Camp, one must note, is a proved culture virus affecting non-deviates as well as deviates.) Seeing Greta gotten up as an innocent country girl in *The Torrent*, one understands better that creeping parody of passion that meant her downfall in *Two-Faced Woman,* her last picture. The 'two-faced' was painfully exact. A split personality may have suited the being termed by Robert Graves the Triple Goddess of archaic times on earth. But for our times, even one extra personality makes *The Divine Woman* (the title of a Garbo film) into a schizophrenic with professional delusion-of-grandeur. Film myths of the making and unmaking of a star began to appear as early as the thirties and their climax, in the sixties, was explicitly labelled *The Goddess* – no accident that an actress with superficial sex-appeal and no real ability, Kim Stanley, was featured in it.

The sex goddess, supposedly, satisfies a basic human need:' she would and should be the sanctified, superhuman symbol of bedroom pleasure, and bedroom pleasure as such seems here to stay. Europe, however, held a more tangible appreciation of sex as sex. Thus, a Brigitte Bardot came as no surprise at all. This legitimate goddess, after fifteen years' hard labor, has faded. Yet while she was at her international peak (somewhat pre-Loren), she had the simplicity and stark presence natural to erotic greatness. B. B., with canonic plenitude up front, facile nudity and long, tumbling blonde hair, was an impressive paradox: a cheerful Magdalene. Repentance and guilt were alien to her if only because her assets (like Jane Russell's before her) were so unmistakably God-given. Unworldly innocence imparted to B. B.'s sexiness a gay pathos; worldly sophistication imparted to Mae West's a more complex gaiety, a more complex pathos. B. B. was a symbol that implied nothing but reality, Mae a reality that implied nothing but a symbol ...

When the self-farcing tendency began overtaking stars and films in the late fifties and sixties, even bouncy B. B. began parodying her rather down-to-earth divinity. As of now, screen nudity (to take sex at its simplest) has begun to be so proliferant as to look common. Arty, self-conscious, coyly denuding camera shots of the sexual clutch (one has had to creep up on body-candor in the movies) has become, by 1969, a cliché. Sex goddesses inevitably were victimized by the big breakthrough toward sexual realism. Currently, we are down to the nitty-gritty of the postures, the pantings, the in-plain-view of sex – down, in other words, to its profanity, including the garniture of those four-letter words. The sex goddesses have become sitting ducks for the exploding peephole of a film frame. In *La Dolce Vita* (1960), Fellini's genius for casting cannily registered the fatal downwardness then true of sex-goddessing. We found a perfect big-blonde-goddess type, Anita Ekberg, playing a parody movie star with a bust like a titaness, a baby voice and the courage of Minnie Mouse.

Sexy even so? Well, yes. Fellini pressed some delicate poetry no less than some satire from the combination of Miss Ekberg's shape, poundage and sweet, naïve femininity. Yet when, in the film, her husband whacks her for moonlighting with Mastroianni and she slinks off to bed, La Ekberg is just another silly woman – and 'divine' only as a young man's midnight fancy. Even when she had answered in kind to the baying of neighborhood dogs, it was more a chorus than a command: the gorgeous bitch fled in an auto when the baying became serious. Fellini thereby branded the explicit profession of sex goddess a benignly comic fraud. Whyever should sex goddesses have fallen so low as to be 'caught out' like that? The way they were caught out is clear enough: their regal posture was shown as an imposture: a fabricated illusion based on physical pretensions and almost nothing else. The method was to expose the base fleshly mechanism behind a grand illusion. In Hollywood, both sex goddesses and other stars were, it seemed, manufactured. Essentially, the goddesses had been lovely hoaxes foisted upon a naïve, gullible and dated public of both sexes: the gaga identifiers (female) and the gasping adorers (male).

It is a pause-giving irony that the truly great among sex goddesses were the first to show glaring symptoms of the decline and fall of the movie line. Was there something too façade-like about the Very Greats? Gazing back, one can detect one of the handsomest, Nita Naldi (who played opposite Valentino in Blood and Sand), unable to be anything from head to foot but a striking mask. In the teens and early twenties, statuesque feminine fulsomeness was still bona fide; it was the sweet and pure star actresses who were petite. Today, like Bara, Naldi must seem a rather puffy anachronism; if not downright absurd, at least strangely pathetic – a period clotheshorse, stunning but quite without humor. And take Mae West as a 'mask' rather than a comedienne: physically she seems made from a mold, as if her whole body were a layer of simulated flesh about an inch thick, with nothing whatever inside. It took wit, humor and an interesting face to make La West a real 'divine woman.'

Historically, humor came into Hollywood supersex with the later twenties in the personnel of Flaming Youth: chiefly the 'It Girl,' Clara Bow. And then, of course, came Jean Harlow, who created a totally new standard for sex goddesses. Jean was a sacred-whore type whose unabashed vulgarity (even as West's) was integral with the spell she cast. Yet a few veils of illusion had been brutally torn off: evidently the sex goddess was no lady if, as Harlow, she could be a downright slut. Nobody sensed it then, I think, but a great symbol was being debunked. There could be no question about *Harlow's* real fleshliness, all over and through and through, if only because nothing seemed to exist between her and her filmy dresses but a little perspiration.

Like Mae, Jean was funny – more professionally and seriously so than Clara Bow, who was only a rampaging teenager with sex-appeal; essentially, that is, Clara was *decent*. Both West and Harlow let a certain middle-class decency (allied with basic chastity) simply go by the board. Both gloried in being, at least potentially, unchaste. They weren't exactly prostitutes (or but rarely) yet that they exploited sex professionally hit one between the eyes. They were Gimme Girls as much as Glamor Girls and quite beyond morality in those vocations. It would be humanly unnatural should beautiful ladies, every bare inch of them, cease to be darlings of the camera's eye. But capitalized Lust is either a mad holiday or a deadly sin. Once, being a sex goddess was to skip all mundane considerations and assume that Lust meant Glorious Aphrodite. In the movies' advanced age (they are well over seventy), sex and other sorts of violence keep the film cameras grinding. But make no mistake: the goddessing of movie sex, subtly and brutally too, has met an awful fate.

In West, parody was a divine she-clown act; in Harlow, sex bloomed miraculously, nakedly, gaudily from the gutter. *The Queen*, a documentary about classy transvestites competing for the title of Miss All-American, offers (at the moment I write) the most eloquent evidence anywhere that sex-goddessing can still be taken seriously. Yet among those to whom queendom is synonymous with homosexuality, the divinity of sex as a public symbol carries a necessary irony and a necessary narrowness. 'Harlow' has become a sort of trade name among professional transvestites. The winner of the contest in *The Queen* calls himself just Harlow, and one of Andy Warhol's home-made films is titled *Harlot* because it features an Underground transvestite's camp act in a blonde wig.

This 'superstar,' Mario Montez, has attached the name of a minor sex goddess (extinct) who was lately honored with an Underground cult: Maria Montez. The camp symbolism of the Warhol film, whose action takes place entirely on and about a couch where four people are grouped – two young men, a 'lesbian' and 'Harlow' – is to have Montez extract first one banana then another from various caches and munch them deliberately, in voluptuous leisure, for about an hour. This is the principal 'action.' Get the picture? If you do, you qualify for the Underground sex scene. It's this way: one is to imagine a camp queen of sex, even when genuinely female, not with an adoring male crawling up her knees, but an adored male with *her* crawling up *his* knees. In her early days, Garbo herself used to slither over her men like a starved python. But she was only combating Old Man Morality: her erotic power, and its authenticity, were never in question.

Today everything is in question about the sex goddess but the blunt mechanism any woman offers a man. Personally, I find the progressive demoralization of the s. g. in females rather desperately saddening. Two acting celebrities, Bette Davis and Tallulah Bankhead (while neither was ever a sex goddess), have parodied neurotic and unconsciously funny females so often and so emphatically that they represent an historic attack on high feminine seductiveness. Sex-parody became, rather early, an integral part of Miss Davis' style till it exploded in her 100 per cent camp films, *Whatever Happened to Baby Jane?* and *Hush, Hush, Sweet Charlotte*. The aging Miss Bankhead's failure as a serious actress was suavely turned into success on the radio as a bass-voiced caricature. In the movies, finally, Bankhead followed suit to *Hush, Hush, Sweet Charlotte* with *Die, Die, My Darling* (Ugh!). Yet she (a handsome woman in her own right) had once in her career, if transiently, vied with Garbo.

We find a rich clue to the fate of the sex goddesses if we look at the way classic beauty currently serves movie sex. If the physical proportions and personalities of Sophia Loren and Anita Ekberg lend themselves easily to light sex-comedy with a wedge of farce and satire, the face and figure of Ursula Andress (taken in themselves) have a pure, invulnerable classic beauty. In the nineteenth century and the first quarter of the twentieth, Ursula would have been destined as a sex goddess of real if removed divinity, surrounded with protocol and awe, a queen of fashion as of sex. On looks and style alone, Andress would do as well in society as in the acting profession. But what, alas! was her fate? To be an ultra-classy foil for a James Bond – a lesbianlike Pussy Galore! A 'destroyer of men,' by all means, but stamped with the comicstrip sensibility (see *Modesty Blaise,* et al.) that informs all Pop versions of camp sex.

The newest archetype of the sex goddess, robbing her of her former dignity and classic authority, inhabits the comic strip itself, where Barbarella (played by Jane Fonda) has been enshrined as the supreme Vinyl Girl of sex-appeal. Fundamentally, she is the oldtime serial queen, *rediviva.* Remember that serials (take *The Perils of Pauline*) were always animated comic strips with real performers. Even more significantly, there has been the completely nude Phoebe Zeit-Geist, the comicstrip heroine introduced by the Evergreen Review. Like a metaphysical idea, Phoebe seemed not to know what clothes are. Her sole function, naked and attractive as she was, was to be camp sacrificial victim *in perpetuo* for the historic villains and most grandiose, come-lately freaks of comicstripdom (for more clarification of this theme, consult the well-thumbed dictionary of sado-masochism at your local library).

Maybe no fate is really awful so long as, like Phoebe's, it's also fun. Yet the point is erotically disputable. To those tend-ing to think the female sex represents a supreme power, like antiquity's Ruler of Men, the latterday Pop versions of sex goddesses partake more of existential gloom than existential fun. The 'fun' is slightly sick. Shouldn't the put-it-on-the-line psychology of sex-presentation be left for the hardcore geeks in the audience? Actually the transvestites, with their delusions of reincarnating extinct sex goddesses, are truer queens of beauty and sex than Ursula Andress – who looks more and more as if she had been cut out of cardboard and achieved her classic volumes by courtesy of 3-D (flesh-tones by Technicolor). I, for one, think it an awful fate that the grand profession of sex-goddessing should have sunk to the petty profession of sex-shoddessing. The robotizing trend of female charms (against which only that cartoon pair of *Playboy* tits seems holding out) must not be underrated. Think, ladies and gentlemen! The supreme goal of male propulsion, as foreseen in *2001: a Space Odyssey*, is a geometric black slab with unproved sexual capacities. Theda Bara would, tacitly, be more negotiable than that; and shapelier.

Come to think of it, Marilyn Monroe came along in those fidgety fifties and altered the whole set-up. There was something genuine about her, and really pathetic, as if she were all too human to exercise the great craft of queening it for the tradition. We know what finally happened to her. Maybe she was the last 'goddess' actually seeming to be made out of flesh rather than foamrubber: something to sleep *with*, not *on*. And that was probably her fatal mistake. Goddesses are to be slept *about*.

3. The Horse:
Totem Animal of Male
Power – An Essay in the
Straight-camp Style

In that informal realm of civilized thought and action where the vestiges of primitive life survive, the horse and the dog are rivals for fame as American totems. 'Civilized' man must have relatively domesticated totems. And it is natural that film, recorder of movement, should be the art pre-eminently glorifying animals. Despite movies as successful as *Lassie* and *Son of Lassie*, the dog must continue to bow, as American totem, to the horse. This ascendency is logical for two reasons. While space was used picturesquely and effectively in Lassie's long journey back home, the range of movement open to what Americans term the 'horse opera,' and the superiority of the horse as power-symbol, determine the issue of rivalry. After all, the dog is a creature more domesticated than the horse; he gets as close to man as the interior fireside and even his bedroom, whereas, in the living-quarters sense, the horse is more intimate at the open camp fire. Moreover, a dog, especially if small, can be embraced more wholly and is more articulately and aggressively affectionate than the horse. This seemingly superior intimacy between man and his dog, however, is offset by the folk experience of the American cowboy – that experience recorded so voluminously by Hollywood. The cowboy *rides* his animal, and at the same time is more dependent on its power than North American man, below the Arctic regions, is on the dog's power. The physical contact between cowboy and horse – an animal bigger than man – provides an emblem, as well as a drama, of mastery that transcends (assuredly in the aesthetic domain) the easier, more urban and commonplace, relations between man and his 'best friend,' the dog.

Obviously, too, the horse gives the drama of good and evil a more distinctive place in story and legend. As a 'wild animal,' the horse may be tamed, whereas wild dogs offer men no temptation to tame them. Temperamentally unruly horses, furthermore, yield mysteriously to gifted individuals. In movies, the horse of evil character, which sometimes offsets the docile horse, has a term in American-Spanish lingo also applied to a man: 'bad hombry.' The best dog movie, in my opinion, came from England, *To the Victor,* which was about sheep dogs. Not only was there the sporting angle (duplicated in the equine domain by racing) but also the drama of blood, moral and immoral. In *To the Victor*, it is not the hero, or totemic, dog who turns out to be the nocturnal sheep-killer, but his rival. This film was excellent precisely because of its moral scope, and because, moreover, this scope subtly reflected the moral struggles in human character. This (like the American-made *The Yearling*, about a fawn) was an extraordinarily *civilized* animal picture. 'Horse operas,' dedicated to a minimum of sheer violence, are more casual and crass, but highly pertinent, nevertheless, to our national mores. Perennially, horse films tend to be inadvert legends – invariably, if also unconsciously, totemic in nature.

As England and Europe are more thoughtfully aware than we ourselves, America is the land of, among other things, 'the open prairie' and 'the lone cowboy'; alone, save for his eternal partner: the horse.* This coupling is a paradigm for the pagan myth-creature, the Centaur. The man-horse becomes a pseudo-organism; a cowboy has a grandeur and a sense of power, with his horse under him, which he could not possibly have afoot. Totemically speaking, this is a merging between the

* In latter days, the 'spaghetti western' shows just how thoughtful a country Italy is.

religious-magical image, the clan emblem, and the work animal. But the *personal* relation, with its imaginative reverberation, makes the mythical importance of the American man-horse. The horse is not only a power-symbol as a fleshly engine but as an extension of the man's personal power and, more specifically, of his sexual power. With these considerations, one can register more accurately the emotional impact of the film image of a beautiful and powerful horse, mane afloat, rearing against an empty horizon: this is a simple traditional emblem as old as the American film industry itself. A man, traditionally, is seen already on the horse's back; the struggle for mastery has been implicitly won, and this mastery brings American man his power over both equine and bovine herds. In more serious films, the riderless or yet untamed horse becomes a symbol for man himself – objectively or subjectively, father or son – and sometimes symbol for woman, the woman to be sexually rejected or obtained. The function of the totem animal in the primitive initiation rite for pubescent boys was a parable of birth from the animal itself. This 'birth' provided a symbolic origin which the youth could identify as absolute, superseding his mother's womb as scene of his father's fruit; in this way, his incestuous rivalry was replaced by a father-identification, with the sexual element of the mother lacking. 'The lone cowboy,' in this perspective, is the initiated youth joined to the totemistic father-animal, which, as the horse's rider, he has symbolically vanquished.

Let us take for granted the regulation horse-operas, or Grade B westerns. These have had their human screen idols who embody this totemistic evolution of man-horse in a strictly static sense; actors such as Roy Rogers, Ken Maynard, Bill Elliott and other, lesser, riders. But of highlighted totemic interest are two films, one of which, *The Outlaw*, because of censorship difficulties, was first seen only on the West Coast and at private showings in New York; the other film is *Gallant Bess*. These two movies must be credited with a degree of originality because of their extremism; even if artistically gauche in their lack of consciousness, they are not uninspired. At the least, they break away from the usual boy-and-girl romance coupled with the winning of big stakes by the boy's or girl's racehorse; a memorable exhibit of this latter type is *Homestretch*, in which the fate of the romance and the winning of the race are duly dovetailed. Let us not be squeamish about the horse race as a symbolic variety of the sexual act, particularly as we must face an analogous, if more complex, symbolism of this kind in *The Outlaw*. The obsessional temper of racing fans and the emotional build-up to a minutes-long suspense (the race itself) accompanied by the wildest excitement and breathlessly climaxed, are factors of racing that testify to its sexual parallel. Moreover, we are compelled, not only in the light of these two movies, but also in the perspective of traditional legend and ritual, to recognize in horse-operas of a significantly totemic kind the presence of the Oedipus-complex. The anticipated result of the initiation rite previously mentioned was precisely the destruction of this complex. This is true in whatever form it may be found.

As I have written much to signify, the mass unconscious is given free play by the Hollywood habit of catering to the most ancient of popular stereotypes, in which – inevitably – lies a basic substratum of primitive superstition; here the stereotype is the western adventure story. In the *Flicka* pictures, Roddy McDowall portrayed the boy isolated on a farm and striving to establish symbolic power by befriending and mastering a horse; first, a mare and then this mare's son. This was a vestigial, purely individualistic effort to achieve totemic initiation through a horse. Roddy plays a moody youth rebellious towards his father but humoured by his mother. Symbolically, of course, the mare's son is Roddy himself in multiplied power and pitted against the renegade stallion, whom he must succumb to or vanquish. In this way the boy's Oedipus rivalry with his father is displaced to the objective equine drama, made doubly effectual by his ownership of the triumphant stallion; *just because* this plot is a modern vestige, the symbolic totem enters reality and has its drama there. The boy alone is spectator of the crucial fight between the stallions, which takes place in the wilds and which involves, naturally, the leadership of the herd and sovereignty over the mares. Roddy's horse seems to have yielded to domestication, but when his adult power is proven in mortal combat, he takes off to lead the free herd. This anticipates Roddy's own eventual voyage into life beyond his parents' world and virtually proclaims the success of the psychological initiation rite. Another film, *Indiana*, portrayed an adolescent romance in which the boy, by stealth, clandestinely mates two fine racehorses belonging to different stables; not only did this incident provide, in the more obvious sense, a symbolic conjugation with the girl he loved, but also a totemic rite in which the boy could eavesdrop on the parental marriage-bed; by the substitution of the totemic animals, his illicit jealousy is satisfied.

If these symbolic readings of film material appear somewhat exaggerated or overspecial, it is impossible to mistake what is considerably more pointed (deliberately or not) in *Gallant Bess* and *The Outlaw*. The former is straightforwardly – indeed, to the hilt – the story of a youth's obsession with his mare and is the strategic psychic foreshortening of the initiation rite into the struggle to overcome obsession with the maternal sex-image. To summarize the plot: the boy, called to war and enlisting as a Seabee, is parted from Bess, his beloved mare. At camp, his pin-up picture is not of a movie queen but of Bess. Hearing that she is about to bear a colt, the boy requests leave to go to her but is denied it until his arrival (from his viewpoint) is too late to save her life in the ordeal. In a kind of delirium, he digs her grave during a violent storm and cannot be persuaded by an old farmhand that 'since you love her, you'll always have her.' Returning to service, he goes with his outfit to prepare an airfield on a captured Japanese island base. There he has nightmares (how oddly literal!) in which he sees Bess – in 'negative' – rearing into space; his tent-pals can't sleep because of his groans and outcries and he is physically chastised by his own buddy (one of those cheerful roughnecks who typically supply humour in American films). Finally, one night, he cannot believe that the insistent, pathetic neighing he hears from the jungle is not that of his dead mare, so he gropes his way into the forest, where he finds on the gound a real horse, seriously wounded; needless to say, a mare. With the connivance of his tent-pals and eventually the toleration of his superior officer (a man whose severity turns to good will, and who obviously is a father-image), the boy revives the new Bess and she is established as a sort of troop mascot. Bess does soldier duty and saves her master's life when a Jap sniper shoots him; she also performs tricks in a little corral, at least one of them (the boy is the ringmaster) being most insinuating. Convalescent from his wounds, the boy is scheduled to leave Bess on the island when his outfit is ordered away, but in an excruciating sequence, Bess breaks leash and swims after the transport, where in defiance of regulations she is allowed to clamber on board: boy and horse are reunited. As a dénouement, Bess (on the American farm) successfully bears a colt. Again, the boy hero is the mating agent, but here no sign of a stallion appears; the boy is clearly master of a totemic birth ritual in which he is both the symbolic stallion and the infant colt.

In case anyone believes that this film should be considered innocent of any underlying meaning, I quote verbatim a remark by the boy's wisecracking pal: 'Maybe there's something to this love stuff besides *dames*.' I submit that my own interpretation is at least free of vulgarity. Furthermore, on the realistic level where such substitutions do take place in the human libido (thus making the film true to life), the story paraphrases in allegory a boy's transference of obsession with his mother (the first Bess) to that with another woman (the second Bess); just so, he might be disconsolate at the death of a beloved mother and then find a girl who would substitute for her. I should add that the emotional tone of the actor taking the youth's role would not have been tolerated had the story been projected in script as about an adolescent crush on a *human* female. In that case, as ironic as the hypothesis is, such an exhibition of masculine emotion would have been condemned as 'morbid' and never have been filmed to set before the public!

The Outlaw, as a straight story, is less ingenuous than *Gallant Bess*, although aesthetically, of course, the Howard Hughes production is profoundly inept. The boy (played by a newcomer, Jack Buetel) is a bona-fide outlaw, Billy the Kid himself, second in American legend only, perhaps, to Jesse James, and even more of a lone wolf, since he sets out singly in this movie to avenge his brother's death. A more or less fragile female, apparently, has killed his brother. Let us pass over the more routine innuendoes, as lewd and nude as these are, and turn to what a more sophisticated censorship might have more reasonably, if less needfully, become alarmed at. In its own oafish manner, the movie extends the power-symbol of the horse to an ambivalent and ambiguous sort of homosexual fixation. Here the stallion, frankly termed a 'sweetheart' by a rival outlaw (Walter Huston) is a bone of contention between Billy and said rival, whom it seems adequate to identify by his nickname, 'Doc,' and who is senior crime champion in the story's locale. Originally, the horse has belonged to Billy; stolen, he has been sold to 'Doc,' in whose possession Billy finds him and from whom, by hook and crook, he wrests him. Billy, by outbraving and outdrawing 'Doc' so arouses the latter's admiration that the two enter an ambiguous partnership, half affection and half enmity. The plot of their rivalry for the horse – obviously, as a stallion, the emblem of sexual power – supersedes their rivalry for said female, and so independently complicated is this major theme that the stallion symbol assumes a realistic value; i.e., the stallion is an actual love-object, a co-extended Narcissus image for each male; certain details indicate that for 'Doc' the attractive boy becomes homosexually symbolic of the horse. At one point, the two males bargain for either strawberry roan or girl; when Billy chooses the stallion, dissatisfaction gleams in 'Doc's' eyes; the girl forthwith appears in a doorway and – in the screen's most unladylike manner – shouts at Billy: 'What! You'd exchange me for a *horse?*' This howler was apparently conceived as brutal realism. Throughout, the action gives sadism a big play. This fact is not least evident in the amusingly exciting climatic sequence of the formal gun-duel between boy and man to decide by death the parlay-prize of girl *and* horse, the survivor to claim both. How ingeniously the sporting atmosphere is preserved! This is curiously pointed because twice in the film Billy has been set to shoot the girl, and once he actually gives her the rope-crucifixion – an invention of the Indians – only to reconsider and come back to release her.

As the rivals face each other for the duel, and the clock gives the signal to shoot, Billy's guns remain hanging in his holsters. As 'Doc' taunts Billy for cowardice, the former artistically knicks each of his ears with bullets. Psychologically, Billy's inert passivity needs explanation; everything, including manly honour, is at stake. Realistically speaking, something *unconscious* must restrain him. What can this be – if not subconscious homosexuality – but the shadow of the Oedipus guilt falling on his trigger finger? He is faced by a man half of whom is as fond of him as though Billy were his own son, and half of whom, in the symbolic sense of the paternal sex-rival, is bent on destroying him. In the former role, 'Doc' – true to his nickname – is the paternal medicine man who, as the rite proceeds, symbolically castrates the initiate by knicking his ears, and yet, as the father afraid of the usurping son, he is ready to literally exterminate Billy. This combination of personalities in 'Doc' might well paralyze Billy through sheer bewilderment as to the proper identification; guilt and innocent faith contend in his heart. That this scene is saturated with a quasi-homosexual atmosphere is proven by a sub-plot of the affections – no less than an old and sentimental friendship between 'Doc' and a fourth character, a rather ridiculous sheriff (Thomas Mitchell) who has tagged along and finally caught up with the two outlaws. During the duel, the sheriff (fleeced of his guns) is a helpless bystander, an emasculated figure who raises loud complaint against Billy as cause of his alienation from 'Doc' and starts sobbing. One might hazard that this disqualified symbol of law is a masquerade for the wife and mother, whose spirit here interferes with the initiation rite because it is *lethally real*, not a true rite. The girl, although present, is purely negative. Despite the sheriff's wails and his own indecision, Billy at last draws and kills 'Doc,' thus fulfilling what is to be identified, finally and specifically, as a symbolic Oedipus destiny.

Accordingly, in this film, the virtual totemic rite has fizzled and become *drama*. What appears on the surface as perhaps the most outrageous 'fairy tale' of all westerns somehow manages to emerge as the most dramatic and least neatly symbolic of filmdom's masked totemic rites. First, the horse is never in the movie as a dramatic factor: 'Doc' himself is a sort of Centaur, a paternal outlaw whose traditional ascendency has been challenged by a stripling novice. Here a mythological parallel is fortunate: Greek myth has it that Chiron, a Centaur, instructed the hero, Achilles, in the arts of peace and war. I suggest Billy's parallel with Achilles also for another reason, for it was Achilles who retired from the Trojan war until he was moved to avenge the death of his bosom friend, Patroclus, and Billy's original motive in the story was simply revenge for his brother's death. Sexual rivalry, however, was automatically thrust on Billy by events. But the significant thing between the two males of *The Outlaw* is that only *one* set of essentials, girl and horse, exists for them. Obviously, the physically desirable female will not suffice either of them: the totemic symbol, the stallion – almost identical with the self – is also necessary. It is the *human* relations, the impersonation of the human father by 'Doc,' that complicates the boy's totemic imagination. It is as though 'Doc' were a medicine man who desired to under-mine the ritual totemic release to be considered the boy's traditional right, and this precisely because, perhaps, 'Doc's' own totemic release, in terms of modern society, has not been completed, rendered authentic. He himself is to be conceived as a 'son' whose initiation once failed, perhaps also became real, violent drama. Are Billy and 'Doc,' after all, not *outlaws*, traditional bad-men who are paradigms for the rebellious sons of the original horde? We must not fail to note that the 'out-law' is a renegade member of the cowboy clans.

Nor must we overlook that, in the trance of the movie theatre, one is inclined to forget too easily that popular fiction represents a vast cultural residue. Yes, movie stories are made up 'out of someone's head,' but because of this very openness of viewpoint towards the chosen material – that feverish in-vention so peculiar to Hollywood – what we term 'super-stition' holds sway. We speak of 'romances,' of 'melodramas,' little realizing, as a rule, the religious-magical vestiges that inhere in the integument of these terms as imaginative forms. So it is with the totemic role of the horse in American films. In one sense, the cowboy and his horse (they were once co-starred in American films) are obvious and simple, like a coat-of-arms; in another sense, as in *Gallant Bess*, ancient totemism is fused with modern neuroticism; in still another, as in *The Outlaw*, the horse is present as a sort of totem fantasy: a coveted power-fetish without which the female cannot seem completely desirable – or completely won. After killing 'Doc' and mourning at his grave, Billy starts away alone on his roan stallion; a few moments before the movie flashes off, the girl is permitted to jump up behind him and the three go off out of the picture.

4. The Costume Romance: Historical Perspective 1

Post-war years in movie production saw a revival of the costume romance as more or less a natural part of popular catering. The charm of 'another time' as often combined with 'another place' has not waned for the movie-goer any more than for the best-seller addict. The war theme as a mere reflection of pressing reality during the years of conflict inevitably appropriated its cinema space, but not without a psychological touch of foreign 'costume' for American audiences. Europe, as Henry James can still freshly remind us, is traditionally an area of covetable mystery. That war and post-war inverted Europe's desirability did not lessen it as a domain of exotic realities. One thing which the costume film brings to mind is the almost total public lack of interest in the native costume romance. *Gone with the Wind,* of course, was an exception; its repeated revivals through the years serve to impress one again with the virtue of a *long* film; a virtue which another costume romance, the French-made *Les Enfants du Paradis*, reinforced. Are the movies always trying to make history stretch to the present?

The romantic tradition of America has not been neglected: *The Scarlet Letter* was made with Lillian Gish; Cooper's frontiersman and Indian sagas were filmed, and there was the rare

All That Money Can Buy (based on Stephen Vincent Benet's *The Devil and Daniel Webster*); *Magnificent Doll*, an unspeakable thing concerning Dolly Madison, can be mentioned only with a bow for statistics. We may note the normal tendency to equate the love romance with the historical, or costume, film. For America, romantic love is a more or less 'historical' or past-time quantity and its basic exoticism was brought straight home to Broadway by Jean Cocteau's *La Belle et la Bête* (*Beauty and the Beast*), which I was privileged to see in its virgin wholeness, without the cuts and imposed reading-dialogue that mark the anglicization of foreign films. Cocteau's film proclaims the survival of romantic love as an ideal of Europe, specifically of France.

During and just previous to the war, Italy was filming the lives and works of its operatic composers. *Verdi, Madame Butterfly,* and *Amami, Alfredo* (based on *La Traviata*), were films which, while meaningless to art, maintained a tone of seriousness (however superficial) toward the dignity of the romantic idea and the authenticity of ethical tradition. What one might term the *conducting-agent* of tradition in these instances was music, which in its operatic form is inseparable from romantic love. However, we find post-war Italian movies *Roma, Città Aperta* (*Open City*), *Sciuscia* (*Shoe Shine*) observing contemporary realism skillfully and with a vengeance. Strangely enough, pre-war Italy supplied a most non-singing version of *Rigoletto: The King's Jester*; only Ferdinand's motif-aria, as I recall, was actually sung in it. Pertinently, *Before Him All Rome Trembled* is a contemporary spy-drama involving an opera singer so that we see traditional romance literally spread-eagled by implacably disrupting reality.

Can we gainsay that both opera and ballet, embodying the quintessential vestiges of romantic love in aesthetic forms, have less spiritual vitality here than abroad? Even the cinema of the Soviet Union put *Russian Ballerina* into the field before America got around to releasing its own version of Benoît-Lévy's moving *Ballerina*. We must scrutinize America's great technological pride to reveal the mechanism of ballet and opera popularity; here, it is less for the romantic beauty of their arts that singers and dancers are admired than for their skill: the *tour-de-force* of their arts. At the same time the unreal, or *illusive*, element of opera and ballet romanticism must be interpreted, rather, as a classicism of the temporally and spatially remote. For example, it was the 'classical' romanticism of *Verklärte Nacht* that the modern choreographer Antony Tudor used for a ballet expressing neurotic love-tensions (*Pillar of Fire*), yet the costume feeling was significantly enough kept to the turn of the century. Ballet and opera are classical symbols of leisure-class superiority and, despite 'modernist' efforts in ballet, are more or less atrophied as expressions of the moral life.

As some classical ballets do, Cocteau chooses the literary tradition of the fairy tale and proves it, it seems to me, a still viable form. This is not the same romantic device as that in a film such as *The Queen's Necklace*, from Dumas' story, or even *Carmen*, both French productions. The difference lies in the obviously greater sophistication of Cocteau's sense of metaphoric artifice; as a matter of fact, he has neatly psychoanalyzed the well-known fable and yet preserved a traditional surface qualified only by a certain gentle irony. In the Cocteau piece, film becomes a direct instrument of the poetic imagination and, as with his quasi-surrealist *Le Sang d'un Poète* (*Blood of a Poet*), *Beauty and the Beast* deserves to be criticized as absolute cinema.

In regard to *Carmen*, the Prosper Merimée story was used rather than the Bizet derivative, with the opera's music as continuous background. The departure from the operatic tradition was doubtless in the service of a grainy naturalism that would provide relief from the overfamiliar clichés of the romantic museum-piece. Moreover, almost any novel plot provides a better working script for cinema than any opera. Viviane Romance, while too highly made up (as French actresses almost invariably are), made her 'Carmen' look more like a Spanish gypsy and less like an opera singer; a talented actress, she gave the role an unexpected verve. Yet as a film, for all its quota of lustiness and costume picturesqueness, *Carmen* is no better *made* than many an American film of the last couple of decades: like these (I am thinking of Von Sternberg's costumish Dietrich films), it is given over more to luxury than to art. One must admit in the interests of precision, however, that in the final mist-clad scene when Carmen and Don José die by a knife in the latter's hands, the desperate evocation of fatal love and the image of death as explicit obverse of the erotic image are things for which one might look in vain throughout the history of American and English movies.

The *modernity* of the costume romance in *Carmen* must be identified as the continuity of a moral tradition, this tradition being nothing but the ascendency of passional love. On the other hand, the noble heroine of *The Queen's Necklace* is a daring, unconscionable schemer who supports an indigent husband with her tricks and uses her lover as an accomplice; *her* modernity is a factor alien to our dominant American puritanism: a tradition of worldliness that is exclusively a European possession. Love as a romantic idea, in the worldly tradition, is but an aspect of, so to speak, moral costume; it goes with the rest in a sphere of heroic striving proper to the aristocracy. Nevertheless, love has the specific transcendence of romantic idea in *The King's Jester*, in which Michel Simon gives an interesting performance of Rigoletto's role. The film, like the opera, tends to obscure the underlying profundity of the story, the former through its costume manners and the latter through its melodrama and musical overlay. As climax, the emergence of Gilda's head from the sack and Rigoletto's terrible ironic laughter have a poetic charge that cannot come across with treatment dedicated to the *romantic narrative* rather than the *romantic idea*. Both *Beauty and the Beast* and *Les Enfants du Paradis* consciously center themselves on the romantic idea of love, thus claiming a mode of 'history' other than literal event.

These two films are equally serious and equally ambitious. *Les Enfants du Paradis* has perhaps the most consistently brilliant cast of any movie I have seen, being headed by Jean-Louis Barrault. He takes the role of Deburau, the nineteenth-century French mime, who pines away after an impossible passion. *Beauty and the Beast* I saw in its uncut entirety, one sequence being omitted even from the public showings in Paris as interfering with the rhythm of the plot, but I saw a cut version of *Les Enfants du Paradis*, reducing its original length of three and a half hours to two and a half. The missing hour might restore to this movie its artistic symmetry;* as it is, it seems jumpy and vague in spots with some of the important action weakly motivated. But the main drive survives, and the movie emerges as an authentic ode to romantic love – not the more conventional type between normal beings, but one replacing the customary mechanism of the clan or caste barrier with the barrier of a pathological fetishism for virtue. As the mime who acts 'Pierrot,' the fantastic role of the frustrated lover, the youthful Baptiste Deburau is considered a sort of simpleton; actually, he is a detached dreamer of a morbid and lyric obsessiveness. His real fancy chances to fasten itself on Garance, a casteless sort of courtesan, whom he cannot love because of her lightness of virtue. The story, which contains some superb miming by Barrault as Deburau in his theatrical performances, recounts his rejection of his object of passion, his marriage to a plain, devoted girl, and finally his anticlimactic commitment to his obsession, which results in Garance's abandoning him after one night together because (she is now a rich nobleman's wife) 'it would all never work out.' The cliché quality of this climax is a little discouraging but a fully rounded film preceding it might have charged it with more conviction. The film remains true to the sterling romantic conventions of a 'fatal love' – to wit; a love containing its own germ of frustration; the mystery of the passional motivation; and the hallmark of the single night of fulfilment.

The importance of the energy and the art which have gone into *Les Enfants du Paradis* is that the supremacy of the *romantic idea* is asserted. What counts is the psychic weight. The film's mid nineteenth-century setting is less meaningful as costume than the fact that Deburau's theatrical expression of love as the clown Pierrot is the paradigm-masquerade for his actual passion. So the heart of romantic love is projected as

* Since this writing, I saw the uncut version and the improvement is conspicuous.

literally a metaphor, which, according to modern conditions, would seem necessarily the law of its behavior. It is an idea, a symbol, before it is an actuality, a moral duration.

The question arises: was romantic love ever destined to be love 'infinitely' fulfilled? Is not its true paradigm, rather, the Romeo-and-Juliet pattern of a tragically decisive realization? Shakespeare's legend (let us try to forget its apotheosis in Hollywood) teaches us, I think, not that 'romantic love' must necessarily be tragic, as it was the prejudice of the nineteenth century to conceive it, but that *it is prepared to undergo tragedy to maintain its purity and passional drive;* that is to say, romantic love is not necessarily tragic love even though tragedy be its only absolute test. Of Romeo and Juliet, it may be said that they died in order to love well. The psychological subtlety of the nineteenth-century conception was its alignment of tragedy with the erotic fulfilment itself: romantic love was only 'rational' to fear physical indulgence as a constantly renewed trap. Owing most probably to the decline of the belief in immortality, fear of death became more important than fear of love-failure. Thus the tragic conception of the nineteenth-century romantic reversed the Romeo-and-Juliet formula: one loved in order to die well.

The romantic importance of *Beauty and the Beast* is orientated to its metaphoric artifice, which its fairy-tale magic and its costume surface carry out systematically. Emphasis is shifted from romance as history (as true or possibly true happening) to romance as absolute idea, even as dreamy fantasy. Yet a study of the movie's psychoanalytic substratum indicates that it embodies a typically French, and presumably still valid, moral tradition: love as the art of elegance, the 'beauty' of nature triumphing over its 'beastliness.' Cocteau's aesthetic maturity is manifest in the structure of the plot, telling in allegory the story of a girl's fear of masculine erotic brutality as a particular result of her father's tender love for her contrasted with the bold swagger of her suitor; ideally, her love for her father is displaced by her discovery (elaborately organized as magic symbolism should be) that her suitor is actually capable of the same kind of tenderness. The film is to be praised for the consistency of its poetic texture and for charming inventiveness in detail. Its French bias also helps it pose a leading question: is the moral drama of feminine virginity and its sexual fears a fairy-tale commodity, 'past history' like the magic era of mankind, or has it validity today? – a question which seemingly demands a corollary: can love any longer be considered one of the social arts? This realigns the concept of romantic love, as subjected to the nineteenth-century hazard of 'incarnation' (so much a mythological throwback!) to the status of idealism and to its medieval origin as a poetic emotion contingent on an elaborate ritual of symbol. If Cocteau's film may be considered a re-examination of chivalric love, his French virility in this respect has drawn to its ethical validation the 'historic' psychological reservoir of the unconscious. Freud too strove after an *etiquette of the ideal*; that is, toward sublimation. It might be considered 'romantic,' at this moment of history, to insist, like the delicate heroine of *Beauty and the Beast*, on the classical erotic factor of an *art of love*.

I think that film critics would profit by investigating the field in which certain moral ideas seem to survive in life *only* through the media of the arts, of which film is one. I have spoken of 'conducting agents,' but these actually apply to the authenticity of the intellectual, or formal, transmission, not to the verifiable mores of our society. My own, more partisan, question would be: what practical validity has the movie myth? – and as corollary: is psychopathic murder the new *practical*, neo-nineteenth-century form of the romantic love-idea in America? In Joan Crawford's movie, *Possessed*, the heroine, whose tragic obsession with a faithless lover leads to her murdering him, would have been romanticized up to the second quarter of this century; now she is a psychopath with hallucinations. *Les Enfants du Paradis* would push the practical consequences of romantic love as absolute moral commitment no further than 1850. From then on, the tendency was toward the strange prophylaxis of a Stendhalian hero or the death-and-disease love-symbolism of a Baudelaire.

That England keeps the romantic idea orientated to moral eccentricity on the one hand and to military conquest on the other, is evident by the lavish costume productions of *Henry V*, *Caesar and Cleopatra*, and *Great Expectations* (their authorship being severally explicit). *Caesar and Cleopatra* always impressed me as a romantic joke, exploiting a literary legend to make cute commentary on love and politics – realms in which modern society is presumed to require Shavian lessons. There is, moreover, a bald effort in *Caesar and Cleopatra* to emulate the Hollywood Technicolor spectacle. The same might be said of *Henry V*, although Hollywood could hardly have achieved the genre pictures of the French court or quite the milieu of the Globe Theatre that Laurence Olivier's English production has given Shakespeare's chronicle play. The transference of Shakespeare to the screen has always seemed to me a semi-barbarism, not because too little respect has existed for the Bard, but because the Bard simply did not anticipate the movies. That film-makers are sensitive to this last point is quite clear from a device used in this very film. The play begins as a production in the Globe Theatre, and then at the point of Henry's embarkation for France, shifts to the actual deck of Henry's ship and remains thereafter in 'true' latitude and longitude. At the close, the formal idea is retained by moving back to the Globe where Katherine, now Henry's Queen, is seen as a boy in a most unlovely wig. The device is there; it works like a clock. But it does nothing to preserve the rhetorical grandeur of Shakespeare's play, to which the battle scenes (with suitable panoramas and suitably embroiled extras) are merely impertinences. *Great Expectations*, an almost equally expensive production, did little to convey Dickens' essential quality to the screen, although its efforts make creditably orthodox luxury-cinema. It is merely that Dickens provided, as did Shakespeare, a 'shooting-script' whose native anfractuosities had to be overcome.

Eisenstein, creator of *Ivan the Terrible*, is aware of the kind of writer who provides the best shooting-scripts; for example, Pushkin. Not that the story of *Ivan* (Part I) is taken from Pushkin (Eisenstein himself wrote the script) but that this director is one with a coherent and – in purely technical terms – complete art of cinema. His *Ivan* is mechanically episodic in the regular saga manner, yet it should strike any spectator as more unified *in style* than any of the films I've been discussing excepting *Beauty and the Beast*; even that has questionable spots the like of which cannot be found in *Ivan*. It is not only that Eisenstein has maintained psychological and emotional tone, as may do the best exhibits of certain other directors, but that he creates a formal dynamics of film in terms of vertical-montage, or exact synthesis of the visual and the auditory elements, including music. Actors are not merely photographed speaking, as in Hollywood and Elstree, their speech is correlated exactly with music and image in the total pattern. This method naturally gives *Ivan the Terrible* a formal validity automatically strengthening its legend of the Russian tsar. By virtue of his *art*, Eisenstein displaces history (let us not be concerned with the bias of the historical interpretation) from the realm of recorded facts to that of pure legend. As such, his Russian overlord (impressively acted by the famous Nicolai Cherkassov) becomes a hero as fictitious, if not as profound or meaningful, as Odysseus or Siegfried. Reviewers have balked at the extreme stylization of the movement, extending to the measured gestures and facial expressions of the actors, but these critics do not realize that such stylization not only enhances the noble character of the action but likewise gives body to its symbolic character; in this respect the period costumes are brought within the artistic scheme: metaphor, film style, and historic event are brought within the same sphere of pure fiction, of which *the costume* (even facial make-up is formalized) is the literal token.

Like Dumas' history, Eisenstein's makes love the mere accessory of worldly success, if however a success quite official and, indeed, feudal in essence. Aided by a perfectly loyal tsarina, Ivan's political consolidation of empire provides, assuredly, an ethical opposite of the modernized psychological chivalry of Cocteau. After all, we can say of *Beauty and the Beast*, with its final flight of pure lyric beatitude, that it is merely a boudoir dream, transcendently romanticized and questionably *au courant*.

5. Revival of the Matriarchic Spirit: Historical Perspective 2

The modern arts have not been poor in acquainting us with the recrudescence of matriarchic ideas more or less in connection with the Oedipus-complex. In *The Infernal Machine*, Jean Cocteau recreated the tragic idea of *Oedipus Rex* with elaborate emphasis on the role of the Sphinx. His sphinx is a female devil, the extant beast of physical and moral corruption, even of death, which every young man must conquer as a threat. Because the hero must triumph inwardly as well as over material temptations, the Sphinx appears as a lovely young girl, or lust personified. She is, precisely, the witch-like lure of the beast-god, Anubis. But in Cocteau's ambiguous design she is also the virgin destined to entice young men – benignly and not malignly – from the incest situation. As we know, even Oedipus as the wandering hero, the dragon-slayer, cannot avoid the incest peril because of his unique destiny in the tragic pattern, which Cocteau preserves.

The forfeit of life for those who do not guess the Sphinx's riddle reminds us of the Oriental legend of the princess whose hand had to be won through performing a feat or guessing a riddle. Anubis, then, is also an image of the legendary king-father who puts the unsuccessful suitor to death according to precedent. '... my thread coils round you,' chants the Sphinx to Oedipus, 'with the volubility of honey falling upon honey.' These are the legitimate love coils surrender to which, if he but knew it, would rescue Oedipus from half his unknown crime. Cocteau's Sphinx knows as little of Oedipus' double crime as he knows until, having given away the answer to him, she is told by Anubis that she is no other than Nemesis, goddess of vengeance. To keep the tragic pattern and yet show the Sphinx as a young girl desirous of Oedipus' love, Cocteau had to give her two personalities. Vengeance is the attribute of the Furies, mercy is Minervan; these emotions of the Sphinx qualify each other in seizing on Oedipus. In freeing him through what seems a sublime personal love, the Sphinx actually frees him to commit the second half of his crime. That Cocteau reserves the vision of justice for the matriarchic figure and denies Oedipus even his demonic wisdom is a point whose general significance reappears in his film, *Les Parents Terribles* (*The Storm Within*).

Both this and Vittorio De Sica's film, *Ladri di Biciclette* (*Bicycle Thief*) bring to the screen notable examples of the revival of the matriarchic spirit. The presence of the female fortune-teller in De Sica's film arises circumstantially from the rapid post-war growth of this ancient institution in Italy. It seems justifiable to speculate, therefore, that its source is a reaction felt in the depths of the Italian people, and confirmed by De Sica through Bartolini's novel, against the failure of the combined patriarchic symbols of church and state (the Pope and Mussolini) to have created a prosperous destiny for the nation; thus, plausibly, the seeress has a precise function in the film's artistic plan. Organized labor, church, and police, fail to provide effective aid in the hero-worker's search for his stolen bicycle; these institutions are inutile, indifferent, or actually obstructive.

In the long-term sense the old-fashioned gypsy fortune-teller (still with us everywhere) is but a degraded vestige of the antique principle of female wisdom, a vaguely discernible elision of the Furies, the Sphinx, the Gorgons, the Fates, Diotima, Sephira (or Sophia), and Athena. Socrates accepted Diotima's answers to his questions with the implicit psychological credulity with which today one might accept the words of a clairvoyant. And of Madame Sosostris, the fortune-teller in *The Waste Land*, Eliot says that she 'is known to be the wisest woman in Eruope.' In view of the whole poem, his irony seems not altogether flippant. Part of the furor against the sibyline manner of Gertrude Stein, as well as part of the worship she received from young artists, was owing undoubtedly to the combination of her rather abstract maternal image and the quasi-mystical nature of her utterances. Moreover, the confused homage paid by the poet Yeats, and the unqualified devotion of other men as well as women, to the seeress Madame Blavatsky, existed side by side with hostile criticism of her by scientists and proper snubbing by the legitimate church. An exemplar of the professional medium appears in Noel Coward's *Blithe Spirit* (play and movie) as a comic image. But this role, if acted so overwhelmingly as it was by Margaret Rutherford, has an odd power to evoke transcendental feelings apart from the film's hocus-pocus surface. Madame Arcati, the medium, becomes a witch of traditional, authentic cast when she uncovers the mediumistic housemaid and finally exorcises the ghosts. This scene speaks of sinister depths in the human spirit as well as of the magic power peculiarly associated with women since the Middle Ages.

The struggle of patriarchic authority against matriarchic rebellion fills history, myth, and literature. Mozart's *Magic Flute* provides a distinct echo of the old sexual hostility for divine supremacy. Its Freemason motif places the patriarchic idea in a fluid, unofficial realm of popular imagination, and reflects the actual domestic situation in which often the ruling parent of the two must be decided. The opera's matriarch, Queen of the Night, is inevitably brought to submission by the temple priest, Sarastro, though not before she flaunts her demonism in competition with his benignity. It was natural for Merejkowski, the author of *The Romance of Leonardo da Vinci*, to depict Leonardo, patriarch of the emergent scientific spirit, as a symbol of white magic opposed to the black magic of a witch. Carl-Theodor Dreyer, the Danish film-maker, has recorded two imaginative, stylistically differing studies of the priesthood's struggle against witches: *The Passion of Joan of*

Arc (1928) and *Day of Wrath* (1943). *The Scarlet Letter,* of which there have been two American screen versions, embodies the same tradition in American literature.

De Sica's seeress in *Bicycle Thief* is the witch rendered benign and surviving largely by pressure from the primitive masses; not at all a society professional, she is actually a simple woman of the humble class. Cocteau's obscurely domestic matriarch is a 'gypsy' only symbolically. As a naturalistic drama with clever underpinnings of symbolism, *The Storm Within* is about the crisis in an ingrown middle-class family precipitated when the only child, a boy, falls in love with a girl who turns out to be his father's mistress. The older man has sought his affair in the normal course of a cooling conjugal love as well as, more specifically, because of the utter absorption of his wife in their son. The mother's sister, a onetime fiancée of the father, is domiciled with the three of them as friend of the family. The action concerns how the elderly trio is determined to frustrate the son's intention of marrying the girl (whose connection with his father is first known only to his aunt), and then how, moved by the spectacle of the lovers' grief, the aunt persuades the parents to revoke the conspiracy and admit to the young pair the fraud that has been imposed on them. When the lovers are dramatically brought together again, all seems about to culminate happily when the mother, unnoticed, slips away and swallows poison. Her deathbed scene, unexpectedly moving, turns the sophisticated comedy into a transcendent tragedy, of which certain preparatory signs have not been lacking.

The intimate scenes between mother and son are as obvious to the casual eye as Hamlet's closet scene with Gertrude as played in Olivier's film. But the son in Cocteau's film, with his forthright, romping, childish temperament, seems innocent of incest motivation; in fact, the female members of this family are clearly wiser than the males: *they* are the really ingrown ones. But unlike *Hamlet*, *The Storm Within* lacks a positive atmosphere of guilt. Every 'guilty' impulse in it has been neatly absorbed into common types of neurosis, whose homey edges Cocteau has been at pains to gild with his witty dialogue. The dialogue is nuanced to show, for instance, the conventional degree of consciousness which a contemporary mother, morbidly fixated on her son, may secretly and, as it were, decently attain.

For once a rather familiar situation among civilized beings is exhibited in an artistic spectacle without obliging the spectator to hesitate in deciding how much the people really know of themselves and each other, and how much the author may have allowed them, through misguided tact or tactic, to *seem* to know. Cocteau's characters (the triumph is not too minor) seem to know what they really know, no more and no less. But the poet Cocteau knows something more than they do without allowing them to learn it in the film's duration except in the most oblique sense. The mother and her sister are just conscious enough of their inner motives to justify the symbolism, which as a result does not appear artificial. In her supreme moment of crisis the mother, after her husband and sister have persuaded her to give up her son to the girl, suddenly becomes clairvoyant. A door has slammed; they think the boy has left the apartment, but the mother declares he is looking for sugar in the kitchen; she repeats his every movement aloud and as she announces that he is about to open the door and appear, he does so, munching a lump of sugar. The character and tension of this scene prepare the audience for her suicide and its subtle revelation of passion and tragedy.

The stricken woman explains her act by telling the other four, including the girl, that they looked so satisfied as a group she did not feel herself necessary to their happiness. It is the fatalistic note of a self-doomed personality and a final realization of that rhetorical threat of suicide with which the family is but too well acquainted. The mother's death is arranged like certain violent and sudden trances of mediums except that the human faculties, both earthly and 'unearthly,' are now annihilated. Ironically she has displayed a serious example of that clairvoyance of which mothers playfully boast to their children so as to establish the hegemony of their wisdom, and which obviously has been an element in the relations between this mother and son: she experiences 'second sight.'

Cocteau has not omitted crying clues to the explication of his climax. Not the least important but one easily neglected is the son's personal nickname for his mother: *Sophie;* that is, the legendary name of divine female wisdom, Sophia or Sephira. The unkempt household is nicknamed 'the Caravan' and the mother refers to herself as a gypsy. As the camera recedes from the deathbed in the final shot, Cocteau's own voice is heard intoning that gypsies have no home on earth: 'The Caravan moves on!' The prominent lack of appreciation suffered by this movie was certainly not caused by the film-maker's lack of consideration for his audience. He meant to present a naturalistic Jocasta as a matriarch who relives the religious destiny of her sex, feeling fated in this era to yield to the patriarchic conspiracy; in substance, this means the present custom of the male's initiative in perpetuating the human family. Similarly, as a timeless personality rather than the pro-tagonist of Sophocles' tragedy, Cocteau's young Oedipus has to obey the sexual law and in turn become a 'Laius.' The actual Laius of this tragedy is not in himself strong enough to cope with the matriarchic magic of his wife; he has been made an unsuccessful inventor, that is, an 'amateur' in modern patri-archic magic. To win out for the present system he had re-quired the aid of the presiding spirit of the plot, his wife's sister, the Minervan friend of the family. It has been she who invented the idea for separating the lovers and she who initiated the merciful exposure of the fraud. Like Athena in the climax of the Orestes trilogy by Aeschylus, she formulates the play's philosophy of justice. Of course, Cocteau's human subtlety has motivated her also with revenge against her sister for originally stealing her fiancé.

We should not overlook Cocteau's exact implication with regard to the surviving matriarchic spirit. The wisdom of the mother's climactic illumination is that, in rebelling against the dominant system, the matriarchic spirit creates disorder and usually acts in vain. The better course is precisely Aeschylean: the Furies in wife and mother should quiet their passion, what-ever its cause, and the mother-wife should become Minervan, be serene and poised as the father-husband's obedient partner rather than his rival for authority over the male child. The *mère terrible* in Cocteau's film seems to yield to her husband in form what she refuses to grant in substance; all the more interesting her supreme moment of self-abnegation which, proud and egoistic though it is, implies the objective judgement that her sister would have made him the more practical kind of wife – and she will, indeed, from now on.

This judgement by the self-doomed mother is an apotheosis of gnomic wisdom. Like the purer example of the seeress in De Sica's film, Cocteau's anachronistic matriarch is sibylline in the mediumistic sense, and as did the pagan priestess, she habitually takes a drug. It might be supposed that the fortune-teller in *Bicycle Thief* is introduced merely for local color or perhaps (since the worker's wife has employed her to foretell if her husband will get a job) to show how silly and futile a woman may be. But the film's testimony amply proves such suppositions wrong. The correct prediction that the job will materialize is only the beginning of the seeress' role. The bicycle necessary for the job is stolen on the worker's first trip into the field. The long, gruelling search for it finally comes to nothing; the worker, who has previously scorned the fortune-teller, now visits her in a kind of bewildered, numb despair. Their interview is brilliantly managed. The seeress' answer to the question whether the stolen bicycle will be recovered, while succinct, is as cryptic as sometimes were the answers of the Pythian Priestess herself. It is: 'You will find it right away or not at all.' When the worker professes that he doesn't understand, she will only repeat the same words.

Quite unenlightened, the worker walks out vaguely with his little boy, and the first sight he meets on the street is the loitering figure of the bicycle thief, without the bicycle. He gives him precipitate chase, finally collaring him, but is now threatened and bullied by the thief's neighborhood pals. A policeman advises the frantic worker that no case exists against the culprit whom both the audience and the worker have identified beyond doubt. He starts for home and is tempted, while waiting for a bus, to steal a bicycle he sees leaning against an isolated doorway. The dramatic fatality of the bicycle's image here has been superbly approached by the director. After a brief inner struggle, the worker gives way to his impulse and pedals furiously away on the stolen machine, but becoming involved with pedestrians leaving a stadium he is overtaken almost instantly and seized by an angry crowd, who rough and insult him. But the bicycle's owner decides not to press a charge. This time the worker really starts for home with his little boy. The movie fades out as they merge with other pedestrians.

It seems to me that this ending, beautifully managed as it is, would be only half as effective, and lack a clue to its essential meaning, were it not for the fortune-teller and the exact text of her second prophecy. Curiously enough, this text is literally fulfilled in the traditional cryptic manner. What the worker finds at once is the thief but not the bicycle. We are to assume that he never finds the bicycle if only because it has virtually been established that it was sold and taken apart shortly after being snatched. It is true that the bicycle which he himself steals might have turned out to be, by miraculous coincidence, his own. This would be a nominally divine sort of good fortune, yet as with the oracles of Oedipus' time, De Sica's seeress does not bother in this case with the recovery of stolen articles but with the realization and the recovery of the spirit. The film's climax has been taken generally as having a social message: the common worker is more or less helpless under the present system, and fortune-tellers cannot rescue him from real dilemmas. But luckily De Sica and his collaborators are profounder than to have desired such a simple, superficial content.

The enigma of the prophecy is to be solved by noticing that the worker finds the bicycle thief, loses him, and then, himself becoming a bicycle thief, takes his place. Thus fulfilling the seeress' words, he does regain the bicycle 'right away,' but symbolically through impersonating its thief. But as his own bicycle *immorally* became the original thief's, it is immorally that the bicycle he proceeds to steal becomes his. The law of personal property supersedes this way of fighting theft with theft. The Furies of vengeance have spoken in the worker as they spoke in Orestes, who paid back murder with murder, and they have further spoken in the spontaneous rage of the crowd that pounces on the worker as he flees. It is the universal fury of mankind with a grievance but it is not the high form of civilized justice. Balance is immediately restored in the Aeschylean manner by the bicycle-owner's 'Minervan' pardon of the worker, who receives his spiritual apotheosis through the grace of this instruction by example.

The film-makers have invented nothing to show us this fact dynamically through the personal aspect of the worker, but I think his natural inarticulateness has been replaced by the nobility of the plot, across which falls the ancient, benevolent shadow of the presiding matriarch, the fortune-teller. As Athena, she casts the deciding vote for Apollo, the worker's implicit patron, who represents the beauty of a moral truth: man's labor of universal guilt. Orestes, by killing his mother, the mariticide, assumed her guilt. The worker, by stealing a bicycle, assumes the guilt of the original bicycle thief. As, with his little boy, he gets lost in the crowd, one senses about him the unseen glow of his inward enlightenment.

As Cocteau romantically and symbolically suggests that the incest feud be dissolved, if necessary, by the inspired act of its chief motive-force (here the *mère terrible*), *Bicycle Thief* suggests, in more realistic mood, that the economic feud among the underprivileged is a total loss, a matter of dog-eat-dog. Lesser films might conceivably contain or suggest the same social messages. What makes these exceptionally eloquent examples of their medium is the form each has been given, and this form in each case is notable for *two* reasons: the use of the matriarchic role as survival of an occult wisdom and the manipulation of the old tragic plot of criminal guilt. In Cocteau's film the gypsy-matriarch is in the center of the action, its veritable vortex; the Minervan matriarch, her sister, is subsidiary but potent. In De Sica's film, the matriarchic spirit is a symbolic embodiment, the fortune-teller, who has somewhat the role of a priestess or chorus. The common keynote of the matriarchs is second-sight: a divination of fate unavailable to ordinary perceptions. This use of spiritual intuition should be taken, I believe, as a healthy sign in a milieu inclined (through the movies as through other media) to place far too much faith in surface facts and the mere pictorial image.

The two films that have formed the nucleus of my theme, as a matter of fact, by no means exhaust the contemporary symptoms. Cocteau's chief revision in adapting his *Orphée* (*Orpheus*) as the currently seen film was the strength of the role he gave Death, who is a woman. At the moment in New York a public controversy continues over *The Miracle*, a brief film by Rossellini which has been selected as a 'best' for 1950 by the New York critics but whose exhibition is stiffly opposed by religious groups. This tale of a goat-girl who imagines her illegitimate child has been immaculately given her by a saint, and is thereon cast out of her village, is obviously the old legend of the devil-visited witch revamped to give it a sacred atmosphere. Aside from the extraneous problem of social conduct, its mythic and symbolic emphasis is securely in line with the matriarchic revival. We are naturally reminded, in this connection, that the Roman Church admitted the Virgin into godhead in 1950, and that *The Miracle* was not banned in Italy where implicitly it has the Pope's approval. Another current movie, *The Mudlark*, pays a spectacular tribute to the queen-mother Victoria, placing opposite her a little boy whose dream is to sit for a moment on the throne. Imagine a reversal of sexes in this situation and you will see how much more readily acceptible, on an esthetic-mythic basis, is the royal person as female.

During the current theatre season in New York, several plays have unambiguously exploited the matriarchic theme. If the musical, *Call Me Madam*, is a political joke at the expense of a matriarchic delusion, it is nevertheless a valuable symptom, inasmuch as positive and negative faceting of a trend precisely establishes its viability. At the opposite extreme is Lorca's *House of Bernarda Alba*, staged by ANTA for two weeks on its subscription program. This play, like the same author's *Yerma,* represents, among Lorca's variations on the fertility ritual, the dissident inwardness of a virgin-cult. The ruthlessness of the matriarch, Bernarda, who turns her manless house into a nunnery, leads to the suicide of her youngest daughter.

Jean Anouilh's *Ring Round the Moon* pivots on the presence of a rich, worldly-wise old matron who finally sets in order, like a dea ex machina, the confused romances of the young people. This play, and Jean Giraudoux's more successful *Madwoman of Chaillot* of the previous season, present the matriarchic image equally on an inspired, not to say illuminated or possessed, level. So the farcical destruction of the reigning patriarchy by Giraudoux's madwoman inevitably absorbs, through its special texture, the poetry of a revival of matriachic 'magic.'

To visualize Cocteau's possessed matriarch, Sophie, is again to identify a dually symbolic and realistic image, and in this case one created by an artistic intelligence presumably as intimate as any other with the profounder vibrations of the *zeitgeist*. All of which is not to make a judgement of these filmic and extra-filmic symptoms as necessarily portentous. At the same time, the announcement by De Sica and Zavattini, his collaborator, that their next film is to be orientated to *the fabulous*, coincides with the image of the seeress in *Bicycle Thief* as symbolically relevant. As a kind of pilgrim's-progress or initiation-rite, *Bicycle Thief* is already instinct with the fabulous; its humble fortune-teller parallels those disguised fairy-godmothers who watched over heroes in the old *contes*.

6. Pornography and Truthfulness: A Report on *I Am Curious**

1. *Re Art*

The film in question, *I Am Curious* (Yellow Version), being demonstrably a serious work of art, should not have to answer to the charges of being obscene and unfit for public exhibition, however limited the exhibition. But since it *is* answering to these charges, it can be specifically defended against them simply as a document, though it is also a work of art.

2. *Re Appeal to Prurient Interest*

The definition of prurient interest is covered by the term, lewd and morbid curiosity. While often associated with sexual matters, prurience covers anything that may be deemed morbid or impure in thought. This gives the term a wide latitude. Now, in judging the prurient interest as involved theoretically with any one film work (whether or not the said work pretends to be artistic), we have to consider the kinds of film which,

* The author (among others) was asked by Grove Press, which wished to distribute this film in the United States, to prepare a statement in defense of it as a serious work of art. The courts denied it exhibition as 'obscene', a verdict later reversed by a higher court.

despite being open to the same charges as *I Am Curious*, are allowed public exhibition.

Popular contemporary films, seen by spectators of all ages, are full of scenes of gross sadism and killing (to name only two: *The Dirty Dozen* and *Bonnie and Clyde*). Such scenes are getting longer and more detailed all the time, whole films being devoted to them. In my opinion, films containing such material are far more offensive and more truly morbid than contemporary films having unusually frank erotic scenes. It seems to me that it is more immoral to kill than to commit rape and therefore more immoral to show the same; note that murder involves a stronger legal penalty than rape. But in this case, rape is not involved, nor is it involved in most sexual scenes in contemporary films.

As to prurient spectator-interest attracted by sex films in general: many cheap commercial films featuring sex, and allowed public showing in New York City, are entirely phony, and produced in a low-grade spirit just to make money. They may not actually *show* as much nudity or sex as does *I Am Curious* but what they do show leans far more toward prurience in the strict sense than does anything in the film in question. Like hardcore pornography (that is, sex-act films illegally made and privately shown) it is quite transparent that so-called nudie films regularly shown on 42nd Street are phony. Sex acts are clearly indicated in the latter but by actors who are very inferior and, like prostitutes, are working for the money alone. It is moral prostitution to film-making. On the other hand, the actors in *I Am Curious* are sincere and professionally competent and show us a fictional version of life as it is. As for the effect of this film on the spectator, there is bound to be a certain proportion of the public that will find evil and lewdness in the slightest suggestion of sexual performance: the lewdness is already implanted in them, and partly by numerous legally shown films that are far less candid, less honest, than *I Am Curious*.

If it be a matter of direct appeal to this preconditioned section of the film audience, I believe that a film such as *Psycho*, which combines violent murder with sexual motivation, is far more obscene and generally immoral than either the commercial nudie films or *I Am Curious*. In *Psycho*, the male protagonist is pathologically fixated on his dead mother and has a related impulse to murder women; he is shown stabbing to death, in a shower bath, a naked woman. This was so vividly enacted that a young man who saw the film proceeded to do the same in actuality, and when caught, and confessing the crime, he said he did it because he saw *Psycho*. It would, then, be most improper and unfair to prohibit the exhibition of a film such as *I Am Curious*, whose most violent scene between people is an erotic quarrel, which ends in nothing more terrible than a healthy act of sexual passion.

3. Re Contemporary Community Standards

Contemporary community standards, as everyone knows, have much changed in the past decade and are still changing. Gradually, through the decades, puritanical and Victorian moral taboos have yielded to realistic recognition of the facts of life. We must bear in mind the swift mutation of moral standards when attempting to judge the permissibility of showing *I Am Curious* to the public. Unquestionably its showing would be a landmark victory in the crusade for moral freedom-of-speech in visual terms. This freedom has already been won in literary terms.

First, *I Am Curious* is automatically to be placed in the 'adult' category which already has legal status in the exhibition of films. One implicit meaning of this category is that enlightened standards prevail in it. Adults usually know (and should know) what sex really is. However, some adults have vestigial moral prejudices and are shockable by such things as are shown in *I Am Curious*. We must respect all *seriously* held prejudices. At the same time, in the interests of world sexual enlightenment, we must argue that not only is it widely agreed that so-called sexual perversions between consenting adults of opposite sexes take place as a routine part of sex life, but also it is known that these acts are part of the most ancient heterosexual heritage coming down from highly civilized peoples.

One need mention only ancient Greece and ancient India. Fellatio, cunnilingus and sodomy, for example, which apparently take place in *I Am Curious* between the hero and heroine, are not necessarily always *accomplished* acts, but rather, are regular excitations preliminary to the basic copulative act; in other words, they help this act. Sexologists call such things pre-coital play. Although the protagonists in one sequence of *I Am Curious seem* to commit sodomy, there is a possibility that the male is achieving normal vaginal entry from behind the female.

No contemporary adult community standards in the world, valid as they are, are so good that they cannot be improved. I believe they can be improved in the direction of still greater candor about what really happens between the sexes. Only if science, the study of existing facts, be competent, can there ever be a really competent morality. Millions of adults can attest that such things as are seen in *I Am Curious* do happen between adults – and they don't only happen in sexology textbooks. One thing I have always lamented about commercial films (I wrote about it in *The Hollywood Hallucination*) is that, in the old days, they were so vague about what really happened carnally between two people in love. 'Did they or didn't they?', at a certain point, was often an enigma in film romances. Vagueness about intimate sexual behavior in films makes vague, foolishly inadequate character-motivation.

It has been about three-quarters of a century since Freud and then others actually investigated behavior in the bedroom through dreams and spontaneous fantasies, and published the results to the universal benefit of mankind. It is time to improve contemporary adult community standards by publishing the results of parallel candor in serious contemporary films (fact or fiction) about sexual behavior and sexual fantasy.

Re this point, the heroine of *I Am Curious* has a nightmare in which she imagines herself shooting and then castrating her lover (the latter act is indicated but not literally seen). *Why* does she have this nightmare? Because she is violently jealous. *But it is only a dream*. She then purges herself of her violent jealousy by repeated sexual intercourse with her lover. Thus, as to the nature of sex shown in this film, it is unquestionably healthy in that it releases the young woman from the morbid hate that momentarily obsesses her. Contemporary community standards would be bettered by showing this moral process, which is so true to life. It is well known that the sex act effectively patches up violent quarrels between lovers and married people. Regardless of its form, the sex act is an *act of peace*.

4. *Re Redeeming Social Value*

The whole story of *I Am Curious* has so much social value, and up-to-date social value, that I would not even recognize the qualifying term, 'redeeming', but strike it out as irrelevant. The honest sex of this film does not have to be 'redeemed', it is self-redeeming by showing that the female protagonist is redeemed, through it, from violent jealousy and hate-motives. It is because the morbid protagonist of *Psycho* did not have a proper sex life that he committed his horrible murder. However, the fact of the present case is that we see a young woman dedicated to the modern political ideals of non-violence and civil disobedience: this is very plain. As the film begins, she is against 'class society' and apparently in favor of such questionably 'peaceful' acts as sabotage. She is, in short, a member of the youthful Independent Left or New Left. The plot of *I Am Curious* then does something very important and, so far, unique in contemporary films. It shows, by what eventuates, that the heroine is a fanatic Leftist through ignorance of experience and in particular of sexual experience. Though she is by no means a virgin by the time the film starts, she is erotically frustrated. As soon as she achieves free and positive sexual expression, she realizes that sex is itself an act of violence *but with one important qualification*: sex, in healthy people, breeds hatred only transiently; in fact, sex requires only the repetition of its own sort of violence – that is *passion* – to create a state of peaceful satisfaction.

In retrospect, then, the young woman tacitly judges her political and social stand, where the so-called creed of non-violence leads to violence *and an indefinitely prolonged violence*. We can verify this by well-known contemporary events outside of films. Technically and theoretically, according to the radical creed, a sit-in or take-over such as happened at Columbia University in New York is 'non-violent'; nevertheless, it was legally a trespass and led to stealing, defacement and finally clashes with the police. The same story is being enacted the world over. Martin Luther King's own group was split by those who began to feel that true non-violence would accomplish nothing since, in any case, non-violence somehow leads to preliminary and intervening acts of violence, as it did in King's murder.

5. *Summation of the Film*

I Am Curious is the story of the heroine's conversion. Her most violent act, when at the end she wrecks single-handed her own apartment, is symbolic of the erotic purgation she has already experienced. Ethically, it has been a question of one kind of violence or another and she is symbolically clearing her own ground for reconstruction. In healthy people, sexual violence can be quickly controlled and instrumented; hate prompted by jealousy can be purged by the sex act. At the end of *I Am Curious* we see the lovers firmly reunited on this basis.

It may be inferred that *I Am Curious* is morally and politically controversial. Some Leftists, I feel sure, will consider its whole thesis morally untrue and improper. Thus, insofar as the contemporary political creed of non-violence is viewed by *I Am Curious* with satiric criticism, and a criticism from the standpoint of sex, the film is indeed controversial. Sex enables the young woman to discover that she herself is momentarily capable of violence. Therefore she is humiliated by the pretence that the aggressive creed of civil disobedience and sabotage can really avoid violence. Every day we see in the newspapers that indeed it cannot avoid violence. Eventually the creed of non-violence, if persistent and aggressive enough, may earn for the world a peaceful socialist society. *But how long will this take?* And how much violence must intervene? According to the optimistic Russians (as reported by this very film) it will take *thirty years* through revolutionary methods; through civil disobedience methods, say the Russians, it will take *three* H U N D R E D *years*.

In *I Am Curious*, peace between a man and a woman is accomplished in a few days, and through sex alone.

Part 2
The Modern Psyche

7. The Psychodrama

The Psychodrama, which I capitalize gratuitously, is a distinctly minor form of clinical practice. But I think its moral motivation and express theatrical pattern far more significant in American culture than its psychiatric limits technically suggest. Actually, it is the private therapy of the mentally and emotionally handicapped individual turned into a collective enterprise. In what may be termed the ritual of the Psychodrama, the individual patient tries to explicate his dilemma in terms of pantomime, possibly words too, before a small audience of others like himself: those with similar difficulties. The psychiatrist functions as a stage-manager director without script, more like the moderator of a discussion panel than like a stage director. Group therapy is but a less theatricalized version of the Psychodramatic session, which may take place on an actual stage or platform. In group therapy, a round robin of storytellers (groping autobiographers) replaces the actor-patient in the spotlight.

However fragmentary, even chaotic, a session of either sort of therapy may be, its social implications are fairly obvious and simple. It is a form of communication among individuals, each of whom has the right to be both hero and critic – critic of another as well as himself. Historically in terms of drama as an art form, the monologue may well come to mind here. Because the subject matter of *Hamlet*, for instance, is deeply involved with psychological mysteries, that play's soliloquist may spring up in the same thought. Is not Hamlet acting out a sort of Psychodrama for an uninitiated audience, the court of Denmark, and is not the Ghost, to this audience, an express element of Hamlet's imagination? Many features of this hero's fame attest to the conclusion that he is a prophetic 'Psychodramatist.' In this century, however, the uniqueness of his historic enigma has been permanently altered by Pirandello's plays.

Pirandello's *Six Characters in Search of an Author* are members of one family, ordinary people with ordinary problems, who feel the strange need of acting out their difficulties before a public audience. Like the people who used to expose their private lives in the former American radio program 'Court of Human Relations,' they wish to be judged by something beyond the moral standards prevailing among them as a family because their domestic conflicts have balked, defeated and sundered them. If they cannot be put together again, they at least wish to define themselves as individuals, so they can be free to act, to begin their lives anew. But even this, in the case of Pirandello's 'six characters,' is in doubt owing to the power of the family idea that has such a grip on them.

Here we have only a description of many a clinical patient's more or less overt dilemma. In a curiously direct and persuasive form, the Psychodramatic motif has invaded American movies by way of a film called *The Savage Eye*. It is significant that this offbeat film emanated, some years ago, from the very heart of commercial filmdom, Hollywood, having been made by Hollywood professionals as an independent, presumably very sincere, expression of feeling. It concerns a young woman whose private life seems ruined by a recent divorce from a husband with whom she is still in love (or thinks she is still in love) but from whom divorce was necessary, apparently, for reasons of personal dignity. In the erotic sense, she has been 'robbed.' She therefore has to reclaim her lost integrity, her lost pride, and invent a new life. The conduct of the young divorcée in this film, however serious as involving a recognizable human problem, is open to the suspicion of what is known technically in psychology, and loosely in society, as 'exhibitionism.' In a sense, Hamlet himself attracts this suspicion.

In a time of publicity-seeking by nonprofessionals as well as professionals, exhibitionism is a highly charged word. It becomes oddly supercharged by *The Savage Eye*. The relation of its story to old-fashioned 'soap opera' (surviving today in certain comic strips) cannot be missed. It has a corny naïveté of its own. You may feel that what the hopelessly confused, growingly cynical heroine needs is a 'Mary Worth': the matriarchal fixer on the loose. In this light the style of the film becomes remarkable. First of all, it is photography, not popular illustration; second, it is *candid* photography for the most part; that is, while many scenes are obviously staged, there are many which are such social 'documents' as the camera has long been providing. Some stretches (for instance, in a department store and at an airport) seem taken on the sneak, the work of a hidden camera. Others seem the result of invading certain commercial establishments (a beauty parlor and a yoga studio) with the proprietor's permission and a simple direction to the customers: 'Just act natural, please!'

According to news stories, the final 'Psychodramatic' form seems to have been an afterthought to haul together, shape presentably, the findings of this 'savage eye' of the truthful film camera. But why a specifically *savage* eye? Candor, as brutal, is a well known aim of documentary trends and likewise a constant ambition of certain schools of still-photography. What modulates *The Savage Eye* in the midst of its journalistic candor is its soundtrack, which carries the stream-of-consciousness of the young divorcée, this being varied in turn by the voice of a self-identified, smooth-talking Guardian Angel who sounds (he is never seen) like one of the more voice-cultured radio announcers. I suggest that the function of the Guardian Angel is parallel with that of the Psychodrama's stage-manager director; he succeeds in being romantic and supernatural only because of his archaic descriptive tag of 'Guardian Angel.' Objectively, he is merely the voice of private conscience that issues 'warnings' and otherwise tries to 'help.' Having definitely drifted from his supervision, the young woman tries out a Faith Tabernacle. After absorbing a prodigious amount of its antics, she rushes hysterically out to her car and speeds off – nowhere. On the highway, not unnaturally, she has an accident, from which she is carried unconscious into an ambulance. In her fight for self-rehabilitation, she seems to have lost the last round.

The Savage Eye, attempting to be realistic, uses reality to show some of the orthodox social maneuvers of the masses to solve loneliness, old age, disappointment and other personal problems. One maneuver is the Social Bar; another is the loose-change Gambling Casino where, win or lose, one may have one's lunch. Another is the Yoga Studio, where one is introduced to passive body-distortions as interesting replacements of normal postures; another is merely the hat shoppe where ladies go to acquire one more lure to obtain a new husband or a new lover. All this, according to the divorcée's reactions on the soundtrack, is repellent, sometimes (as at a strip-tease entertainment and a 'drag' ball) downright vicious. In the climactic spectacle of the Faith Tabernacle, it is as horrifying to the heroine as would be the sight of a Black Mass to a Catholic. The heroine's recuperation from the accident strikes a note of hope and the movie concludes with a sentimental fillip of optimism. Apparently, the row of blood donors is a symbol of the group's healthy re-absorption of 'lost' individuals through a return to simple humanity and its basic needs. Beyond that, the film's makers have thought of nothing save an echo of 'avant-garde' dream somnambulism to state that the heroine has escaped some delusive vulgar solution through shock treatments administered by 'the savage eye.' Before she tries 'life' again, she actually seems ripe for the Psychodrama as the next step.

The English industry once did the story of a young concert pianist who suffered an auto accident in the course of searching, vainly, for true love. It was not till a psychiatrist started giving her a drug, under which she could relive her past, that she realized her true love was her former piano teacher; then she could also remember how to play again. The fact is that the divorcée of *The Savage Eye,* seriously speaking, could well take up The Method after being discharged from the hospital; that is, she could take up theatrical performance as the individual's perpetual 'psychological problem.' *The* Method, derived from the Stanislawski Method, is an institution in the American theater: the Actors' Studio in New York. Many directors and actors of stage and screen are its successful graduates, and at least two great stars, Marlon Brando and the late Marilyn Monroe, are widely thought to have been 'made' by it. One may observe of these two popular actors that their private difficulties in past years have received some very open publicity. In the case of Miss Monroe, her private life and her professional life overlapped at a truly Pirandellian angle inasmuch as the star's relations with her husband, Arthur Miller, came to a crisis in Reno while she was making there *The Misfits*, a film about a neurotic woman's divorce.

What is proudly termed The Method runs into some trouble with veteran actors as well as, allegedly, into some trouble with itself. Ingrid Bergman, after playing in television with a new American 'Method' actor, Rip Torn, told a newspaper reporter that she thought Mr Torn's acting very good but that, nevertheless, a Method actor seemed to make 'trouble for himself.' It was widely reported by the press that John Huston, who directed *The Misfits*, had some difficulty with the star, who at one point abruptly absented herself from work on the film. Anna Magnani, of all actresses, cannot be called hardened in the mold of the professional tradition. Yet, according to Tennessee Williams, it was Miss Magnani who (rather unfamiliar with English, the language she was using) became flustered during scenes in *The Fugitive Kind* by Marlon Brando's habit of being behind her cues and even inventing lines she had not heard before. This was how Mr Williams accounted for his view that, in this film, Miss Magnani gave a performance below her usual level.

All this may be somewhat mysterious to those uninformed of the nature of The Method. The Method initiates the actor into a strong rapport with the role being played so that the edges between life and artifice, the private individual and the actor, necessarily become fluid and vague. This means that the given script, as such, is subject to change. In *One-Eyed Jacks*, a film which Brando directed and whose lead he played, he was reported by *Life* to have instructed his actors (in scenes re-shot and re-shot) to make up their own lines with only the gloss of the plot to guide them. He coached them by showing them how well *he* could get along without memorized lines. Surely, in a film molded by the classic saga of the good-bad outlaw of the Old West, one can appreciate the worth of something intending to make it look fresh. But the hero-myths of nineteenth-century fiction – such as, for example, Natty Bumppo's – are so archaic that The Method, as a form of resuscitation, looks touchingly naïve.

The treatment of *One-Eyed Jacks* is, in a way, as naïve as that of *The Savage Eye*. As judged by modern experience – that is, by its standards of moral reason – the story of the good-bad outlaw of a bygone day erects 'fictions' fully as sentimental and redundant as those vulgar efforts of modern society to create ideal and efficient moral goals such as *The Savage Eye* exposes. If the romantic fictions of the former are deliberately manipulated to seem attractive rather than repellent, they are just as absurd, just as sentimental, as those from which the heroine of the latter has an understandable revulsion. The major difference between these two theatrical fictions seems to be that one is very broad and monolithic, a 'mass entertainment,' the other a set of small populist cults whose theatricalism is divided from the big professional theater. My theme is that the Psychodrama is the nexus between the one theatricalism and the other. The Method is really an agent or vehicle of this nexus.

What has Brando been able to do with the old-fashioned Western of vintage period (1880–85) through The Method? He has logically touched the spirit of the Psychodrama. The Psychodrama is, so to speak, a one-man theater with an audience of potential actors under the charge of a new-fashioned psychiatrist. The Psychodramatist's own unconscious helps and so does the 'coaching' of the psychiatrist; so does the spectacle of other Psychodramatists engaged, it is likely, with very similar 'scripts.' Let us consider in passing the professional one-man theater, whose American exponents have been monologists such as Ruth Draper and Cornelia Otis Skinner. Of course, they adhered to given scripts. But sometimes these were written by themselves; moreover, their 'theater' was a succession of imaginary selves so that their art was limited to ever renewed effort to be 'somebody else.' The abstraction from drama as a collective form of expression is the same as in the Psychodrama. But according to The Method, this abstraction is the actor's *normal* way of *participating in* a play. He makes up his own speeches in given situations *as though* he were playing 'himself,' *as though* he were living 'life.'

A professional phenomenon that helps us comprehend the Method actor's viewpoint is the existence in popular art of performers who always 'play themselves' anyway. This is true of most film comedians; one need mention only W. C. Fields and Charlie Chaplin as men whose personalities (and this was even true of Chaplin when he invented a double) were the public images of their private temperaments. Mae West is, and was, simply Mae West, and so was Mary Pickford till she had to mature. Then there was Garbo. Her public had been so much in love with her romantic mystery, abysmal voice and eyes haunted by a past and shaded by sinister black eyelashes, that both she and her public became confused when she tried to be 'somebody else.' Marlon Brando, because of distinct personal traits, has come to be in much the same position as Garbo. For him to 'act roles' in the sense that Laurence Olivier does would not only be intolerable; it would seem unnatural.

Brando's personality fits so well into his role as Rio the Kid in *One-Eyed Jacks* because he plays a grown-up, permanently rebellious child, strangely isolated in a brooding privacy, perhaps nursing some profound, elusive hurt, beautiful physically, and as tender as he is tough. To some extent, all these qualities are familiar as those of the American 'criminal hero.' But Brando is supercharged with them. He is a criminal in this film and a quasi or potential criminal in past films; he simply carries the atmosphere of the 'innocent sinister' like Mark Antony's mantle. There have been lots of Western heroes, with the seamy side plainly written on their faces, who have had to be reformed in their maturity or have carried their lonely good-bad ambiguity into the distance with them. Brando's image, on the other hand, is that of the juvenile delinquent whose rebellion has survived; the grown-up 'boy' still mystified by his responsibilities as an adult.

Brando is instinctively right to coach himself in the stance of the Method actor, for in this way he stays closest to the personality-type I have indicated. He is quite old enough to have seams in his face (as candid shots of him prove) but in *One-Eyed Jacks*, excellently photographed in color, he wears a seam-suppressing make-up, dramatically lit and registered by a cameraman who knows how to bring out the actor's ideal qualities. Hence, the truth is that Brando's face and his person are seen with the maximum of artifice. He is so graceful that at moments he looks balletic without losing virility: the male dancer's ideal achievement. He even has the lightninglike rapidity that defines the brilliant balletic style when reaching its climaxes. This accomplishment is the more remarkable in that it is precisely when Brando shows sudden violence, indeed explosive *savagery*, that his stylish brilliance, in *One-Eyed Jacks*, comes to the fore.

In his case, The Method provides that tension of inner alertness that projects character spontaneously, with *inspiration*, to the audience. 'Living one's role' has long been a part of the theatrical idiom. But an extra dimension is given it by The Method. Both in psychology and fiction, modern researches in personality and behavior have revealed the presence of the involuntary act arising from the unconscious and completed without the consent of the conscious. Albert Camus, in *The Stranger*, created a hero whose personality and fate are entirely governed by such an act. The pattern of the 'involuntary' act can easily be seen in *One-Eyed Jacks* in those cases where Brando, after a period of more or less conscious brooding, uncontrollably explodes into action – always wreaking destruc-

tion. This pattern, of course, has many ancestors in the repertory of romantic fiction. Here it has a special, very channelized
function.

It is a 'sign' which an initiated audience perfectly understands both because of Brando and the thinking customs of our
time. Event by event, Rio's conduct becomes increasingly the
result of being more 'put upon' than 'putting upon.' He has
learned all he knows as the result of bitter experience, the experience of outraged 'innocence,' and his character is simply a
carefully coached reflex-action to the aggression of others.
There is no secret made of the fact, from the film's very beginning, that Rio the Kid is a bank robber who often shoots to
kill. Then he is betrayed by a close confederate, and starts out
(according to the Western stereotype) on his revenge-mission
after suffering enough in prison to lend this mission the color
of righteousness.

No mature movie-goer can complain that there is anything
unorthodox about the plot and look of One-Eyed Jacks. The
plot could not be more type-tailored; we have seen it literally
thousands of times and its settings here are simply glorious.
Yet its manipulation is subtly marked with still further novelty
by The Method. In the dialogue, a great deal is made of the
fact that people lie. The original betrayal of Rio is the withdrawal of a promise to rescue him from capture. Even before
that, Rio is portrayed as a fraudulent love-maker who tells a
woman he is giving her a ring worn by his mother when he has
just stolen the said ring. Later, when inevitably he meets his
true love, a really pure girl, he proceeds to seduce her by a similar deception in which a necklace he has just bought plays the
same role. This time the seduction is successful and the girl
conceives an illegitimate baby. But she lies to her stepfather
(the object of Rio's revenge), and though she confesses to her
mother, her mother in turn lies to her husband. This world of
fraud, this round-robin of lies, is familiar in crime films; it is
supposed to be there. But no one is prepared to deny its moral
viciousness, or the moral viciousness of bloody cruelty which
may go hand in hand with it.

I maintain that The Method has done a great deal to make this familiar world of fraud more acceptable without changing it a jot. Rio is duly dissuaded from his revenge by the love of the girl he has seduced, eventually wins the underdog's smashing triumph – and tantalizingly departs at the end on his perpetual flight from the Law, promising the girl that he may turn up again some day. Why should this incredibly tarnished stereotype deserve all the 'trouble' taken by Method acting? One reason I have already given: the hero is Brando's one-man part. He played it in *The Fugitive Kind* with a guitar instead of a six-shooter; if the role was different, the person and his moral reflexes were the same. These moral reflexes, as I have noted, are communicated through the graces of The Method. But inevitably, roles in films are self-chosen when a great star plays them. Rio the Kid is played to the hilt with innocence aforethought. He is made to live (and speak) in that quasi-Pirandellian climate where the 'plot,' by its nature, is a suspect quantity (perhaps even a 'pack of lies') and its true usefulness is the simplest test of one's private integrity. If the style is the man, so, in Method acting and the Psychodrama, is the plot.

One must note the significance of the title in *One-Eyed Jacks* The slang epithet is spoken by Brando to characterize duplicity, being based indirectly on the proverb that, if a man's eyes are too close together, he is not to be trusted. Rio's betraying confederate has become a flourishing town's sheriff, hence a model of virtue whose criminal past is unknown. Both men, meeting again at last, deceive one another by pretending to be friendly; actually, they remain enemies. If Rio, too, is duplicit because he has a grudge-mission, one senses (for reasons already given) that he alone rebels against the world of fraud to which the plot has condemned him. Isn't he oddly like Hamlet in this respect? It is the world of fraud, which hides a crime, against which Hamlet rebels. Moreover, we sense in Hamlet his rebellion against the very revenge-mission to which he has dedicated himself.

Bluntly speaking, Hamlet's world, too, is full of 'one-eyed

Jacks.' The term comes from the profile of the two Jacks on playing cards, who keep the other sides of their faces hidden, 'and in this way establish a plastic relation with the man whose eyes 'are too close together.' Symbolically, a liar's true face is the motive which is hidden behind his visible face. Rio himself must be a one-eyed Jack, but he is a one-eyed Jack 'with a difference.' What is the difference? The difference is that self-promoted 'innocence' of the plot which a Method actor *pretends to have*, and which a Psychodramatist, at least according to theory, *really has*. The world as a fraudulent plot is imposed on Rio no less than it is on Hamlet. The substance of their similar protests against it is consciousness of an original innocence, which has been tricked into being a medium of violence and bloodshed. The whole theory of the Psychodrama is that its uncertain, confused protagonist has also been imposed on by a plot he never made, and thus his chief business is to free himself from its entanglements. To do this, both the Psychodramatist and the clinical patient have to invent words and acts. Each invents them as he goes along. In being an 'antagonist' of himself, he is an antagonist of a certain plot, a given plot. This is just the way the divorcée of *The Savage Eye* is pictured: as the antagonist of a given plot. She lends herself in desperation to 'a world she never made' and thus develops toward it a fatal allergy. The Psychodramatist of clinic or theater starts out with the idea he can turn this allergy into its own antidote: he can discover the new world of his own truth. The Method actor is debonair about the plots in which he finds himself; they are all external artifices in which the lie is basically the lie of the actor's pretense; therefore stage characters who lie offer the same problem as stage characters who tell the truth. For the Method actor draws only upon the hidden truth of *himself*.

If the sources of this contemporary American 'Method,' as a theater motif, are Russian and otherwise European, this is only what is true of American social origins. It is perfectly apt that, to intellectual Europe, our nation traditionally should be Cowboy-and-Indian country. The gangster was simply an urban version of a world picaresque hero who was revived here.

In England, Robin Hood became a scholar's archaism after being enshrined as a romantic legend; over here, he raised fresh dust as the Lone Ranger and the fleeing gangster. Such lively vestiges as he now shows seem oddly alien in this global, and notably psychiatric, era. Yet these vestiges, via The Method, have sneaked back on to the Psychodrama's clinical stage, where the 'lost' individual attempts to reintegrate with the group.

Robin Hood was a mythical gangster who might have chosen (as even the Knight Errant) to go 'on his own.' As a sheriff, he was put on his own, in a sociological sense, in *High Noon*, when a whole town denied him cooperation. In *One-Eyed Jacks*, he rejoins society as a cousin of the audacious district attorney of another urban myth: the hero (maybe tainted himself) who tackles, alone, organized political corruption. What survives as the moral emblem of this hero-type? His magic individualism as one who wishes (like a Huey Long) to lead and reform the group: one who has renounced it out of moral disgust, out of his own inherent virtue. The mount he always rides is our country's undying cult of personality. This cult is the Psychodrama's 'ghost horse.'

A newly publicized situation of the lone-wolf hero (or heroine) is that of the person of Negro blood white-looking enough to pass as a White. The pioneering film *Shadows* displays this heroism as if inadvertently. The film is declared, at its close, to be an 'improvisation.' So The Method as a plot has come into its own with very little help from the Popular Formula. The plot was seemingly an organic growth from a given situation which is quite commonplace; in other words, it is of the Psychodramatic kind; the motives form spontaneously in each person's breast, the words jump to his lips. *Shadows* graduated from film society and art house showings on to Broadway, and yet the consensus of newspaper critics, while finding some interesting realism in it, felt that many stretches of its dialogue were flat and trite. Of course, the relation of *Shadows* to Chekhov's plays and short stories, in terms of style, has received almost no mention. Yet obviously, the vaguely discontented, compulsively talkative, idle semi-bohemians and small-time theater-people of *Shadows,* on the fringe of the Beat cult, are very like Chekhov's rurally isolated, mindloose, also compulsively talkative people, whose chatting and soliloquies are projected into the ambiguous echo-chamber of the Psychodrama. I don't mean that *Shadows* achieves the finish, beauty and depth of Chekhov's art, but that it is a remarkably fertile and living work in the true experimental sense.

The white-looking younger brother and sister, presumably half related in blood to a big-brother type, dark Negro singer who supports them, form an authentic duo in unconscious incest, complicated by the element of race-prejudice, which we see ruining the girl's first love-affair and crystallizing the younger brother's brooding frustration. Both brother and sister feel unconscious resentment against the African-looking 'big brother' who is the soul of kindness to them, but who represents (in this world they 'never made') an overt handicap. It is no accident that the plot tends to explode into violence just as *One-Eyed Jacks* does – and just as Chekhov's plays do. The pattern of violence always rises from a ferment of protest just beneath the social surface. The younger brother and sister are a pair of 'One-Eyed Jacks' showing white on the outer side, black on the under. They do not *mean* to 'deceive' but their very physical appearance leads people, who do not know their brother, to think them 'white.' *Shadows,* in the movement of its plot and dialogue, succeeds admirably in conveying the *quality* of the lives of brother and sister, their unique situation as members of society. The Psychodrama could do no better in this way. But in the end, there is no true revelation of the individual to himself, no elucidation of the terms of his problem, much less of its solution; that is, there is no *tragic* revelation, no *untragic* revelation. *Shadows* begins and ends like many of Chekhov's works, without dramatic emphasis, as though fortuitously.

It is not modern, and I daresay it is not even American, to be tragic. The agonic American's self-revelation is too theoretical and experimental in life to be represented as final in art. Proof of this is furnished by two very significant American novels of recent decades: *The Great Gatsby* and *All the King's Men*, whose 'heroes' are, respectively, a bigtime gangster and a bigtime politician. In both cases, there is an observer for whom they become objects of hero-worship as well as virtual alter-egos. The 'stage' of their careers (both of which end disas-trously with their assassination) is a platform where a sort of Psychodramatist-hero acts out a vicarious life for the hero-worshipper. In another of Scott Fitzgerald's works, *The Crack Up,* he performed a 'Psychodrama' that literally predicted his own disastrous end. We may glance aside at the unfortunately publicized private life of a strictly contemporary novelist, Nor-man Mailer, to see the same thing taking place, not on a printed page, but in the immediate flow of life. Apparently, according to Mailer's reported statements, the explosive event that once took place in his home was an act as 'involuntary' as that of Camus' 'stranger,' Meursault.*

I suggest that the Psychodrama, as an American theater motif, is a precise sign of the search for a new operative identity by no means confined to individuals, but of which the individual (in the theater and elsewhere) becomes a conspicuous medium. This motif has a markedly experimental cast, of which The Method is the theatrical formula. The degree of public atten-tion gained by an off-Broadway repertory organization, The Living Theatre, tends to show the general influence of the hidden Psychodramatic aim. In one original play, *The Marry-ing Maiden*, the actors' lines were partly determined by a throw of the dice (based on the Chinese system of *I Ching*) so that they had the effect of projecting in echo-chambers of the hid-den self. An element of the fate of the personality thus be-comes *chance* itself, which here is another name for uncon-scious impulse. The directorial techniques of The Living Theatre (whose very name suggests an experimental fusion of reality and artifice) tend toward audience-participation and thus improvisation, or at least the illusion of improvisation.

* Lately Mailer has begun to make films himself. The latest, *Beyond the Law*, has some vitality as *cinéma vérité* and perhaps serves for Mailer as Psychodramatic self-therapy.

Today, the world is very consciously concerned with systematic 'curative' measures of various scopes. There are wide-range programs that, if successfully carried through, will settle social problems of far-reaching extent. Necessarily, with so many economic and political factors involved, the 'experimental' note of these programs is unavoidable. For this very reason, there are ever-renewed parleys that are expected to produce, happily, some inspired idea that will have the magical effect of uniting dissident factions, of making pacific what was unpacific. Small wonder that what are known as 'plots' in the theater should reflect this positively experimental and improvisational motif. Meanwhile, in our tight, tortured world, embarrassing 'explosions' of discontent take place, 'areas of danger' suddenly raise their alarming heads.

The value of the concept of the Psychodrama is to show us a theatrical motif that is a direct key to social truth. Perhaps we may take an ambivalent pride in the fact that this motif is peculiarly American. It is in our plays, novels and movies, where what I may risk calling the Method Hero bluntly exposes himself. I think no one represents this hero better, in the theatrical medium today, than Marlon Brando. He (this 'hero') is mainly concerned with establishing, as a moral and prevailing quantity, an original *innocence* – and he does not care how much violence this aim entails. The 'conquering hero' is already an anachronism. No matter how many fist-fights or gun-battles he wins, he typically remains a fugitive; he lives on the loose, unraveled end of life. What he infallibly needs is a New Start. It is for this reason that the Juvenile Delinquent is far more than the label of a classifiable social problem, far more than an under-age, vestigial 'romantic hero.' He is the very form of the deep moral predicament which *a hero*, by definition, must represent in our age. He is the first state of the ambiguous good-bad hero, the gangster and the racketeering politician, and in essence, in the United States, *he has replaced this hero*. In brief, he is the *maturest* hero, this man armed with a Method, that we have.

The Method, it appears, is one limited way out of the social trap, the labyrinth of confusion which is this hero's moral climate. It is *not* a given script in art or in life. *Wisdom* is a given script. The *tragic catharsis* is a given script. These are not blessings for him, the Method hero; nor are they simply models of behavior which he consents (even as theatrical make-believe) to follow. They are social platforms for the beginning of a search for personal truths that will form a practical identity, a 'working' identity. In this light, a stereotyped 'character' or a freshly minted, creative one are much the same in the theater or in life. The Method is superior to madness and effectively updated from the inspiration of Hamlet's creator. It accommodates anything from a punch on the nose to a dirty word; from bloody murder to murdering the script. It is an already formulated American 'freedom' that has given us propulsion, and might well give us pause. In our midst on two kinds of stages, the clinic's and the theater's, it brings 'acting' into attunement with life.

8. Maze of the Modern Sensibility: An Antonioni Trilogy

Antonioni is not merely one of the film-makers with the new spirit; he is one who has rightfully earned the reputation of being 'new' in the best sense of the word. As might be expected, he has achieved his novelty through re-emphasizing an old, and true, trait of the film; if today we can call this trait 'advanced,' it is because, at an historic moment, the visual strength of the film was adulterated – or at least complicated and theoretically compromised – by the introduction of sound dialogue as an integral part of the form. Antonioni's style – best visible in the trilogy, *L'Avventura, La Notte* and *L'Eclisse* – is a return to the visual as the medium's prime instrument.

Let us consider this proposition. Suppose none of the above three films had a soundtrack, that the dialogue was quite missing, either as spoken words or subtitles. Isn't it true that each film, certainly *L'Avventura* and *L'Eclisse*, would still come across with basic significance intact? I don't mean that the dialogue between the actors does not, in all cases, enrich the meaning. In *La Notte* the dialogue is especially important toward the end. All the same, while speech is an integral part of each film, the eye of the camera has always been charged with telling an eloquent story, unusually meaningful for the hour in which we live.

What the camera in each film relates is an articulate skeleton for Antonioni's incidental message. Each film thus has a plot made exclusively of visible action in the ordinary physical and human sense, and this action remains foremost in meaning beyond what is said by the dialogue.

Take *L'Avventura*. Assuming we were to ignore the dialogue, we would still be well aware of the relationship between a man and a woman, Sandro and Anna, and that a second woman, Claudia, is a friend of Anna's, perhaps (ironically) her best friend. Actually, at first, the dialogue hinders rather than helps. Through the mere pantomime of Anna and Sandro in the house while Claudia waits outside, we guess an odd tension between a pair of lovers. Then the three go on to the yachting party. Obviously these are well-to-do upper-class people, rather frivolous, rather bored, taking it easy while they try to enjoy an outing on the water and give their more private urges an airing. Again, pantomime alone is sufficient when Anna makes a gift of a dress to Claudia – a symbolic anticipation of her replacement, by Claudia, as Sandro's lover. Anna's subsequent disappearance, the search for her, the anxious gloom of everyone, are all very much on the visible surface. Sandro's attraction to Claudia, her resistance, her suspicion of him – all this is conveyed by the pantomime alone. There are many wordless stretches where only musical motifs or fragmentary speech reflect the quality and meaning of the physical action. The rest of the plot is structured just as optically.

Much the same is true of *La Notte*. Of course, without the dialogue at the start, we would not learn the dying man's very special relation to the married couple, Lidia and Giovanni. But we would know Giovanni's manner of being unfaithful to his wife (as in his encounter with the nymphomaniac being treated at the hospital) and that this denotes a rising crisis in the marital relationship. It is even arguable whether the dialogue, though interesting and revealing, adds very much to the serious depth of the situation. That Giovanni is an author, we learn at the party for his new book. All remarkably 'optical' for a film issued in 1960! The lavish party at the rich magnate's home is self-explanatory, to say the least; again, we find Giovanni philandering as the tone gets sexy, though in this case the ladies resist: the magnate's daughter, Valentia, won't be seduced by the husband, Giovanni, and his wife, Lidia, won't let a roving Don Juan seduce her. All is said with a crystalline camera. However, at the end we do need the dialogue between Lidia and Giovanni to receive the full flavor of ambiguity in their emotional crisis; still, if we lacked it, we might well assume that the sudden fit of love-making after their little scene at dawn may be a stopgap for a lifetime of quarrelsome togetherness.

I think our third film ought to be considered just as specifically. In *L'Eclisse* two lovers have just quarreled, and at one point we realize they have stayed up all night to do so; most of this first stretch is, significantly, quite wordless. What is said when this couple, Vittoria and Riccardo, do converse, clinches the matter. She is breaking off their affair. She doesn't say exactly why, for there is often no reasonable explanation when love comes and goes. We see, rather than hear, how apathetic she is; she conveys a certain 'modern' feeling. He is very unwilling and does not 'understand,' but she disengages herself, won't see him again. The days go on; she scarcely knows what to do with her life. . . . There is nothing the camera has not been effectual in telling.

Vittoria seems not to want a new lover. But then she meets the young man at the Stock Exchange. The Stock Exchange needs no sound mechanism to let us know what *it* is, although its sounds make it more exciting, more itself. Its mad, monotonous music goes with it as song goes with sexual longing. Step by step, we see the new couple, Piero and Vittoria, getting together as he starts persuading her to make it an affair; he has not quite succeeded when a crucial rendezvous is scheduled. Antonioni now brings off a striking anticlimax. There is a stretch of the simplest action – and it is altogether background action. It is the general scene of the rendezvous, which neither keeps, the particular street corner where they have held hands, languished at each other, hesitated, brooded, kissed; at least Vittoria has hesitated. Though Piero seems finally to have won her consent, it is *her* mood which prevails. Shot after shot shows us the familiar street corner and other things we have seen, a nursemaid, a horseman, some playing boys; as twilight comes, a bus emptying itself of commuters from the city.... That is all.

I have sketched out Antonioni's three films this way not merely to draw attention to their highly filmic nature but also to lead to a comprehension of their significance and of the film-maker's views of modern life and love. Antonioni has become one of the most intellectual film-makers in history. He used to write scripts for Fellini but now directs as well as writes his films, the latter with script-collaborators. He has been induced by interviewers to talk at length about his films – his approach to their technical problems, his motives, the conceptions he wished to express. What he has said is enlightening yet, I should say, not enlightening enough. A concrete reading of the films themselves, as corroborated by Antonioni, will serve us better, I think, in grasping them objectively.

Antonioni's views, the substance of what he has said to interviewers, is actually not very startling to those already initiated into modern novels and modern thought in general. Without affectation, this film-maker is saturated in the contemporary mood and viewpoint we know as Existentialist. Unfortunately, his reasoning, while provocative and full of cues, is not nearly so concise and lucid as his films themselves. What stands out most clearly in his ideas, seen through his work, is a direct grasp of men and women in relation to a landscape: what amounts to an interpretation of modern love through actual environmental symbols.

Consider our trilogy as suites of fluid, panoramic pictures. Of course, one remembers them as more intricate than the versions just outlined. The main impression, surely, is of *figures in a landscape*, just such as exist conventionally in landscape painting. It is rewarding to glance at the large tradition of landscape painting. Even the most conventional and insipid romantic painting, or academic painting, is more than just decorative, does a little more than utilize human beings as mere details of a large pictorial pattern. Figures are present in landscape painting not just to diversify a vista or humanize unpeopled nature; they are there to point up a certain relationship between humanity and its environments. True, in the Western World until Renaissance times, nature might have been called only 'background' in painting. But then men began to appreciate 'picturesque' nature for its own sake: a nature where man was a mere spectator, included for the sake of 'documenting' his own presence, a nature that (though man might be absent) imitated one of the vistas he had begun to consider aesthetic.

By and large, in all pictures of nature *and* man, their relationship to each other is somehow implied. *L'Avventura* is a perfect illustration. How crucially vivid is the relation of the wild island of volcanic rock to the party which invades the waters around it, how crucially vivid is the island as a symbol of desolation in regard to the lost girl Anna! This volcanic island is *barren* nature – a kind of open, unattractive labyrinth without clues, frightening, causing the searchers to seem alien nomads. Antonioni, discussing his films with students and teachers at an experimental film school in Rome in 1961, mentioned something vital and central to his method and his source of inspiration. He said that in making his first film, *Cronaca di un Amore,* he found it interesting, spontaneously, to keep the camera going on his actors after a scene had ended; in short, he filmed them behaving 'out of character' while in the same fictitious environment. It was a psychological inspiration to be expected of the race that had produced the playwright Pirandello. The interesting element was that the actors had become detached from *any* environment, momentarily, and walked as it were in a no-man's land, a special sort of moral vacuum, being not wholly out of character and yet not in their own lives.

A director's passing impulse became a creed. Antonioni would make a style, a moral way of life, by showing men and women detached from their environment – something in the manner of actors as they work themselves out of a role while remaining in the environment that has been responsible, so to speak, for creating their roles. One can see how in this director's four later films, *Il Grido* and our trilogy, a lone person or two lovers wandering about become an integral part of the story: a part of its *suspense*. The image of individuals mentally detached from their surroundings constitutes a typical and telling concept of modern society.

Apparently on the other hand, Antonioni has never drawn any very definite or satisfying conclusions from his subject, preferring to investigate it as a motif of modern behavior. The hero's vain, unhappy odyssey in *Il Grido* shows it in a rather primitive form, being only a long prelude to his suicide. It is equally visible, and more complex, in Anna's disappearance in *L'Avventura* and the unsuccessful search for her; in the wife's lengthy wandering in *La Notte* and the prolonged, wistful pursuit of consummation by the pair of lovers in *L'Eclisse,* ending with the anticlimax of an unkept rendezvous: scenes showing *only* the environment.

To Antonioni the typical situation of his loving couples lies in what he calls their 'irrational and desperate attempt to make physical contact.' That is radical wording; in fact, I think, a bit wild. As for physical contact, we can assume lots of it in the trilogy. So it would be precise to revise Antonioni's wording even if we have to assume a deal of speculativeness as to why two people, as it were, find it so difficult, in his films, to 'get together.' It could be a matter, as seems true in *La Notte,* of *re*-establishing physical contact between a wife and a husband; then it could be a matter of physical contact as a purely moral value: a morally sanctioned contact; then, too, it might be a complex sexual problem of contact: sexual consummation as thoroughly satisfying. Yet just because Antonioni's stories leave us to speculate about the nature of his lovers' contact, what he really seems to be after is a quality for which none of the foregoing definitions would be an adequate explanation. What he is pointing to is an indefinable vacuum in which it is easy to make love, any kind of love, but that once this vacuum is attached to reality and enters an order beyond vacuums, it is hard to fall in love – to make the contact Antonioni basically means.

Love as an instinct, the Eros of mythical culture, has failed. In romance, in poetry, even in magical religion, the emotion of love, its ecstasy, has stood warrant beyond any everyday, secular sanction such as that of marriage or what we call fidelity in love. Antonioni does bring something into drastic and unavoidable question: the erotic ecstasy itself. What has seemed supreme to poets, to the heroes and heroines of love tragedies, seems to have lost all credit in the world evoked by Antonioni. His films show simple eroticism as base, as in the incidental seduction of the young painter in *L'Avventura*, or psychopathic, as in the hospital incident in *La Notte*. In the world of sane and serious women, says Antonioni, making physical contact is a great problem. Sandro and the girl, Claudia, who has supplanted the lost girl, Anna, try to make contact in this spirit, their failure and desperation reducing them to tears at the end. Making love to a fancy whore has been easy for Sandro; what is hard is for him to have a serious affair. Asking how true is this viewpoint is the same as asking how true, how wide and how valid, is Existentialist philosophy.

On this ground very large issues must be considered. Regardless of wars, for example, regardless of national hatreds and national rivalries, nature, as such, does go on. Men and women are duly attracted to each other, they mate and produce their kind: mankind. For the present purpose, we can assume the same is true of the rest of nature: the lower orders and their reproduction. Yet man – man alone – is conscious, it would seem, of an obstacle to the satisfying achievement of this supposedly eternal and properly natural process. His fears and doubts, in general, have made him lose faith in every aspect of it – even in love – as a great physical experience: the heroic moment of ecstasy. Antonioni's own term for the moral situation of lovers is stalemate. Good enough. The description is even true of the less believable lovers in *Last Year at Marienbad*. Antonioni has made an interesting statement in connection with his avowed theme. While morally conscious, man today, he declares, 'has no fear of the scientific unknown,' he is 'afraid of the moral unknown.'

As Antonioni's specific explanation of the stalemate in *L'Avventura*, this gets him in very deep water, far over the heads of his characters in their conscious concerns. But what does the statement in itself signify? Man, I suppose, is to be considered unafraid of the scientific unknown because he is invading far space so dauntlessly and defying the moral consequences of opening some of nature's deepest secrets and harnessing them. Ah, but the moral unknown! This he is thought to fear, and his fear leads him, if we believe Antonioni, to stalemate. What is striking about this formulation is its assumption that human morality is an 'unknown.' The future is necessarily implied by the term *unknown*. To some extent, the future is by its nature unknown. On the other hand, in terms of life, the future also contains a program established by two things: natural facts and human morality. There are orders, systems, of both. For many thousands of years, human morality has been an accumulation of wise, that is to say, practical agenda governed by social and religious rules. Why should morality therefore appear as a bogeyman of the 'unknown'? Why indeed? This much, Antonioni has established: his characters are rendered helpless, and eventually defeated, by fear. But why should they be so afraid? Like children, they seem afraid of – *la notte*.

Perhaps Antonioni, I suggest, has placed a greater burden of concern on their shoulders than average human experience justifies. Be that as it may, I think they appear credible and valid if we assume they represent a certain modern kind of fable: they suffer from a certain pathological condition of mind whose explanation can be found in Freud, who called it paranoia. (Although I do not fasten on Antonioni's characters – or on Antonioni, for that matter – the technical strait-jacket of being paranoiacs.) They simply illustrate this type of emotional imbalance and mental disorientation. Antonioni lets them loose in a moral landscape – the landscape of the agoraphobe where openness is the sinister, the frightening element. Why should these 'figures in a landscape' be so relevant, so much a part of our problems as a race today? Precisely because the 'sinister' element in open places today is the element of radioactivity. In the moral sense, the threat of extinction by atomic explosion or fallout becomes latent and is easily transferred to symbols. As certain films in a recent New York Film Festival told us, tranquilizers, sleeping pills and drugs are assoc-lated threats as things also undermining human health and capable of destroying it.

One film at the New York Festival * made drugs into a moral necessity in the world of the future where atomic war had driven the surviving remnant of humanity into a miserable underground existence with no hope for individuals then alive. Thus drugs and other stimulants are no longer voluptuous vices, aids to sexual ecstasy and the refuge of aesthetes and eccentrics, but the very last resort of humanity made desperate. I refer to the existence of a psychic milieu, a milieu that encompasses the scare of a drug such as thalidomide, with its threat to human generation, and of insecticide on a massive scale when it becomes potentially harmful to men and animals as well as insects.

I don't think I exaggerate by filling out the psychological factors that go to make up the overwhelming fear of the future – the moral unknown to which I believe Antonioni refers. One might protest that after all, in the case of Antonioni's films, the troubled people (who apparently have no recourse to drugs) seem well-adjusted, leisured types, and high in the professional world; attractive, with a better than average chance, one might say, for ordinary happiness. Why should *they* fear the moral unknown so much as to be radically stalemated by it? As I say, Freud's paranoia supplies the answer. The roots of paranoia are not on the surface; we can only guess and identify it by its manifestations.

Paranoia is a psychological affliction manifesting itself in extreme fear or delusion of grandeur, so that the sufferer is detached, at last, from the actual conditions of life surrounding him. This state can originate only in some early experience of shock, some major dislocation of natural desire or drastic assault on the self-esteem – some hopelessly frustrated yet impassioned need. The hero of *Il Grido* is a perfect example. The insult given his sexual ego by the loss of a woman's love is something from which he never recovers. This woman has given him an erotic delusion of grandeur; no other woman thereafter can fulfill his need, with the result that he destroys

* 1963.

himself out of prolonged hopelessness. Antonioni had not found his true stride in *Il Grido*: its hero is too obviously a maladjusted individual to partake of the agoraphobia of the *moral landscape*. Yet his sexual temperament suggests that of Anna in *L'Avventura*. At first Anna strikes us as a sort of nymphomaniac, unable to let a private moment with her lover go by without the impulse to make love. Nymphomania is a state inspired by various fears: fear of impotence, fear of losing a lover, fear of injury to the self-esteem. Maybe Anna senses the ebbing of Sandro's love, not specifically because Claudia has won it away, but perhaps because of her own overdeveloped eroticism, her own delusion of sexual grandeur, vulnerable to the first whisper of suspicion.

Freud pointedly, and I think truly, says that to the paranoid personality, nothing seems indifferent, everyone and everything seems involved; the world itself is in a conspiracy to exalt or damn the paranoid individual. This is an autointoxicated state familiar to modern thought and profusely verified by phenomena quite outside Antonioni's films. The morally starved lonely paranoiac, guiltless of crime, imagines that detectives follow him everywhere. Sex-starved, unstable women visualize rapists in every dark corner of house and street. Any shadowy, unseemly or ambiguous aspect of nature is apt to arouse a paranoid sort of fear. May not the huge island rock, desolate and forbidding, symbolize to Anna the ultimate desert of her fate as a sexual being – that is, unsatisfied yearning, the humiliation of desertion or desolation? Thus, getting lost, she contrives suddenly to abandon all struggle. She falls or deliberately drops to her death; or, what would be more significant, she may have allowed herself to be kidnapped by a stray band of smugglers, committing herself at last to prostitution.

According to this scheme, what Sandro and Claudia then come to fear is the shadow of paranoia which Anna's disappearance has obscurely thrown over their lives in the tragic search for her into which the pair are drawn. They step cautiously and encounter unexpected, ominous things: the closed 'ghost town' where they knock in vain, the roaring train that passes so close to their embraces. Antonioni mentions the symbolism of Mount Aetna in the far distance of the last shot in *L'Avventura:* Aetna is a sleeping threat, its eruptive power a symbol of sex as delusion of grandeur. The sex impulse has been taken into a vast landscape beyond its local habitation in men and women.

Antonioni is important because the human predicament he evokes is profound. We should not be facile in judging his version of that predicament, either its principles or its facts, if only because around his work a certain vagueness, a fog of motive, hovers. A moot aesthetic question is how mysterious one can be about what is already mysterious, how vague one can be about what is already vague. Antonioni's heroes and heroines (however decisively we might classify them as paranoid) are mystified, hesitant persons, and characteristically vague in communicating themselves. The conclusion of each film of the trilogy is, one might say, suggestively vague. That of *La Notte* is the least vague because, however desperately, it throws in its lot with the act of sex as something definite, at least externally.

Suppose we were to rate Antonioni's distinguished trilogy as an inspired begging of a great question. He does not show his characters as actually psychopathological but models them to intimate the presence of the danger, the total perversion and alienation from the reality of sex. This is his note, his mood, his music – this threat, this forecast of doom. We can see how individual Antonioni is by comparing him with his countryman, Pirandello. The latter was much more excited about the same sort of moral problem; he made human doubt and indecision root itself in individual identity and its moral drive. Pirandello, however, came before the age of the threat of racial extinction. The deepest moral problem affecting human beings, in the age to which we have come, would not be the identity of the *individual*, his specific and organic and functional personality, but the identity of the *race*, which may become extinct before it has perfected itself, before it learns just what man is, how much 'god,' so to speak, is in him. We could term this problem that of man's universal identity, his identity with time and space and all other beings. Many religions, of course, are sup-

posed to have solved this question; on the other hand, however content men have been to live by the rules of religion and
philosophy, war is a great human hurt which has never been
eliminated.

Tentatively, Antonioni may well have this same issue in
mind, this 'atmosphere' of question and inescapable peril, and
so his vagueness might be thought proper. When other people,
such as those represented by his characters, become aware of
this perilous atmosphere and cannot explain it, they merely
register the quandary of it, the embarrassment, the risk. They
come to know much about its terms, its circumstances, its
way-stations; about identity, they know nothing – it is as if
they dared not look. ... They can only suffer and perhaps give
up. Is the situation not merely hopeless, but also hopelessly
paradoxical? Perhaps not. Antonioni's consciously held views
may give us a useful clue. He says that he means to represent
people hopelessly 'detached from their environment,' while
Freud, we recall, takes his analysis of paranoia a big step further: the paranoid personality becomes *de*tached from the real
environment, from what is immediate and actual, only to become *at*tached, through psychological delusion, to the whole
universe (nature, society, individuals) which he assumes is involved with his private affairs. Good. But under what precise
aspect does the universe 'concern' itself? Only under a delusive aspect. All the while, the universe is not really involved,
concerned – not its men, its animals, its stars, its winds, its rain,
its earth. Underneath his delusion, the paranoid knows this and
it bothers him a great deal. Freud's and Antonioni's interpreta-
tions of modern society in its paranoid motives exactly
complement each other. Antonioni is really carrying out a
necessary implication of Freud's hypothesis. The paranoid's
inner desires are not being fulfilled; moreover, his condition is
the direct result of his belief that they can never be fulfilled. But
this vision is so terrible that he refuses to believe it. He evokes
the very skies and total strangers to help him prove it untrue;
the proof of world phenomena is entirely delusive but he
accepts it, in nightmarish fear or delusion of grandeur, as positive and final.

As I have implied, this is not Antonioni's explicit formulation when questioned as to the meanings of his films. He imagines his people have got at the reality of things, and that this means alienation from the world that seems made for them. The up-shot for his characters would seem to be: how true, how typical, is the conviction of civilized beings that one is apt to be alienated from personal love today? The answer to that, I think, is that it depends upon the response of individuals to the aggression of external conditions in the world; this aggression tends to create a general insecurity in the individual, to pro-mote all his moral fears. Granting the truth of the moral situa-tion between two lovers in Antonioni's trilogy, there is a sen-sible effort in lovers, today, to escape from the problem with dignity, to yield to its insolubility, but not without being aware of its crucial importance.

In the climactic *L'Eclisse*, the enemy of love is understood by the heroine as signified by the Stock Exchange; the inward and spiritual luxury of the senses is opposed, and fatally, by the outward and materialistic luxury of money and animal appe-tite. The most insidious danger, as Vittoria in her long hesita-tion seems to realize, is that the symbol replaces that for which it stands. Sensibility is finally ruled out; luxury becomes the desert that is suggested by the wild party at the industrialist's home in *La Notte*. When the collapse of the market takes place, Vittoria observes how a 'ruined man' behaves, being struck by his 'hygienic' mildness under the blow. Virtually bankrupt, he takes it philosophically, has an alka-seltzer and occupies his mind with doodling at a café table. I think that at this mo-ment, Vittoria realizes that she, too, as a lover, is bankrupt and that her flirtation with Piero is, probably, a form of erotic doodling.

The erotic fatality hinted here would be an Existentialist despair in love without making visible all its inward struggles but showing them as if documentarily. On the philosophic level, we are obliged to refer to myth and its moral significance in human history. It could be argued, with Antonioni's trilogy as proof, that man is in permanent exile from happiness, not that we are merely passing through a bad phase in this era. In short, Adam has permanently been driven from the Garden of Eden.

It is interesting to note, in an issue of the *Cesare Barbieri Courier* (Vol. III, No. 2), however, the opposing existentialist stand taken by the Italian school of philosophers in modern times. This is an optimistic rather than a pessimistic Existentialism. Despair may exist but it does not automatically develop as paranoia or as a confirmed philosophy of pessimism. Professor Abbagnano says that the Italian school rests its hope on possibility, that is, on changes possible in the future. In other words, the idea of the perfectibility of man is not dead but vital. This Existentialism, says Abbagnano, views the human situation from a scientific viewpoint. Social morality is a laboratory where experiments will be followed through on the premise that improvements can be made – general improvements in moral and physical health that will affect individuals.

I did not want to close without offering this larger light in which we can estimate and further think about Antonioni's trilogy. Cannot we suppose that, accordingly, these good-looking people, so eligible in most ways, might have more courage, a better education one might say, and shake off the contagion of the Atomic Age of paranoia and its ambiguous landscape? Maybe it is possible to make the best of the worst of all possible worlds by doing a little better than Kierke-gaard's successors, provided we can take them seriously in their despair. In effect, we find men and women stranded in a kind of mythological country in Antonioni's films. This country, if it be only psychopathological territory and not Existentialist territory, might be 'saved' for better things. How deliberately fashionable is Antonioni being as a teller of tales? His sensibility, in any case, is a most interesting gauge, a veritable barometer and seismograph. Antonioni's filmic genius may have 'vamped' us a little into imagining we have more in common with his human situations than is necessary, or than we really have. Yet, just in putting the question before us in so rich and competent a way, this Italian film director's achievement is a major one from any view.

9. The Messianic Complex

Above a line cut of his signature, Robert Penn Warren wrote a statement about the film version of his Pulitzer Prize novel, *All the King's Men*, which appeared in New York papers as an advertisement. After praising the independent authenticity of the screen characters and story, he says: 'In this picture, I think there is intensity without tricks and pretensions, and always a sense of truth: such a thing as this could happen in a world like this.' With what a magnificent sideways motion Mr Warren has pointed a steady finger at the dark mysteries of Hollywood – yes, 'a world like this' is, and could be, nothing but the local spot, the very scene of the crime, where American movies are largely made and almost totally conceived.

If Mr Warren, because of his peculiar position as the author of the novel, must be gingerly, there is no reason for me to be. I ask bluntly: If Jack Burden, the narrator of both film and novel, is caught in the mesh of an action which it takes dearly bought experience to induce him to believe he understands, isn't Mr Warren under the same burden of compulsion with his novel in the stark hands of Hollywood? Mr Warren's generous tribute to the Hollywood vision of things covers a multitude of modifications, big and little. These might appear slight or random to someone with reasons, but to someone without reasons, such as myself, who has respect for the novel but none at all for the screen version, they make all the difference, indeed, between a world like Hollywood's and a world like Mr Warren's. The major revision will indicate the degree to which everything must newly conform: Judge Irwin of the novel becomes Judge Stanton of the screen, an uncle of Adam and Anne Stanton; as such, his secret paternity of Jack Burden, in vanishing, disposes of one of the crucial elements of the novel's plan.

On the silver screen, all adds up to a considerably solid defacement. The casting of the character of Willie Stark himself is a key to the web of artistic mayhem. The screen type is well known: he is a burly man with a flattened nose who, if cast strictly to Hollywood type, would appear as an ex-pug, possibly a strong-arm man in the bodyguard of a big-city politician; he is not a Southern hick lawyer or a surrogate for Huey Long, he is an old-fashioned 'gorilla.' And he talks like one, straight from the boss's (not his) mouth. The accent is East Side, moreover, not Deep South. I am trying to say, more directly than did Mr Warren, that Broderick Crawford as Willie Stark is not in any respect convincing as the character in Warren's novel, and scarcely even as a human being, unless you find good, round, unpretentious Hollywood ham to your taste in the theatre.

Some literary critics complained, I believe, that Mr Warren liked Huey Long's surrogate too much. But if he did, his novel justified his extravagance to the hilt. If Willie has a certain essential elusiveness to Jack Burden, who is Mr Warren's mouthpiece, he has the same for the reader. But this elusiveness has a suggestive contour and a clear poetic substance. Willie talks with some of the color of the Bible and the Elizabethans, and it sounds natural because, as Jack Burden believes, in a way he *means* it. (Mr Crawford has been told, of course, that Willie doesn't mean it; people only think he does.) How did Burden know Willie meant it? He knew because Mr Warren conceived these passages of Willie's speech in inspiration and they relate to a center of intelligence one couldn't find in the film with a squad of detectives and a search warrant.

To what is Mr Warren referring, then, with such perfect dis-
cretion when he speaks of the film as 'a world like this'? He
refers to a world without coherent ideas, but more than that, to
a world without any intent to make ideas cohere, for it is a
world whose profession is to understate and if possible avoid
the intellectual consciousness of the real world.

Whatever Mr Warren accomplished in his novel, either as
work of art or as social commentary, he took the real world
for his inevitable setting, for he wanted to state something sin-
cerely. Jack Burden's role as moral chorus for Willie's quasi-
tragic career as demagogue, as well as Willie's own role of
people's messiah, are stated succinctly in the film as truthfully
as orthodox Hollywood can hope to say it. This statement
occurs in miniature when a sort of 'March of Time' newsreel
within the film is made of Stark's career, and the commentator
declaims at the end fortissimo: 'Messiah or Dictator?' The
conversion of supposed life into formal terms is scientifically
accurate here if we accept, as the world of this film adaptation,
the world we are in when we sit in a newsreel theatre. What
happens to Willie Stark's life by way of the newsreel-short is
the same as happens to the novel – to Jack Burden's continual
struggle with himself and his search for Willie's true meaning
– on a more elaborate scale in Robert Rossen's screen story.
The latter is streamlined, consciously reduced in dramatic and
intellectual stature, and converted, in brief, to the terms in
which assiduous readers of *Time* and *Life* regard everything
from the atom bomb to the writings of Gertrude Stein. These
terms are those to which a state of goggle-eyed detachment is
all-receptive.

A sure-fire system of reading the misreadings of the film is
in respect to the screen's dialogue, where paraphrases and dup-
lications of the novel's words have been used. Screen synopsis
has a cute way of rejuggling situations, and thereby compli-
ments itself on prodigious feats achieved in the interests of
condensation as well as convenience. But everywhere that one
may identify condensation in the film version one may just as
clearly perceive falsification. Now Mr Warren himself has
opened the way (in gentlemanly manner) to considering the

filmic *All the King's Men* a separate entity, perhaps as though it bore something of the relation of *Alice in Wonderland* to the life of a real little girl in Carroll's own era. If, by some curious move of fate, the *Iliad* were to be translated into Ojibway, I suppose there might be valid grounds for concluding that, so far as the Ojibways went, a very satisfying job had been done on the Homeric epic. But I dare say not every soul who sits in a movie theatre is an Ojibway or first cousin to one.

Though I put myself in the position of one with a Homeric rather than a Hollywoodian attitude toward Mr Warren's novel, let us be perfectly fair. Eric Bentley's criticism of the novel's shortcomings should be studied and expanded.* For Mr Bentley went so far as to place Mr Warren's world grazingly close to what came to be Mr Rossen's world: 'The worst thing you can truthfully say about *All the King's Men*,' observed Mr Bentley, 'is that the almost Hollywoodian thriller which is Warren's vehicle is all too easily separable from his theme.' Indeed? Is Mr Warren, one may wonder, trying to dissociate himself from the very deed he helped to perpetrate? The existence of the film brings into sharp and inevitable focus, then, the literary problem itself. If the film had achieved this focus on the grounds of asserting jealously its true filmic rights, a separate if genuine artistry, it would be different, but what it asserts is the mere existence of the literary-filmic type of the 'thriller.'

One is inclined to appreciate the delicacy and underlying gravity of Mr Warren's position in the matter. What have the Jack Burden and the Willie Stark of the screen done, in crystallizing characters less valid and interesting than their novelistic prototypes, but likewise crystallize, in Mr Warren's direction, the pejorative elements of melodrama and journalism that, according to Mr Bentley, inhere in the original work? In the literary perspective, Jack Burden has not only his own complexity (embodied chiefly in his ambition to write Cass Mastern's story rather than Willie Stark's) but also a special complexity in relation to his counterparts in other works of

* Eric Bentley, 'The Meaning of Robert Penn Warren's Novels,' *Kenyon Review*, Summer 1948.

Robert Penn Warren. Mr Warren has publicly hinted that this negative functioning of the film be disregarded in favor of something it does on its own – does for the masses who care not at all for any of his characters who live only in print, and who care just as little for the subtlety of Burden's relation to R.P.W.

I suggest – with, I confess, some timidity – that Mr Warren may suspect that in the routine Fascist toggery with which Mr Crawford as Stark is gotten up may abide as much or more of 'the truth about Huey Long' than he has put into his novel. And I suggest – with decreasing timidity – that this state of honest confusion may exist in Mr Warren because he embarked on his project as something more of an allegory than its actual guise gives one leave to assume (hence the pertinence of Mr Bentley's comment, that, as for naturalism, Mr Warren's is 'not naturalistic enough'). But if this is true, and if Jack Burden's ambivalent feeling for Stark reflects (as I should say) R.P.W.'s ambivalent feeling for what a Huey Long represents, Mr Warren's glad hand for the movie might well be attached to an arm with a mourning band. The novelist certainly knows that where he has a thousand ways of touching off, bodying forth, the inner irrational that is Willie Stark, the film has three or four: the rest is stereotyped façade, paraphernalia, the rush of sound and matter through space.

I should identify the innate drama of the novel as based on a contest of poetic attitudes. Willie Stark's rhetoric is not the only 'classical' element in his nature. As a Homer of the Redneck's consciousness, he is also a Pisistratus, a 'benefactor of the poor,' and his methods are much as Pisistratus' are reputed to have been. If Huey Long was not so eloquent as Warren has made Stark, Long's personality had an inevitable cultural equivalent of mass mythology, where the legend of a Messiah, indiscriminately politico-religious, is embedded. If Jack Burden can never say outright of Willie Stark that he is a charlatan with histrionic talent, neither can Mr Warren say it outright of the deceased Long. But why? Visualizing the premises of his novel, he cannot say it because Willie Stark is patently the incarnation of a poetic vein of politics; he engages the imagination of the people on the same basis that even Jesus engaged it, and that Napoleon and Hitler – for good or evil – engaged it: he gives them hope in the idea of a leader who shall save them in their distress, a leader who opens to them a new way of life. Perhaps the ambiguity of this political-literary legend lies, really, in a modernly vague distinction between body and spirit. When one delivers the body from want, is the spirit truly benefited through this means?

This ambiguity, on the level of a superior culture, must inevitably be translated into more refined terms. That is, such a 'humane tyrant' as Willie Stark is perhaps too much dedicated (by whatever methods!) to the relief of 'the body,' to the relief of the materially underprivileged. Dr Adam Stanton's compromised position becomes entirely credible in this light. Yes, Stark's monument to personal vanity, the hospital, *will* do a great deal of common good. But there is too – as Adam knows –the soul, which also must have 'common good.' But when Adam Stanton says 'soul,' is he not a little prejudiced – doesn't he really mean the souls of a limited, privileged class who have gone to big universities in both North and South and as adults brood over the meaning of life and literature more than they concern themselves with the sufferings of the poor? When a surgeon cuts, he cuts for money, for private fame, and for science as much as he does for others and for human life. Such seems, when all is said and done, the ineluctable reality of human nature. And when Jack Burden must criticize Willie Stark for 'doing good' by questionable means (though none seem so bad as the screen Willie's are made to be), doesn't he perceive that everyone who acts must, in a way, act selfishly? Burden, indeed, defines Stark's genius as interest in self (see *All the King's Men,* page 134). May we not conclude that, as Warren's mouthpiece, Burden is actually defining here a typical, even *indispensable*, characteristic of genius?

In such a case, Warren is as selfishly interested in the phenomenon of Long as Burden is, however subconsciously, in the phenomenon of Stark. And how is Burden 'selfishly' interested in the phenomenon of Stark? He is – as we learn fully by the end – actually practicing for the book he has been unable to write on Cass Mastern, his ancestor, and his training in Stark's 'school of research' paradoxically issues, as the novel ends, in his new-found power to go ahead with the Mastern story that long ago he laid aside. So what purpose does Stark serve for Burden? His career as savior of the people has at once disillusioned and initiated him. It becomes the old story of the man of action in relation to the man of thought. Stark combines thought *and* action in that he combines a poetry of traditional culture (the Messiah role and its accoutrement of eloquence) with successful politics. Warren observed the career of Stark's prototype, Long, and considered the *Republic* of Plato. He decided, in all honor to his class of creative intellectuals, that Long must be proven false to poetry as well as to the State. Napoleon's epigrams didn't make him a Homer. Nor did Hitler's rhetoric make him either Vergilian or quite decent. At the same time, to speak in sheer respect for reality, Long was a dynamic realization of an age-old myth and he understood the *poetry* of a life of such ambiguous dedication. Warren could not resist this inevitable poetry, even though his loyalty to it, like Burden's loyalty to Stark, led logically to the moment of downfall, to the final 'criticism' of the assassin's bullet. And who is the assassin? It is the absolute, unyielding amalgam of idealist and practical man: Dr Stanton, the surgeon. He, too, is annihilated because he *competes* with the Messiah. And one cannot compete with the Messiah.

Unless, that is to say, one is a *writer*, the man who acts not relatively, but absolutely, through words; the man who has, as Mr Warren has had, the last word. And literature's Mr Warren, not Hollywood's Mr Rossen, has – make no mistake! – had it. The screen Stark's eloquence (both in words and substance) is to the original Stark's as Walter Winchell's memory picture of the graveyard scene in *Hamlet* must be to Shakespeare's verse. I wish to emphasize here that Warren's selfishness was antithetically constructed to convey the charm and mysterious human challenge of such a person as Stark-Long, for it was against the practical man-of-words, the poet-politician, that he pitted the legend of the pure literary creator, himself, even though he stacked the plot so that the frustrated writer (Burden) should become less frustrated (Warren) precisely because of a now worm-eaten fact, Louisiana's 'little dictator.'

I submit that we should not evade, nevertheless, the question of the influence a priori no less than the influence a posteriori of the movies on fiction. For these influences exist apart and together – the latter when the a priori influence clicks in Hollywood. If it is a necessary humiliation to literature that, however less than perfect it be, its faults be scientifically isolated and shown up by the movies, the fact should be a lesson to all writers, especially to the epic poet that Warren is by way of being in the novel form. The lesson is perhaps that the epic quality is not to be bought at any price and that the creative writer must make his decisions more decisively, and in advance of writing his work rather than at its conclusion. It is more than three centuries since the murdered 'benevolent tyrant,' Julius Caesar, was made a tragic hero in great dramatic literature, and earlier in the present century a gentleman soon hired by Hollywood, Orson Welles, devised a dramatic commentary which helps to make the film's Willie Stark the more credible as a 'March of Time' hero. About three decades ago, Welles streamlined the Shakespearian text and put Caesar and the play into Hitlerian mufti. Isn't it high time either to reject or accept the socio-moral, or broad cultural, truth of the contemporary dictator-type?

The question is not whether the Dictator is politically desirable. The question (in that limited sense in which the creative writer *can* be legitimately selfish) is whether the Dictator is desirable as a hero of the imagination. I don't say that Mr Warren's novel has spoken 'the last word' in the theoretical sense, but according to his view of the matter there is a contradiction between the Dictator's validity in the imagination and his validity in society – a kind of contradiction which did not exist when kings and messiahs had 'divine rights'; that is, when evil as well as good was privileged. Today, because the Devil's work is supposed gradually to be yielding to the implacable advance of scientific ideas, evil no longer has its ancient privileges. It no longer entitles the hero to that very 'agony of will' which Burden at last attributes, but without ethical definition, to Willie Stark. Evil shows signs of being absorbed neutrally, scientifically, into an especially stark Promethean tragedy, in which any creative effort automatically entails both evil and good. In any case, evil is, somehow, still with us. It may be the destiny of Hollywood merely to note this fact in passing. Responsible creative art, in whatever medium, should judge it. The film, *All the King's Men,* underlines that Mr Warren hasn't, quite, judged it. And what I mean the novelist should judge is whether political evil deserves the tragic stature.

10. *La Dolce Vita* and the Monster Fish

While I have made no consistent effort to keep up with either American or foreign films in recent years, I am inevitably keyed up (even as politicians and business men) to 'reading the signs.' When *La Dolce Vita* began playing in Paris, I was there, and all the signs said: 'Go.' Of course the most articulate sign was Fellini himself; to date, I have seen, besides his latest, only *La Strada* and *Cabiria,* but these convince me that he is easily (being much more interesting than Ingmar Bergman) the foremost commercial film director of our time.* I know about the Nouvelle Vague, whose signs are around for all to read. As typical of such 'waves' (it was true of the Italian Neo-Realists), the NV is comprised of one-third pretension, one-third promotion and one-third arguable merit.

Consider the Nouvelle Vague's especially repercussive *Les Quatre Cents Coups (Four Hundred Blows)*: What 1960 film could be more trite in terms of both message and technique? That it was done with 'conviction' only makes its futility sadder. Ostensibly belonging to the classic lean-economy school of French style, it is an over-burdened, intentionally formless documentary treatment of childhood legend – the same

* Since *The Silence* and *Persona* (see the next essay) I have changed my mind: no one ranks above Bergman today.

childhood-legend genre which the French have given some distinguished interest and grace in the past (for example, *Jeux Interdits* (*Forbidden Games*), and further back, *Poil de Carotte* (*Redhead*)). Truffaut, maker of the nouvelle-vaguish *Blows*, might have used a chemical agent to de-Frenchify his theme. What is left? Something, even so far as it is authentic, remarkably flat.

At large, one might say that the fashionableness of this film consists in doing exactly what the much more imaginative *La Dolce Vita* avoided: falling in shrewdly with the 'intellectual' trend of 'abstaining' from aesthetic responses to experience. Politically, so much seems to have been lost, in late decades, by the humanist forces of society that many of the 'sensitive,' in grieved reaction, are heroically prompted to embrace prophylactic sensations and to uphold that sub-rational sphere of human instinct which is paraded in another nouvelle-vague exhibit, *A Bout de Souffle* (*Breathless*), a clever film that strikes me as being a dry, if undeliberate, parody of all the 'baby gangster' films that ever were. I think that the fashionably timed arts are in the midst of a moral hunger-strike against the deeper emotions. Just here is where *La Dolce Vita* (literally, *The Sweet Life*, which may be, after all, the best translation) is modernly unfashionable. *La Dolce Vita*'s inner juice is *there*.

Let us be more precise about the French-ness of the Nouvelle Vague. France also gave birth to the anti-humanism of Dada and Surrealism, which made cults out of social disorder and the irrational. But there is a vast difference between the aggressive assertion of principles of 'disorder' and what I denote by the term 'abstention.' The latter, as an attitude, is immunizing to all intellectual and emotional animation. All that is left to 'excite' are the vulgar responses of moral cynicism and the naked nerves. For instance, in *A Bout de Souffle*, sex seems to be nothing but a complication of the nervous system. Can it, as an activity, be further demeaned? I think not.

The Nouvelle Vague is full of concealed 'sick jokes' about the serious feelings; at least, greeting-card shops put these jokes out in the open. A case in point is the sick Wagnerism of *Les Cousins*, which in its way is a smart little film. It might even be an involuntary travesty of Cocteau's mythism as this was particularly illustrated in his Tristan-and-Isolde piece, *The Eternal Return*. All the animal feelings in *Les Cousins* are on the adolescent level in people who technically are past adolescence. The 'city cousin' is a camping, Wagner-loving semi-fascist, brightly dedicated to a hectic priapism which is somewhat compromised before the film is over; the 'country cousin' is a simple youth with the 'natural' desire to fall in love with the first woman he can take seriously in bed. The unavoidable point of the story, ending tragically for the cause of romantic love, is that old-fashioned natural desire (monogamously inflected) is just too good for a cynically citified world. What is it that here beats romantic love so badly that the film automatically aligns itself with the Beat style of wailing, without taste or dignity, in sheer moral desperation? Here, in fact, is where the voice of the Wagnerian opera grows 'sick' as though (we literally hear it played) it were an outdated record interpreted by a defective needle.

The reason that one is prompted to discuss *Les Cousins* in relation to *La Dolce Vita* is that, in both, the wild-party is adopted as society's moral and emotional gauge. In *La Dolce Vita*, its function becomes archetypal; in *Les Cousins*, it is merely a sex get-together with liquor, and in this respect could not be more 'classical.' There is no try for subtlety in *Les Cousins* (catch the Nouvelle Vague going in for French 'corn'!) and the film's main shindig could not be more orthodox if it were meant to portray the eternal Greenwich Village orgy. Broadly speaking, a wild-party is where the several sexes let down everything, including their hair, where 'heteros' may become 'homos' and 'homos' become brazen. In sum, it is the risky, excruciating crucible of bedroom habits in which many a battle is lost to individual and group sex-loyalty. In *Les Cousins*, the wild-party is specifically the vehicle for the poor country cousin's discovery that, apparently, Eligible Priapism Rules All.

The conventionality is egregious. But just because it is, and because the only one who resists it loses, people enjoy it all –

and particularly so because (in a time of indomitable masochism) the winner, the city cousin, looks as 'sick' as the loser. *Les Cousins* tells us, though not consciously, that the enthusiasm of a Baudelaire for Wagnerian heroism in the sphere of love is not just sick, it's *dead*. What remains (shade of Des Esseintes!) is only a vulgar dandy's fetishism for party stunts. At last the dandy, the city cousin, inadvertently kills his relative just when the latter has decided *not* to commit suicide. As the scene is Paris, the Ivy League irony is imported. No moral heroism, no moral tragedy – just 'beat' luck for everybody.

The truth is, setting *La Dolce Vita* as a wild-party classic beside *Les Cousins*, Fellini's film assumes *validly* Wagnerian proportions, for its plot-burden is to be defined by the hero's tacit lament: 'Wild parties made me what I am today!' Unlike the Nouvelle Vague partying, *La Dolce Vita* holds much more than the exhibition of students rallying round the priapic maypole; Fellini has propounded a serious, competent and long look at all the significant sorts of wild-party thrown by the world today. In our time, *all parties*, he cannily notes, are a little 'wild.' He does exclude, if only because Rome doesn't have them, the ritual Bridge Club and Country Club dissipations, which perk up or peter out only in parked cars. He properly isolates, as significant, the common celebrities' bout, with jazz and champagne into the wee hours; the sophisticates' intellectual debauch, with longhairs, quasi-Catholics and exotic Negro singers; the high-society séance of titles, worldliness and decadent aristocracy, with all the true *preciousness* there; and lastly, a supreme synthesis of rollicking Middle Bohemia, excluding neither drag-queens, professional freaks nor the more eminent leaders of local wassail – of whom the protagonist is now one.

The content of Fellini's film is avowedly autobiographical: he himself was the journalist whose profession, in the film, leads him into all the party traps to whose spell he gradually succumbs. One is aware of first-hand observation recreated with more skill and persuasiveness than even Fellini might have been thought to have up his sleeve. I am inclined, while fully conscious of my daring, to attribute his achievement to moral inspiration. I think that Fellini's moral sense, no less than his aesthetic sense, is far from being fashionably dead: a conclusion also justified by his previous films, *La Strada* and *Cabiria*. In a day when being fashionably dead is virtually the *sine qua non* for success, Fellini has made an abundantly bold and personal gesture. I believe that it clicks.

If there are some points in it for cavil or dispute, these are minor. The film's power was proven by a most amusing dénouement in real life when it was premiered at 1960's Cannes Festival, whose chief prize it carried off. Alain Cuny plays the film's disillusioned 'Catholic' liberal who regrets his worldliness so acutely that he kills himself and his two small daughters. While at a night club in Cannes, this actor suddenly took fire from the memory of his role and sought to stop the act of a rotund comic whose look and routine were irritating him. The unseemly incident was headlined in the Paris papers, which then were reporting the Festival.

Apparently bibulated in a manner from which the character in the film had abstained, Cuny stood up and loudly rebuked the astonished entertainer, telling him that he looked just like the monster fish which Fellini had made the moral emblem of *La Dolce Vita*'s climax. The charge by no means lacked its basis. The fact is that the end of the all-night party is beautifully handled by Fellini as its personnel, in ones, twos and threes, dribble on to a great beach at dawn. The pace and verve of the party itself (like the use of visual/auditory counterpoint in the film's other parties) should make Orson Welles pale with envy and von Stroheim wince in his grave. If any had missed certain implications while viewing the end of *La Dolce Vita*, Cuny's misbehavior should have arrived as a blinding revelation for them.

On the beach, the attention of the exhausted revellers is at once drawn to some fishermen who are hauling in a net on the otherwise deserted expanse. The catch is a huge fish which seems all head, and whose remarkably human and lymphatic eyes stare ambiguously back at the spectators, though not so ambiguously as to avoid producing, on these quelled quasi-Dionysians, a transiently Medusan effect. Beyond question,

Cuny understands the paramount moral of the film in which he played: the monster fish is an image of the wild-partiers' lust for entertaining the animal sensations, a lust that compasses, inevitably, all more or less obsessed forms of human cavorting, among these being – with double-edged satire – the *professional* forms.

In an age when publicity is a megalomania, it is hard for any emotional obsession to avoid, in action, the 'professional look.' Aren't juvenile delinquents, getting their pictures on the front pages of tabloids, eager candidates for movie-star publicity? Society has professional hostesses as well as professional snobs and welcomes at its doors the journalists it is lucky enough to attract. Why not? Parties have their professional 'lions' and these are requisitioned to oblige with their 'acts.' The parties of both *Les Cousins* and *La Dolce Vita* have their surprise 'numbers,' spontaneous or scheduled, one of which is an elegant visit to an elegant haunted house. Moreover, an age of free speech licences one to say that the voyou and the cocotte, even as the gigolo and the courtesan, stage their little charades wherever the style of the party permits.

Fellini has really offered a film that is a *roman à clef*. The *clef* is stunningly touched with phenomenally bosomed Anita Ekberg, who takes the part of a pixy-minded professional sex-symbol (i.e., a movie star). At the turning point of an evening of whoopee, she spontaneously answers the howl of a dog with a series of dramatic yodels from her own throat, whereupon her call is caught up by all the dogs in the Roman countryside, to which the journalist-hero has lured her for a self-apparent purpose. Of course, this is a moment of relative privacy, and yet the lady's reflex is not to keep her presence a secret from the night. Poor journalist! (You are right: the sex-symbol goes back to her hotel unseduced.) This episode is not only amusing but also, like most of the others, impressively true.

Fellini's wild-party line signifies that sort of exhibitionism which, today, never seems able to separate itself from the mirror of the newsman's camera. The *clef* is this 'eye' of publicity. And the moral would be that, even if the orgiastic cast of the modern wild-party is somewhat faked, is much more hysterical than ritualistic in substance, its surface may be maintained in the way that the photograph of two voluptuous female breasts – regardless of what obscure pathology may rule the heart beneath – proclaims the incontrovertible existence of two voluptuous female breasts. Everyone knows, beyond the shadow of a sexual doubt, *all* that such breasts imply. So, if contemporary orgiasts cheat themselves and others, basic appearances may be kept up as long as there are shocking news-pictures and headline scandals.

I am reminded, by the way, of the bitter charge directed at a contemporary nymph by the moralistic hero of Tennessee Williams' play, *Orpheus Descending*, that she has spent the last fifteen years of her life 'at a goddamned ball.' The *clef* here, though only a figure of speech, is the same as in *La Dolce Vita*. But it is the italicized perspective of our publicity-crazed era that gives Fellini's film its main force. The swarming news photographers are an essential ingredient of its style; metaphysically, they are easily translatable, cameras and all, into nightmarish apparitions from Bosch's 'Hell.' This is especially clear from the lightning-like brutality with which the newsmen invade the premises of the 'Catholic' aesthete's hideous suicide, and even ambush with their cameras, outside the house, his still unknowing widow. I fancy (and I hope I do not exaggerate) that Fellini extends the wild-party as a trope for our society, to the Medusan eye of the monster fish as the lustful Eye of Publicity: the news-camera. In fact, I am tempted to have an even deeper confidence in Fellini's insight. As an epigraph for *La Dolce Vita*, I would paraphrase the outcry of a certain morbidly passionate heroine of Oscar Wilde's and Richard Strauss's: 'Well I know that thou wouldst have publicized me, and the mystery of Publicity is greater than the mystery of Death.' In case anyone has forgotten, it was *love* she was comparing to death.

Some, however, may prefer to say that it was 'lust.' The two schools of thought about this general issue have never, to the satisfaction of all, settled their dispute. Freud's emergent *libido* seemed to weight the scales in favor of lust, and if this indicated a basic truth, the lust for publicity and its tangible agents

might be, these days, a highly plausible phenomenon. By insinuating that the orgy embodies our age's only remaining
'authentic emotion,' Fellini would be surveying the field of
love-as-lust (the film's journalist, incidentally, makes a merger
between marriage and the bacchanal) and so the viewpoint in
La Dolce Vita becomes the more persuasive as sex seems to
overlap on the lust for publicity.

Was the orgy not once a very public, no less than sometimes an *official*, occasion? Maybe the orgy is more all right
than a certain satiric light in Fellini's eye seems to infer. Maybe, ritual or no ritual, God or no God, it is society's eternal
health-measure: a medical form of purging the beast in us.
Well, then, love is all the more a special, and personal, problem
as well as an aesthetic gauge. It seems truer to conclude that
none of the higher or deeper emotions, which put life on a
really livable plane, can exist without ritual as a conscious intellectual discipline: wild-parties form just the comfort-station
phase of ritual. Thus, in the modern sense, the 'orgy' would
be sex-ritual reduced to the phony inflation of commercial advertising. This is, perhaps, Fellini's true *clef*. And if there are
intellectual 'orgies' of this kind? Well, draw your own conclusions, brother thinkers!

11. Masterpieces by Antonioni and Bergman

It is useless to pretend that the film is not still the Cinderella of the arts. Insofar as this is true, the other arts (without themselves wishing it) take on the look of ugly stepsisters whose affability and condescension tend to caricature them. Rather self-consciously, well-known novelists have undertaken to analyze the spell cast on them by this vulgar medium or to point out, dutifully, why the disadvantaged 'movies' can never, never rate with the medium whose practice *they* so obviously enjoy. Serious-minded specialists of the film have written respectable, even intelligent books on the craft, the aesthetics and the theory of the brave medium. But these books, despite enduring circulation, remain peculiarly isolated. From the viewpoint of universal schooling, they afford an orthodox branch of instruction in the arts; from the viewpoint of critical practice (film reviewing and so on) they are nevertheless oddly removed from the specific problem of deciding how good a given film is. I consider, and I am not alone in the opinion, that Bergman's *Persona* and Antonioni's *Blow-Up* are especially fine films, quite exceptional among recent works; so highly exceptional that, in view of the separation between film theory and the practice of film criticism, their ways of utilizing the technical nature of film to express attitudes toward human experience should come to the widest notice as major advances in the film's artistic sophistication. In brief, they are masterpieces.

Yet from the casual reviews of them I have read, I don't think that the particular eloquence they share has been thoroughly assessed or even identified; thus the applause given them lacks persuasive cogency. A few critics are serious enough to have recognized the allegorical character of *Blow-Up* as an irony involved with the widespread naïve belief in the photograph as conclusive testimony to the existence of 'reality' as distinct from the existence of 'illusion' (or art). It was historically inevitable that, once invented, photography would take supreme place as witness to the world of things, to 'things as they are.' The gullible sentimentality of this myth of convenience has been punctured hundreds of times in hundreds of ways and yet it persists. *Blow-Up* punctures it creatively on a level far above the average. Our society's materialistic and statistical structure, all conscientious objections to one side, has preserved the truth-telling myth of photography as an indispensable feature of the larger myth of science's super-efficiency. The very point that so much fictional fudge is passed off in the film medium draws between 'fact' and 'fancy' a disconcertingly evident line with a false validity.

Making films and thinking about them on almost any level, in any economic sphere, is far too sophisticated in the trivial sense; so sophisticated that Bergman's and Antonioni's originality in creating two anti-science legends may pass in general for arty-smartiness. This would be a true pity. Back of much hostility to film 'trickiness' is the sodden documentary cult, opposed to creating 'illusions' with the medium and forever attacking imaginative work by pressing the claims of the camera as the sole true eye of truth. Hence a tangible embarrassment to those committed to the creative faculty of film was the late Siegfried Kracauer's *Theory of Film: the Redemption of Physical Reality*. Unquestionably a scholarly work, it kept implying with an unpardonable ambiguity that film 'can be an art' but, in effect, it borrows art for an occasion, like a costume concealing its actual identity. Amid mercilessly massed evidence, we learn that film is a visual medium whose overwhelmingly ideal function is reporting the boundless facts of the physical world.

The existence of such a theory can be explained only by the curious if involuntary isolation endured today by all criticism on the subject of film art. Certainly, Kracauer knew a ready-made audience awaited his book and would hail a formidable thesis reassuring everyone dedicated to the idea that truth-telling in film means what both science and the newspapers call documenting the facts. Yet why, one may go on asking, could such a theory register so convincingly (his book has become standard since it was first published in 1960) when a sizeable array of books elevating film as an art in its own right is also on library shelves, and when the validity of the photograph as statistical evidence of the truth has so often been called in question and refuted? The facile answer is that Kracauer's book is very informative as a technical inquiry; that is, it goes to much trouble to demonstrate the catholic resourcefulness of film: its ability to show both how an artist may develop a pictorial idea and how, without surgery, the inmost sanctums of the live body may be visited; so, in sum, photography is a leading aid in the study of art as of science. Indeed, if Kracauer were alive, his reaction to *Blow-Up* might be that it is an ingeniously simple fiction illustrating his own thesis with highly impressive point.

This, I say, is the *facile* answer and, in its way, irrefutable. Why, I feel bound to object, such a patently split view of film as an art and film as relentless investigator and ingenious reporter? Why, furthermore, the constant effort on the part of certain film enthusiasts to downgrade film as an art – a tactic which is tantamount to isolating the creative faculty of film as mere popular entertainment? Among hardcore intellectuals, one regularly runs up against an automatic condescension, a reflex of sheer suspicion, consigning creative film to a small corner where it must be heavily screened by the most sceptical experts to earn the nominal title of art. If we scrutinize the practice of film criticism, even in superior places, we find the better fiction films frequently reviewed as if they were novels cast in sequences of pictorial and aural illustrations. Naturally,

critics don't always consciously commit themselves to an inevitable parallelism of film with literature and the stage. Yet
the truth becomes plain when a novel or a play has been
turned into a film and the issue is broached on the basis of film
as a pyrotechnic art of translation – an interpretive, rather than
a creative, art. A whole book has been written by a well-mean-
ing and cultivated scholar about the methods by which film
converts a novel into its own technical idiom.* But the value
of end-judgements (just how good an independent work of art
a given film may be) remains in curious suspense despite all the
lip service rendered, even in literary quarterlies, to film *as* film.
Overconscientious film critics may become so attentive to technical quantities as never to decide just what a given film says.
By its own dynamic reflex, the film art is to be observed in-
veterately trying to disengage itself from the debris of con-
fusions caused by its reputation as a synthetic medium with the
emphasis on the *non-creative* side. Filmic and semi-filmic
photographic experiments shown at Expo 67, the World's Fair
at Montreal, were bald exploitations of technique (multiple
screen and 'environmental' photography) having only a token
implication for serious artistic use.

Film's unique position as a quasi-art is mainly due to a
reversible Janus-faced situation. The historic idea on which
Kracauer based his book, and which compasses an enormous
tacit prejudice about film, is that the photograph is rightly
only a mirror of the optically apprehensible world, no matter
what degree of materiality its subjects have. This becomes a
crucial point when in some fiction film a ghost is supposed to
materialize or when dreams (those optically unverifiable facts!)
are projected as if their figures had material existence. In Bergman's *Persona* a psychiatric nurse, isolated with her female
patient as an experiment, develops acute neurotic symptoms
that can be regarded only as hallucinations; meanwhile
her patient would be doing nicely were it not for the nurse's
growingly violent hysteria. Since this film has no supernatural atmosphere, we have to consider the nurse's hallucina-

* George Bluestone, *Novels into Film*, University of California Press,
1961.

tions as simple projections of the mind expressed through an optical medium. Bergman has been astute in devising a scene with three participants, all of whom have the usual physical aspect of photographed persons but only two of whom (the patient and her nurse) are supposed to be present: the third is the patient's physically absent husband. In other words, as in Surrealist films where the imagined action is dreamlike, the physical world is here photographed out of natural context in a purely psychic dimension. It is exactly this creation of a non-objective world with objects (here, people) that the physical-reality dogmatists most deplore as foreign to the film medium.

Persona is thoroughly involved with a clinical situation. In the psychiatric clinic (where the main action of the film begins) the general condition is for the stuff of dreams to be tangible, for dream narratives to be treated between analyst and patient as if they were 'live action' – as actually taking place. To the analyst, as to the poet and all visionary artists, the mind is as much a place as the world, with laws that derive from those of the physical world without being the very same laws; accordingly, the dreamer himself and those perceived in dream seldom obey gravity and material bounds strictly; they fade in and out as material bodies may do in film; they come 'on stage' and go off as arbitrarily as if in some Expressionist or Surrealist film work. It could have been due only to the position of dreams in the context of psychoanalysis that another scholarly theorist of film, the philosopher Suzanne K. Langer, should have ventured, however cursorily, to define the narrative action of film as 'dream mode.' The harmony and discrepancy between Kracauer's and Professor Langer's specializing theories form, as it happens, the Janus-face to which I alluded above.

According to one of these theories, the moving photograph is properly a guarantee of the physical world in which we live and the way this world behaves; according to the other, the film properly guarantees just the opposite, contravening the laws of daily physical behavior so as to reproduce the image of the same world in its dream mode. Yet of Professor Langer's theory I ask: why doesn't it specify the filmic 'mode' as the psychology of spontaneous association – a stream of consciousness like, for instance, Molly Bloom's, conscious but irrational, flitting about in time and space with no responsibility to chronological narrative or any other convention? It is interesting that in the mediocre, quite uninspired film made from the text of Joyce's *Ulysses*, Molly's interior monologue is done in vocalized excerpts accompanied by illustrating passages of film. Indeed the whole film is a visual/aural excerpt from the original work. The point of our awkward, Janus-faced pair of theories is that *both* assume that the film's dominant function is *reportorial;* one reports the physical aspect of life, the other reports a special mental aspect – or, if you will, seeks to duplicate its 'mode.' The only difference between Langer's dream-mode film, on one hand, and certain types of poetry and prose fantasy, such as Molly Bloom's, on the other, is that the former alone depends absolutely, it is supposed, on the nature of its communicative medium (the film); in fact, according to the theory, it is *strictly limited* by that medium.

Yet why, one bluntly asks, should this be so? The novel, one may grant, is made of words (a 'communication medium') but there is nothing in the nature of language to restrict it to the uses of the novel form, or lyric poetry or the dramatic form. Language can absorb a great variety of formal modulations. So why should there be anything self-limiting about film to restrict it to the statistical form of physical documentation (Kracauer) or the mental form of dream mode (Langer)? – especially when, by juxtaposing the two theories as Janus-faced, they become diametric contradictions establishing themselves exclusively on the same territory? Sophisticated film artists such as Antonioni and Bergman, fortunately, are not incommoded by these heavily scholastic theories; quite the reverse: for in these films of theirs, both theories might be viewed as pompous shadows lurking back of the film-maker's serious playfulness, which tacitly, with a sort of impertinence, involves the scholarly delusions as themes for irony and parody.

Let us go even deeper. Back of most published discourse on film is the reactionary human impulse to make of everything –

from metaphysical philosophy to common dreams and day-dreams – one of science's matter-of-fact attributes. The nineteenth-century phenomenon of the photograph was seized by this same reactionary impulse and developed as a supreme weapon to attack the higher functions of the mind. This is clear if we consider that the appearance of ghosts and ecto-plasm from mediums in trance were, at one time, to be 'proven' or 'disproven' by resorting to photographing them. For the Kracauer and Langer theories, the moving photograph has become willy-nilly a symptom of the degeneration of classic philosophic postulates into a quasi-scientific metaphysics. Typically this is an obsession with reality as process, method and passing aspect rather than as a domain of permanent or total truths. Two such degenerate postulates are Kracauer's 'flow of life' and 'open end,' which he proposes as criteria for the true filmic function. But here his theory, not surprisingly, is found facing the same way as Professor Langer's. Her dream-mode film also implies the 'open end' and 'flow of life' as necessary traits of a disorderly, uncontrolled world without true climax, sustained rhythm or firm spatial orientation. The obvious difference seems that Kracauer has assumed what every rationalist assumes: the physicality of life exists under a variegated, containing and efficient *order* – social, economic, political, etc.; in short, logical; otherwise, as irrational, as irresponsible to mental logic and objective order, the world of things as reflected by the mind would perforce overflow into the absolute fantasy of Langer's shapeless, unmanageable dream mode. Hence psychiatry, as a modern phenomenon, appears as another instrument of the aim of science to press the free-association aspect of imagination (of which dream is the unconscious function) into a quarantine of statutory disorder. Professor Langer thinks, if less obviously, as much within a framework of scientific logic as Kracauer does. Without being rude enough to use the terminology of the mental clinic, she assumes that film is the technical medium expressing directly and purely the content dealt with indirectly and rationally by dream-analyst and psychiatrist. Professor Langer is generous enough not to take a view of her dogma as correctional or inhibitive, and in this respect her companion theorist is equally magnanimous. Their liberalism is their strategy: she is as willing to let the dream mode flow recklessly on in the film as he is willing to let this medium of 'physical redemption' simulate at will the imaginative tactics of the other arts.

The practical point, nevertheless, is that film does not 'simulate' or 'assimilate' fiction and fantasy any more than the dictionary simulates or assimilates the novel, the poem and the play. In positive terms, there is no common basic fact about exposed film except the camera mechanism that makes possible an optical result (the photograph) just as there is no common basic fact about the literary medium except that it is composed of the vocabulary. There is, indeed, as experts have stressed, a 'vocabulary' of the film, or (as one scholar has expressly put it) a grammar; thus, film has no given moral or aesthetic function, no absolute principle or technical limit, aside from precisely the sort of instruments given language by style, rhetoric and grammar. To assume anything else of film is to be *partipris* without the smallest justification except the dogmatic obsession of science cults to win dominion over all 'reality.' The general label for the science cult of film is Documentary. The only question is whether film shall 'document' the disorderly flow of life (free mental association) or the orderly flow of life (mirror reflections of the objective world of matter 'as it is').

I trust I do not seem to overemphasize the importance of theoretic background in approaching the excellences of the two films I wish to praise. The empiric situation in criticism is such that I believe such considerations very vital – indeed integral with just what *Persona* and *Blow-Up* have particularly to tell us. *Persona*, I repeat, deals with a psychiatric situation in recognizable terms of the clinic. *Blow-Up* deals (seen in the same superficial light) with the documentary, quasi-legalistic validity of the photograph. Yet each film gives its theme a profound and specific modulation. *Persona* has turned ordinary plot order and meaning-content inside out; first, by encasing the main action in a kind of amnion of visual irrationality, and second, by sending the course of regular psychiatric therapy

utterly off its track. The film's opening sequence introduces
the spectator without ceremony to a shockingly irrational set
of briefly held images; that is, the sequence begins, minus any
credits, without the least token explanation of why these particular images are shown or why they have the sequence they
do; in themselves, they are only obscurely 'associational.'

Their shots of action are overquick in pace (one is from a
very dated film farce with an actor in skeleton masquerade);
antithetically, their shots of inertia approach the quality of
stills. In fact, when the animated cartoon of a little fat woman
doing setting-up exercises on her back suddenly 'freezes,' we
have a probable satiric reference (becoming more certain later
on) to the current film mannerism of suddenly introducing
frozen single frames into the cinematic flow to accentuate a
climax or sub-climax. Here the 'climax' is accidental and might
be due (as a literal shot of the film strip slipping from a whir-
ring reel suggests) to some technical mishap that stops film
during its projection. Another apparent technical mishap is a
shot of objects momentarily so much out of focus that they
assume abstract form. There are also random shots of quiet
natural scenery, the palm of a human hand pierced by a nail,
profiles of dead, sleeping or anaesthetized persons. Finally,
when a nude boy, his thin prostrate body draped with a sheet
to his neck, awakes at the sound of a bell, turns on his stomach
and starts reading a book, we suddenly realize that the preceding potpourri is more than some spliced film clips gathered
from the cutting-room floor. They have been 'plays' upon the
faculty of film deliberately and accidentally to animate and de-
animate as well as to 'report' animacy and inanimacy and to
identify things through optical concentration – to *focus on*
them; the demonstrated process of optically focusing and un-
focusing implies that extreme relaxation of mental attention
which drains all meaning from objects that technically are still
in clear optical register. While reporting live movement, this
prelude to *Persona* says, cinema may impose on such movement an artificial quietus (the frozen frame) that in one sense is
a parody of death and in another only the conventional super-
speed still of a person in live movement; cinema (as we find

when the awakened boy sees on the wall next him the huge head of a woman going in and out of focus) may also conceal, reveal or transform the identities and qualities of the objects it mirrors. Here is the camera's *active* faculty as opposed to its *passive* faculty of simple reporting.

Bergman, in effect, is whimsically parodying the Langerian dream mode, but not in order to make a Surrealist construct; rather, to inflect the meaning of the ordinary world of 'physical reality' which he now proceeds, paradoxically, to report. The catch is that this world, as he further reveals, is typically compromised by mental phenomena that tend to transform normal appearances and reorient normal behavior. I have already mentioned one incident in the action that follows now: the imagined materiality of an absent person. There is not one facet in the film's little prelude which does not have its place in an orbit of metaphors about a master metaphor. The latter is presented immediately after the ensuing credits and it is the crux of Bergman's psychiatric theme. An actress (who may be playing in a film or on the stage) 'goes dry' during a speech in *Electra* – which *Electra* the narratage does not say – stares awestruck into space, then gives a suppressed giggle. She never willingly, during the entire film, speaks again except for two parrot-like words she is induced to murmur by her nurse: 'No, nothing.'

The terrible blank she has drawn in the midst of the tragic speech has been parodied by the open, unmoored and enigmatic antics of the prelude: particularly the freeze of the little female clown doing setting up exercises and a swift, inexplicable interlude of 'white leader' – the unsensitized film at both ends of a reel which the audience does not see, or glimpses only subliminally, but which here is a briefly sustained light flash dazzling us from a blank screen. We also recall that during the prelude the awakened boy (who may be the son the actress has abandoned) has seen a woman's face going in and out of focus, a face whose features he begins caressing. In line with the close-ups of objects so out of focus as to be abstractions, the actress's mental blackout may pass for the model of the whole opening series of metaphors that arbitrarily identify, or fail to identify, familiar objects. Thus it is the world itself, her private and professional life, everything about her past and her present, which the actress fails to identify (i.e., focus on mentally) when she forgets her lines and is immobilized for an instant.

After apologizing for ruining the scene, the actress presumably goes home and from there, as we find next, to a hospital room where she stays as an unusual 'withdrawal' case. The female psychiatrist in charge is a mature, hardbitten number who crisply, suavely informs the mute actress that doubtless catatonia is a new 'role' for her and that eventually she will tire of it as she seems to have tired of her stage roles. The actress, Elizabeth Vogler, has abandoned a loving husband as well as a loving child and she has steadfastly refused to see either since the incident which has fatally isolated her. However, the presiding psychiatrist tries an experiment by sending her patient off to her own cottage by the sea in the company of the attractive young nurse who has been assigned to the case.

Here the two young women begin living in pleased contentment the simplest rustic life although the actress responds to her nurse's one-sided running conversation only by a smile or a casual, apparently 'innocent' caress. We soon witness, as the nurse develops hysterical symptoms, the kind of narration characteristic of Surrealist and other fantasy films: abrupt transitions of mood, leap editing, and scenes involving the nurse, the patient and the latter's absent husband as performers of a sort of psychodrama automatically projected, it would seem, by the nurse, not the patient. I say 'automatically.' Yet, since she duly snaps out of each breakdown or episodic trance, returning to her rational personality, we may wonder how genuine these hallucinative fits are. Speaking psychiatrically, the nurse may have stumbled on a method by which she hopes to provoke the other into responses that will lead her out of her speechless withdrawal. But the nurse's hallucinations seem too spontaneous and private to relate to a conscious psychiatric manoeuvre. Each of the women reads books and Alma, the nurse, sometimes reads to her patient; the actress is calm until she is forced to react to Alma's increasingly unsuppressed agitation, which might well be Lesbian in impulse.

By the time the nurse has a chance to read a letter from Elizabeth to her psychiatrist, disclosing that she takes Alma objectively and lightly, it is clear that Bergman has been indulging in ambiguity by offering a version of a case history whose true depths lie in the imaginative domain, not in the statistical realms favored by either of the simplistic schools of film thinking: Kracauer's or Langer's. Of the greatest aesthetic importance is the impression one may get, toward the film's end, that the prelude has been a parody of the well-known pastime of dial-twisting on TV and radio. This conclusion crystallizes by way of two similar incidents. In the early stage of her withdrawal, Elizabeth, having a small TV set in her hospital room, is willing for the nurse to turn it on; once, however, when some romantic drama is being broadcast, she repeats her crucial giggle and the nurse turns the set off. And again, quite alone, she is nervously pacing the room when a TV newscast, which she has been ignoring, flashes on one of the ghastly self-immolations of Buddhist priests in Vietnam. The newscaster's hortatory voice has that provocative tonality that some of us condemn as blatant sensationalism. Now *all* voices, to this withdrawn actress, have a repellently blatant urgency.

News photographers, of course, have been on hand when the priest set himself afire. Past the seated figure enveloped with flame, TV watchers are seeing still other photographers snapping pictures and aiming film cameras. The world of suffering, violence and grief has become an awful intrusion into Elizabeth Vogler's consciousness while, in the view of millions of other inhabitants of the world, this intrusion is not only welcome, but craved. For countless numbers, turning on or off the sight and sound of life's 'tragedies' is simply a matter of dial-twisting, an obsessive distraction entirely frivolous even as it flatters the twister's power-fantasy. Perhaps, as Elizabeth shrinks away from the vision in horror, there was never a more stringent satire on the way modern society untragically and amorally regards its own woes and sorriest scandals. To the actress what is modishly called 'electric circuitry' has brought back in objective, for-true form the grim image of human disaster for which classic tragedy provides a traditional catharsis – that catharsis which was interrupted when without warning she 'ran dry' in the midst of a speech ...

Whatever the technical cause, Elizabeth has been victimized by a *retroactive* function of the tragic catharsis; in the light of modernity we may say that, for her, the *cleansing* tragic madness has turned into the *defiling* communication madness. Art, we might also infer, has failed this actress in a great private crisis. Just why does not matter in face of her utter abnegation of the persona of social consciousness. The further action of the film implies that the collective issue has overtaken and replaced the strictly private one. Elizabeth Vogler may have given up the world's life; the world's life has not given itself up, or her, and the therapy of the psychodrama now taking place proves this. By some strange twist, the nurse is now the willing patient, the actress the unwilling doctor-psychiatrist.

For Alma either will not give up the idea of her patient's cure or, what seems more likely, is seeking a cure for her own suddenly exposed dilemma. After having confessed her own erotic excesses (technically heterosexual) and gone through her hallucinations, the nurse proceeds methodically to impose on her 'patient' in verbal form a psychodrama that is supposedly the actress's but that well may be a product of the nurse's imagination. Bergman's plastic use of film leaves the truth ambiguous. During the pseudo-clinical session, Alma's monologue is repeated in toto, the camera on Elizabeth's face the first time around, on Alma's the second. The schizoid dimension has been anticipated by the visual, seemingly 'physical,' accident of splitting Alma's image in two at a crucial moment when she identifies with Elizabeth, who has stepped with naked foot on a broken glass and given an outcry. During the invented case history, Elizabeth's face has shown signs of dismay and guilt; is it her story or the nurse's? The question is resolved, rather than answered, by a plastic device. Suddenly the screen fills with a still photograph of a woman's face: one side Alma's, the other Elizabeth's. The thrilling effect is that of a mask and the classic calm of catharsis seems to close the agony.

But has there been true catharsis? – for either: both? The nature of modern experience seems to suspend any certainty and the remaining action is only tantalizing. The 'mask' has reminded us of the also colossal, but vaguer, woman's face that appeared to the reading boy of the prelude. Actually the affair resumes its turmoil to reach a kind of catastrophe: the electric circuitry of modern life permits catastrophe but not catharsis – not, that is to say, *consciousness*. The plot itself draws a blank. Goaded by Elizabeth's stalwart resistance, the frantic nurse has traded slaps with her, threatened her with boiling water and at last vindictively cries that she loathes her. Therapeutic psychodrama has exhausted itself trying to replace cathartic tragedy. The end is redundancy. Alma simply resumes her professional face and matter-of-factly, as Elizabeth too, starts packing for departure. It is clear the actress will not forgive her last insult. We then see nothing more of Elizabeth; we see only Alma closing up the cottage and taking her packed suitcases to board a bus ... and the boy, caressing the huge enigmatic face, returns. That is all.

Persona and *Blow-Up* are brilliant tours-de-force illuminated by a special negative dimension that functions as lucid irony. If Bergman's film demonstrates the absurdity of the dream-mode theory of film unless there be some intellectual framework to sustain it as a creative entity, Antonioni's vividly projected adventure of a very young fashion photographer is a devastating sarcasm indirectly commenting on the just as naïve physical-redemption theory of film. We perceive, if we detect the true meaning of Antonioni's device, how vain would be Kracauer's protest that *Blow-up* vindicates his conception of the photograph as self-sufficient chronicler of reality. The young photographer's smartness consists in having converted the profession of fashion photography into high-camp fantasy. His studio work is deliberately campy, no involuntary parody of chic but as close to the real thing as its fine satiric edge allows. A great point is scored soon as a rapidfire series of still shots he is making with a posh model ends bang! with her on the floor and him straddling her in accidental mimicry of coitus. The neurotic state of his relations with his craft is shown up by a real, and quite funny, orgy that later takes place with two young novices who have been pestering him for a job. There are strong indications he is fed up both professionally and sexually.

Yet passionate photographers have a nervous reflex so long as a camera be slung from one shoulder: they can't resist a fresh subject. Owing to a subject encountered by chance while the armed photographer is strolling in a park, *Blow-Up* proceeds to give us a real fantasy experience as psychodramatically compelling as *Persona*'s, though not so complex. He has gotten on the track of an adult couple seeking enough privacy, it might be, for love-making and succeeds in taking a whole suite of shots of their progress, which ends in a deep embrace during which the woman detects the photographer's presence. He beats a retreat, but she, leaving her partner, overtakes him and demands the films. Partly because she seems unduly concerned, partly because she is good-looking, the photographer (never named in the film) asks her to his studio for solemn parley. When she arrives, there is some flirtatious verbal sparring. Without much ado, she goes to bed with him on the tacit assurance that, when up, she will get the film rolls. When she is dressed again, the photographer is as good as his supposed word, but what he hands her is a substitute for the films she expects.

Scenting something peculiar in the whole business, he has clung to his interest in what the prints will show. Developing them, he is much arrested by one, of which he feverishly starts making blow-ups: it shows the woman gazing about in alarm as her partner's face is buried in her neck. Is it because she has seen him – the photographer? Every blow-up of sectional details of this shot, getting bigger and bigger, excites the photographer more and more: he is looking for a *visible* clue that will better explain the woman's anxiety to obtain the photographs. Suddenly a convincing explanation materializes. It is nothing less than evidence of an intended crime. The mightiest blow-up of all discloses the blurred image of a man aiming a revolver at the embracing couple from the nearby shrubbery. Now it is night-time and the photographer rushes back to the park. There he finds the prostrate corpse of the man who was making love. A crime *has* been committed.

So it would seem. Having an impulse to act, the alarmed and bewildered photographer rushes back to his studio where he finds, indeed, he has made a decisive error. The betraying blow-ups he has left tacked to his wall have disappeared and so have all the original negatives. The woman and her accomplice, acting too quickly for him, have made off with the evidence. Panicked, he goes back to the park and as he has feared, of course, the corpse has also vanished. The case of retributive justice – the whole position of righteous, vigilant society – has drawn a blank and it is the fault of his own negligence. He seems to reproach himself like a good Kracauerian. He does not seem to apprehend the mere technical and tentative role of the photograph he has taken; it is merely the first entry into a complex human mystery: murder and its skein of motives. Statistically, to be sure, it is of obvious importance; without it, the law must take a wide-open, very handicapped course; the police themselves could not move without a shred of material evidence.

Subjective consciousness, alas! is not a camera and neither is physically unsupported verbal allegation. To the film-conscious, on the other hand, the frustrated plight of things is brought home with a poignant throb. Photography, the mythic all-seeing eye, has been embarrassingly balked. The precise position of our hero as a *still* photographer is especially pathetic. Only one instantaneous segment of reality and the road to the truth would stand wide open! The series of blow-ups should remind the film-conscious that a melodramatic filmic technique of telling a story by a rapidly paced series of stills has entered the scene: the brief film *La Jetée* (*The Jetty*) is an excellent example. In a cinema age, this exciting film looks like a well-edited excerpt from a normally made film: a close-knit succession of dramatic highpoints that individually are merely frozen frames. The possibility of the same technique is cleverly insinuated by the progressive blow-ups developed by Antonioni's photographer.

Now, in sick confusion, the young man visits a painter friend to ask his advice – or rather, just to communicate his sense of frustration. With rather facile philosophy, the painter points to one of his canvases and indicating a detail remarks: 'That's the clue.' One reflects that this painting, whatever its visible/ invisible mysteries of meaning, is a finished work, a total object. Otherwise it is not a true painting. Yet the 'work' the photographer is now imagining is not only highly indeterminate: it entirely lacks optical documentation. It is a floating wispy idea in his head whose irony, as if in 'negative,' seems to gather about his person in space. Thus his painter friend's assurance can only be humiliating. He wanders back disconsolately, camera slung on his shoulder, to the fatal park. ... There he encounters by a tennis court a fantastic group of people he has casually run into earlier the same day. They have painted themselves up and dressed like clowns and apparently are on a binge which has taken the form of crowding in an open, much dated auto and driving all night around the city.

Their deliberately theatrical fantasy is no 'stranger' than his own work with fashion models, no more 'bizarre' than the crime and the way he has encountered it. He sees the car stop by the tennis court and its boisterous occupants pile out. Two, a man and a woman, immediately take the court and begin a mimic tennis game without balls or racquets. Theirs is the art of Marcel Marceau, and as we see, with the photographer, a very skilled and persuasive example. The simple overwhelming truth is that the tennis players are imagining the existence of an absent element of the physical world (tennis balls and racquets) which are not only invisible but imponderable. In brief, they are as absent as Elizabeth Vogler's husband in the psychodramatized fantasy of the nurse in *Persona*; if there is optical evidence of *him* for the sake of perfect clarity, it is only because the situation in Bergman's film is much more specific and complex than the clowns' tennis game. The appearance or non-appearance of tennis ball and man would be equally *conventional* in the imaginative sense.

As silent movies show, and as Elizabeth Vogler's muteness shows, speech in film is equally conventional. Speechlessness in *Persona*, however, has a symbolic role: it signifies total moral abnegation of the world and makes, together with all the other technical stoppages Bergman has introduced in the prelude, a galaxy of automatic discontinuities in reality. But the clowns' mimic tennis game is calculated and positive, not involuntary and negative. It knits up the ravelled sleeve of the film art. The physical presence which it pretends is true is likewise symbolic. No matter how many frames a film may have, no matter how tightly continuous its flow, the very nature of its formal statement guarantees the essential importance, the virtual presence, of what lies beyond any single frame or the sum of all the frames. The image of reality I mean is psychic consciousness, which cannot be photographed in an instant of vision or an infinity of instants, for tacitly it is, even in a painting, an *invisible* totality.

The wise clowns in *Blow-Up* have an inspired impulse to involve this moody bystander who has been interested in their game, for now, his interest ebbing, he has sauntered away. They pretend the ball has been knocked out of court and frantically plead, in pantomime, for its return; supposedly, it has rolled in his direction. At first the photographer seems reluctant or vague; then he stoops toward his feet and pretends to heave it back. The moment is drenched with high filmic splendor. Now, in a conventional *envoi*, the camera begins receding from his still disconsolate-seeming figure till he is quite distant. Before we leave him, however, he suddenly fades out, leaving empty the vista of the greensward. ... It is another film convention given a sharp fillip like some device from *Persona*. There is a weight of sovereign irony behind it and it gives a knockout punch to the physical-redemption theory of film. Like painting, film is imagery and has nothing whatever to do with the existence of physical bodies as such. Film, being a time art, requires a much bigger, more complex unit of psychic consciousness to support it than does the still photograph. It is this purely psychic force – the totality of *Blow-Up* – that possesses the 'empty' greensward and, the photographer's figure gone, endows space with supreme meaning.

Part 3
The Artist in Crisis

12. Orson Welles as a Big Cult Hero

A dialect is a special form of communication, a language set apart for special uses. In the case of film, which in the main uses direct images, a 'film language' may be said to exist. There are many reasons why this dialect, today, governs both big and little film cults. Devoted filmists are still jealous of the medium they admire, especially jealous because, even after films assumed a secure place as a medium of human expression, the arrival of the sound track made words into a major element of film, and thus offers, nowadays, literature as a complement to spectacle. In the eyes of enthusiasts, filmic interests must be guarded *against* words even when the film uses, collaborates with, words – that is, when the sound track has speech, music and other sounds. In this situation, many ironies adhere to the 'pure dialect' of the film language. The figure of Orson Welles suggests to me the chief irony, for he is curiously distinctive and interesting in the light of film history.

If we can consider the big and the little Experimental Film cults as two separate camps. Orson Welles, somewhat like a colossus, has a foot in each. Lately there have been many signs of the stepped-up growth of the *big* cult. It is not only that the commercial film itself, mostly in France and Italy, has recently adopted so-called 'art' devices (conspicuously in *Last Year at*

Marienbad), but also that, on the other side, the little Experimental or Avant-garde Film has manifested a progress of its own toward greater physical stature, and in this respect challenges the commercial film. *No More Fleeing* (1957) from abroad and *Narcissus* (1957) in this country were of short 'feature length' in contrast with the brief Avant-garde tradition of 20 minutes or under: the length of the standard 'short subject.' Cocteau's *Blood of a Poet* (1930) was, so to speak, an ambitiously long short film, as were *Lot in Sodom* and, later on, *Dreams That Money Can Buy*.

Feature films in the commercial field have themselves become longer and longer in recent decades. Thus the newer Experimental Films should not surprise us by their ambitious lengths. One may point not only to Stan Brakhage's work, lately geared to feature length in perpetual motion, but also to essays in the 'major statement' length instanced by *Guns of the Trees*. Of course, there are reasons both economic and cultural for the upsurge of sheer production in the Experimental field – a longer individual possession of the screen being as inevitable as the rise in the number of films. In effect, their makers have procured more and more generous backing. What seems most interesting in this intensification of filmic activity, on the art level, is the way in which the commercial and non-commercial films seem literally to have joined forces. This could not be 'purely coincidental' (nothing of importance is purely coincidental) and if one looks for the reasons, one may be reminded that, as I have mentioned, the two Experimental Cults have really *always* existed. The little one, by now, has had considerable recognition and documentation, while the big one has been rather ambiguous all along. Mainly, the latter has been the preoccupation of the audience we call 'movie buffs': those who cherish the stylistic bents of certain well-remembered commercial directors; those who do their best to pretend that such directors do not fall victim to the demands of the commercial studios; those who believe that the 'big' contributions to the art of the film may be regarded as intact.

That such admired directors – Griffith, von Stroheim, Vidor, Lubitsch, Dreyer, Lang, Pabst, von Sternberg, Murnau, Renoir,

Feyder, Cocteau, Korda, Ford, Hitchcock, Huston, Bergman – have made special contributions to film style and some worthy, memorable films, I readily admit. But that their contributions make an intact art, free of serious blemishes, is most debatable and (I believe) a fallacy. Furthermore, the cult of the Experimentalists – from Dali–Buñuel to the present – is in precisely the same position as its 'big brother.' Though motivated by purer aesthetic promptings, the little Experimentalists have lacked, usually, the imagination as well as the material means to make independent and intact works of art, whether long or short. Paramount, as the Experimentalist or Avant-garde virtue, doubtless, is the drive toward poetic statement, and this by all means has been the special property of the *little* cult.

Inevitably, the question must arise as to what degree the Big Cult – let us capitalize the term – shares in this same virtue, and furthermore what, if anything, the Big Cult has had with which to *replace* the virtue of 'poetic statement.' *Last Year at Marienbad*, while I think it not nearly so important as ostensibly serious people think it, is a very recent proof that a big commercial film can behave just like a little Avant-garde film; that is, it can take a quite elementary situation of human psychology and emotion and treat it in a radically *filmic* way. *Marienbad* does not fear to make the imagination into a filmic instrument, to deliver us into a world of feeling composed from pieces of visible reality, objective nature; in brief, it does what, as to filmic method, was done by the makers of *The Cabinet of Dr Caligari*, by Cocteau in *The Blood of a Poet*, and by Maya Deren in her films. I do not mean that each Big and Little film-maker has not had his own distinctive style and purpose; I mean that a good percentage of both types meet on generic Avant-garde ground. On the other hand, one realizes that, for certain movie buffs, *Marienbad* is to be regarded, for that very reason, as arty and too special; as neither pure, broad nor deep enough. For the same reason, too, Cocteau is still shunned by certain film purists for being too literary, too much a scion of 'classic' ideas about life.

Now who would fit the bill, so to speak, as the hero of the

Big Experimental Film Cult: a type-director of films which maintain touch with real contemporary life and yet are cinematic and inventive and the vehicles of a true film style? I have named my candidate for the honor: Orson Welles. Welles is a darling of the movie buffs young and old, and after more than two decades, he is still operating in high gear. I would agree that he has an indisputable flair for film-making; possibly he outranks, on the international level of esteem, all his competitors in terms of the universal affection aroused in serious admirers of the film art. Yet consider: Welles has consistently been as unfortunate as was another much-esteemed Big Cult man, von Stroheim, at least in the latter part of that departed director's career.

Erich von Stroheim's directorial creativeness ended with a film moulded so contrarily to the way he wanted to do it that he disowned it. This was his version of Strindberg's *Dance of Death*, never seen publicly in the U.S. and a maimed, highly unmemorable film. Von Stroheim's *Greed* (even as preserved to us in its defective state) ranks today as a world classic, close in universal evaluation to Welles's *Citizen Kane* – the only film which, for his part, Welles is willing to recognize as even nearly his own (I except, tentatively, the still unreleased *The Trial*). The plain moral is that esteem, in the Big Experimental Cult as in the Little, is based typically – insofar as separate and 'intact' works of art are concerned – on promise, approximation or intention rather than on achievement.

It seems an illuminating point that Welles and von Stroheim, two of the most valued film directors in history, have produced in the main only 'token' works of art. Thus I think that any responsible estimate of their total output must emphasize, first, its fluid filmic idiom and, second, beware of treating it as a set of distinct and individual films. It becomes preferable to say that these two men are masters of a film style never ideally visible in *one* given work but in arbitrary, uneven pieces that hang together (in each man's case) as a certain trend or emphasis; a certain type, or series of devices. As we know since the publication of Kracauer's *Theory of Film*, there exists a tendency to think of film, not as a group of separable works of art, but as a continuous 'reel' of imagery, revealing what Kracauer calls 'flow of life' rather than 'work of art.' If some are disinclined to accept that theorist's reasoning and strict terminology, it is probably because his viewpoint puts just such heroes as Welles in an overtly compromised artistic position. The movie buffs, that is to say, desire to think the film language an 'art' of its own, regardless of how continuously or discontinuously it 'flows.' Yet, to me, there is pertinence in the flow-theory because it absolves the director from responsibility to the specific and individual work, making him master of a *potential* art: an art visible, precisely, through persistently 'flowing' signs, however well or ill connected.

Does my argument raise doubt in the reader? Well, take two virtually 'intact' works of the revered master, D. W. Griffith: *The Birth of a Nation* and *Intolerance*. The former was badly cut up, so much so in some sequences as to look absurd – how can we tell, even in 'restored' versions, what it was meant to be or should have been? Then, assuming we have the bulk of *Intolerance* and may consider it intact, it is still superficial, and in ways trivial, by any informed standard of history or fiction. Yet among the buffs, the legend persists that Griffith's film style, or film sense if you will, entitles him to be called a 'master.' True, speaking hypothetically, a mauled text or staging of a Shakespeare play still shows 'the hand of a master.' In fact, plays suspected of being *re*written by Shakespeare from pre-existing texts may be said to show just that: the hand of a master. But, in many plays accredited as intact Shakespeare, we have the proof of Shakespeare as creator of deep, true and full works of art, all indisputably one master's. A thumbprint may guarantee an individual but not a work of art; so with film style in the loose sense it is predominantly held. Eisenstein and Cocteau come closest, along with a few isolated works by others. What I take leave to call the Big Experimental film-maker is another matter. His image, as represented best by Welles and von Stroheim, suggests the peculiar and challenging ambiguity of the film itself as a creative art. To me, at least, it suggests that the film director, as incarnated in the Big Experimental Cult, stands midway between the creative artist and the stage director in the theatre, between the composer and the musician in the concert hall, between the creator and the adaptor-interpreter.

In film, editing and style-accents no more comprise a whole and creative art than do rhythm and touch in a pianist playing another man's composition. In many commercial studios, even where distinguished directors are concerned, the final editing is usually taken out of the director's hands (with or without his wish or consent) and practised by a specialist. Poor editing, as everyone knows, can cripple a film's style and its basic message. The same happens, for good or ill, in novels as in films, as well as in such methodical collaborations in the theatre as have taken place between Elia Kazan and Tennessee Williams. No inevitable argument exists against the idea of such collaborations, especially if between talents in two distinctive media: think of Mozart's magnificent *Don Giovanni* with its book by Lorenzo da Ponte. A superb collaboration in avant-garde art was that between Virgil Thomson and Gertrude Stein in two modern operas, *Four Saints in Three Acts* and *The Mother of Us All;* participating in the former with writer and composer, it should be noted, were also the scenarist, Maurice Grosser, who supplied a scenic conception for Miss Stein's bare verbal text, and Florine Stettheimer, who gave physical form to the conception with sets and costumes of her own imagining.

Such complex collaborations as those just mentioned are often the case in films, whatever the creative value of the result. But especially important, in films, is that the director be his own scenarist, and preferably also his story's inventor, *or* that he collaborate as closely as possible with a sympathetic scriptwriter – as did Fellini with Antonioni, Eisenstein with Alexandrov. That such collaborations pay off in artistic gain is put beyond doubt in Antonioni's case because this film artist eventually became a director of his own scripts. Prime and happy examples of collaboration in the commercial film world number those between script-writer Zavattini and two directors: De Sica and Fellini. These observations are made purposely to distinguish between such generic cases and what I mean by the Big Experimental Cult. Whatever Welles's collaborations, whether with Shakespeare or a twentieth-century novelist, or with himself, he remains a Cult hero, a film artist of ambiguous successes; a lone wolf, as it were, whose egoistic failures have stacked up to make him both notorious and famous.

Exactly the same is true of virtually all the better known little Experimentalists. Faults, misfires, technical makeshifts, incomprehensible negligence, can easily be spotted in their works – yet nominally they remain 'little masters.' One is tempted to say that the representative of a film cult establishes the fact that filmic *activity* is being preferred over filmic *achievement*, a filmic *direction* over a filmic *goal*. This does not happen through any basic identification of aim, or even sensibility, between big cult and little cult, or among members of either. Think how hard it would be to equate Welles with von Stroheim (despite 'resemblances') by way of such a measure! Rather, the Cult hero of film necessarily represents the extravagance, the very vice, of being willy-nilly 'filmic.' In short, this hero is one ready to pay any price to be his own 'filmic self.'

On occasion, the emergence of a commercially nourished director as the incarnation of the Film Cult that his admirers dream him, may be attended with anticlimax and embarrassment. Such was Josef von Sternberg's strange 'debut' in the film he made in Japan, *Anatahan*, supposedly beyond the curse of the commercial studio; it was a sort of 'film-maker's film.' Yet *Anatahan* is remarkably weak and undistinguished. The truth is that von Sternberg revealed himself quite uninspired and impotent when lacking luxurious physical means and really dynamic actors. This case of von Sternberg's suggests that the most original and creatively active of important film-makers who have gone in for the 'big money' have operated on the basis of bankrupting their backers. This is notoriously true of both von Stroheim and Welles, who at their peak ran deeper into the red, the more they took over the reins, the more they became wayward 'stylists.'

We might well pause, I think, to entertain a thought from

the opposite direction. Suppose we take two more recently developed directors who are also 'stylists' and yet who combine
financially successful film-making with being 'themselves.' I
mean Ingmar Bergman and Michelangelo Antonioni. At the
moment, both Swede and Italian have arrived at international
renown among the cultists, the buffs themselves. Bergman has
actually replaced his much less active Scandinavian predecessor,
Dreyer, as a cult ornament and big 'Experimentalist' hero. It
is doubtful, surely, if Dreyer's *oeuvre* of the last thirty-five
years has provoked as much intense admiration as some half-
dozen Bergman films have received in the last decade. I think
the reason for this successful breakthrough of the Avant-garde
movement into the commercial film domain is because men
such as Bergman and Antonioni have imitated, in substance,
the best examples of little Experimental film-making, as begun
in *L'Age d'Or* and *The Blood of a Poet*; they take personal
charge of the story invention and the scenario and to some extent the camera itself.

Every striking success in collaboration, visible in recent years
among commercial films, has the marks of Cocteau's personal-
ism or of organized teams such as Zavattini–de Sica, Zavattini–
Fellini, Antonioni–Fellini, Bergman as Sjöberg's scriptwriter in
Torment, Duras–Resnais and Robbe–Grillet playing composer
to Resnais' musicianly *Marienbad*. We had Buñuel becoming his own Dali, Bergman his own Sjöberg. A very tempt-
ing speculation is that the Big Experimental Cult is the
paradoxical result of the failure by brilliant film directors to
find stories or story-ideas by talented collaborators sympathetic enough to work with them hand-in-glove, powerful
enough to send them to school to invent their own stories. For
example, I believe that Eisenstein (whom I regard as the most
artistically successful director in film history) learned much, as
he lived through the years, from both his scriptist, Alexandrov,
and his cameraman, Tisse. He learned better how to invent in
terms of story, dialogue and photographic vision. By the time
of his last work, *Ivan the Terrible,* he knew by practice every
'in' and 'out' of the complex filmic process. Today, Antonioni
and Resnais (not to mention Truffaut and other lesser lights)

have earned more, and more insistent, *bravos* than a Cocteau or a Dreyer did while working through three decades instead of one – and so has Kurosawa, who has been known to the West for only fifteen years or so. Then why is Welles, today, the same toddler among tremendous effects as he was when his startling gift for the stage – revealed by the old Federal Theatre Project – took him post-haste to Hollywood? Partly the answer is that he 'collaborated' with the most culturally backward of the national industries. But it is also because of personal psychological reasons.

Simply what he *is* and *has been* makes Welles the quintessential type of Big Experimental Cult hero – always achieving failure yet bringing it off brilliantly, decking it with eloquence and a certain magnificence; fusing in each film the vices and the virtues appropriate to them. Welles is the eternal Infant Prodigy, and as such wins the indulgence of adult critics and the fervid sympathy of the younger generation, which sees in him a mirror of its own budding aspirations and adventurous near-successes. Beside him, Stanley Kubrick and John Cassavetes look middle-aged, however one adds up the latter two's merits. Welles does 'big things' with fabulous ease and against manifest odds. Careful assessment of the actual results displays, along with the marred success, needless audacity and impertinent novelties. He puts on an intellectual circus even when engaged cinematically with Shakespeare. He proceeded to speak *Macbeth* with a Scottish brogue which ultimately was dropped; also, desiring to place the play in its 'native' barbarous milieu, alien to the refined court verse, he put certain lines of Shakespeare's into a ridiculous light by timing them with lusty bits of staging. Compare the effect of the extravagant headdresses of this *Macbeth* with the equally extravagant ones of the German knights in *Alexander Nevsky*; for the latter, Eisenstein invented a mocking function that was an integral part of the pattern. For Welles, on the other hand, the costume extravagance of the film, like the boisterous irony shed on its language, was a quality of arbitrary wit: a playfulness out of keeping with the solemn intentions of the original dramatic work. Compare, with this Welles film, Kurosawa's flawless transposition of the same play to the barbarism of medieval Japan.

Another Shakespeare play, *Othello*, offers an even better example of Welles at work. Here, chiefly by tracking and a dolly that seemed to be over-oiled, the action is considerably augmented and 'cinematized,' so that the tragic effects, especially at the end, are turned into giddy *bravura*. As another tragic protagonist, Othello has behind him a more brilliant career of success than Macbeth. A strictly private and inward fault is the sole cause of Othello's downfall: sexual jealousy. Psychologically, Othello is very modern because he suggests the explanations of psychoanalysis; that is, he *desires* to believe in Desdemona's infidelity because he *also desires* to 'kill the thing he loves.' Welles, without making it clear whether he understood this complex nature of Othello, was evidently drawn by magnetic attraction to a hero with whom he had a great deal of empathy.

All Welles's heroes are 'big doers' who crumble; *magnificos* who are crushed by secret starvation of personal desires or a cancerous guilt. Fair, hale, noble, with a beard (as in *Othello*) or middle-aged, ignoble and ugly (as in the police chief in *Touch of Evil*), Welles as actor-director shows high human ambition in the grip of an obscure corrosion. The inquisitive reporter bent on searching out the magnate Kane's secret, the adventurer hired by Arkadin (another kingpin of wealth) to discover his own past, bear the same relation to the Wellesian type as Iago does to Othello: he is the chosen nemesis. The hero of *Citizen Kane*, despite all appearances, had been doomed to unhappiness; the reporter's quest simply reveals the technical origin of this unhappiness: a mechanism that has done its work. Welles's hireling hero is the *other self*, enlisted precisely to be the means of revelation to himself and the audience.

This conclusion may be found as a parable on Arkadin's lips when he relates (during the film) the fable of the scorpion and the frog. When *Mr Arkadin*, not long ago, had its American première at the New Yorker Theatre, Daniel Talbot encountered me as I left, and stopping to chat, spoke of this little

fable as a parable of Welles's own life. It is impossible to dis-
agree with Talbot's observation. And what is the parable but
something that applies to Kane's life and Othello's, no less
than Arkadin's, if we think of these roles as masks of Orson
Welles, hero-director? It is a parable for his life as a Big Experimental Cult hero. The scorpion must cross a stream (i.e.,
Welles must make a film) but to do so he must enlist the help of
a frog (it is easy to imagine a producer or a backer as a frog).
But 'Ah,' says the frog to the scorpion, 'your sting brings
death! So why should I carry you across?' – that is, why
should a producer listen to Welles's blandishments when notoriously he is a maker of expensive films that 'sink' their backers?
The scorpion then reasons: 'Now, look. If I sting you, you will
die, that's true, but if you die, I will drown – so why should I
sting you?' The frog-producer (once again!) is convinced by this
wily argument, swims across with the scorpion on his back
('Camera!') and duly gets stung. Before he sinks to his death,
he has time, however, to ask the scorpion: 'Why?' The scor-
pion-director makes this answer, the only one he can make:
'Because it is my character.' Thus, adapted to the present theme,
it is Welles's character to make films, even if he must 'perish'
with his backers.

I have long maintained that film presents an unusually glib
medium for parody and charade of many kinds. As Hollywood
parodies itself and its material (as in *Sunset Boulevard* and
just lately in the unspeakable *What Ever Happened to Baby
Jane?*), Welles does the same in his own line. As a personality,
Mr Arkadin is the summit of the Kanes and the Ambersons:
their melodramatic muse with an infusion of tragic grandeur.
Note that Arkadin wears the most artificial make-up ever
affected by Welles as an actor: he has Rochester's nose (in
Jane Eyre), a palpably false hairline and the beard of a
tragedian. During *Mr Arkadin*, someone compares him to
Neptune; my guess is that he is familiar with the famous
Greek bronze, so marvelously preserved, of Poseidon and de-
liberately tried to reproduce its head.

If we look closely enough at Welles's theatrical disguises,
bearing in mind the above-mentioned parable, we have, I

believe, a perfect image of film as the great adventure of true Experimentalism: a sort of 'confidence game' with laudable motives. Its hero is the substance of film cults at their 'cultiest.' Welles provides the complete Baedeker to failure as to success: an adolescent make-believer is posturing as an adult artist, and doing it so well, at times, that the imitation takes on a fabulous reality. The resultant charlatanry is not deliberate but the product of Welles's supreme confidence that he can overcome all defects of acting and story with his personal gifts. His talent and his remarkable drive are perfectly illustrated in still another directorial-actorial venture, this time on the stage: *King Lear*, played at the New York City Center some years ago.

Again was demonstrated the egoism in Welles that makes the creative wonder-worker into the benign-malign charlatan. I saw an early performance of *King Lear;* it looked under-rehearsed, with no actor in it up to Welles as Lear except Alvin Epstein as the Fool: the two made a very striking team. The production, with its flair and its slapdash, was greeted with moderate enthusiasm, at best, from reviewers and the public. The directorial touch and Welles as actor tended to dwarf the play and to leave most of its actors grounded. Later on, Welles had a backstage accident and appeared in his role on crutches. But then he had *another* backstage accident. ... If the 'scorpion' Welles has no 'frog' handy, he conjures one, it would seem, from the air. However, he refused, so to speak, to be sunk by the second accident and appeared in the role – so I understood – in a wheel-chair! It was enough to give even reserved admirers of Welles a sensation of awe. Surely, the feat set a precedent and aroused some sentimental *bravos* from Wellesians. Yet, apart from the star's fortitude and talents, I doubt that the wheel-chair interpretation added anything to the history of acting in the Shakespearian theatre.

This actor-director's main contribution to acting (as his boyish Othello showed) is a beautiful voice and a prodigal physical presence, the latter of which he invariably over-dramatizes, on the screen, with foreshortening from below. In the Little Experimental field, the same adventurism – let us call it Wellesian adventurism – is repeated again and again with varying, lesser means: the same, virtually automatic, egoism; the 'necessary' self-reliance; the relentless exploitation of the 'filmic' no matter what the material. One could easily list and identify all the parallels. ... Even were Orson Welles to repudiate these parallels, he is their cultural progenitor as much as is Cocteau, perhaps more than Cocteau. Welles, more than any one person in the world at this moment, is a cult incarnate – whether we approach his example from the side of the Little or the Big Experimentalists. He may never do a complete and untarnished work of film art, at once deep in theme and adequate in execution. Yet as a tireless infant Hercules, he has shaken the film firmament, and may (bearded or unbearded) do so again.

Postscript

The issuance of *The Trial*, and a few years later, Welles' adaptation of Falstaff's story from the Shakespeare plays, did nothing to change the cloudiness of Welles' talent as an *auteur* director – the French term has been generally adopted to indicate that a filmic adaptation, whether from an original script, novel or play, ought to rate as an original film if its director has been up to the mark. Welles' interpretation of *The Trial*, in all kindness, ought to be labelled an *auteur* work since it is quite off key as Kafka's work. There are no bravuras, no rhetorical spaces, in Kafka except in *Amerika*, where he seems consciously to have been influenced by comedy films, yet this filmic *Trial* is all acrid, mannered, at times cutely flattened grandiloquence, especially when Welles himself appears as the lawyer to whom K appeals for help.

The presence of Anthony Perkins, fatally miscast as K, can be justified only by the rumor that without him – that is, without a star of the first magnitude – Welles would have been unable to get the backing he needed for the scope of the film. No Welles work is without skilful touches, a true feeling for film language and film narrative, but K is not, decidedly, the hopelessly puzzled, sensibly earnest young man of Perkins' impersonation. The lawyer in the novel is supposed to live in a hovel expressly lit by a single candle. Welles chose the Hollywood scale for this setting and conspicuously employed several hundred candles, making the whole sequence (while, like an eccentric millionaire, he lolls voluptuously in a ducal bed) into a kind of camp that could not be further from Kafka's mood than if it were a spectacle gimmick from a musical revue.

As for the role of Falstaff, it has always waited in the wings for Welles to get around to cinematizing it. His later corpulence and fluid, open, caged-energy manner would seem admirable for Shakespeare's burly, rascally comedian of noble lineage and cowardly temperament. All the outer things of Falstaff, the beard, the encircling fat and windy braggadocio, fit the outer Welles so snugly that little of the inner humor, the savor of a subtly complex character, gets a chance to surface. The greatest nuance Welles could supply was to underplay at times, largely in terms of that slurring, *sotto voce* mumble that is so irritating a part of British acting repertory. The action is put together in a commonplace way and the fighting scenes, while filmically glib, are unduly prolonged and tiresomely 'choreographed.'

Sadly, I must conclude my Wellesian thesis on a pessimistic note. At this late stage, our Big Cult hero is plainly tired out, as his most recent offering, *The Immortal Story,* a tale (not, as the credits state, a novel) by Isak Dinesen, all too poignantly reveals. Reverently manhandling the original, Welles centers on himself as a moribund old man, highly made-up and badly made-up, with too many lines too, too manneredly recited. His direction of very simple atmospheric scenes, laid in China of the last century, is in taste and extremely resourceful; the color photography is also exceptionally good so that Welles' own narcissistic, self-coddling performance, rumbling slur and all, is the photographically lovely film's only downright flaw, Not that its other actors (aside from Jeanne Moreau) could not easily have been better despite the fine voice of the young man playing the sailor. The issue I originally invoked has been settled, I think, by the intervening time. The infant Hercules, in slipping maturity, is egregiously overripe. Now he can shake only a stage-set world, which itself is a rather sorry image of majesty. The Big Experimental Cult has lost an unevenly gifted 'little master' who worked most valiantly – when he could work.

13. Lust for Lifelikeness

Art in America – and above all movie art – tends to be the profession of champions, so it is of the first aptness that Kirk Douglas, whose dull performance as van Gogh in *Lust for Life* may well gain him the industry's annual 'Oscar,' also took the lead in a prizefight film called *Champion*. The idiom of slang – and above all American slang – is studiously avoided in the speaking script of *Lust for Life* as adapted from Irving Stone's novel: a fictionization of the artist's life that attained, worthless as it was, a certain sensational fame a few decades ago. The film is, in a word, flat: as though it were a family album edited (though it isn't) by a vigilant relative of the artist's. Yet so impressed are literate Americans by anything like conspicuous respect for genuine art that even a bona-fide art critic, Aline B. Saarinen of the New York *Times*, was lured into a benevolent attitude toward M-G-M's heroically unvulgar version of the life of this hero – excuse me! – this champion of painting, Vincent van Gogh.

Aesthetic colloquialism really means aesthetic fashions. Ernest Hemingway's style was a literary-type vulgarization of Gertrude Stein's discovery of an occult simplicity, which in the pages of Scott Fitzgerald reached a more authentically indigenous quality: Fitzgerald was discovered for his Americanism, Hemingway for his internationalism. Life as a fight with fame or a bull has an embarrassing monolithism when these two authors are regarded in the same perspective with the movies, not so alien to them at their best as many have supposed. Fitzgerald went through his last hectic Gethsemane in Hollywood, where he ended laid out on a cold stone slab with Dorothy Parker by him to articulate an all too brief and slangy elegy (familiar enough not to be repeated here).

Hemingway has said that he wrote *The Old Man and the Sea* to prove to critics of his previous novel that he could write – or 'still write' – a real book; it concerns an endless bout between a man and a fish and has been purveyed to the public anew in Hollywood's idiom of sea-photography, which luckily can more or less speak for itself. Who can go very wrong with the eternal ocean, especially when it turns out to be the 'winner'? A man's soul is a somewhat more delicate proposition, a fact of which the top level of Hollywood culture was apprised in the not too distant past. Lately, the popular image of the soul has been that which reveals itself when the body is prostrate on a couch and the unconscious is stirred up by questions and suggestions from licensed practitioners of mental medicine. Would Vincent van Gogh, belatedly recognized as a champion of painting, have been helped in his private problems by Freud and his colleagues? The doctors who did try to help him are certainly portrayed by this film with conscious, even selfconscious, dignity. But everyone knows that, as kind as people became to van Gogh, t was not a doctor who was to turn out the champion, but the poor man who cut off an ear and not long afterward shot himself rather than go through the ordeal of insanity before an audience of fellow creatures; an ordeal which, by visual and aural proxy, has just been given him.

One seriously wonders what, as a ghost, van Gogh would think of this re-enactment of his life and this incidental exhibition of his work. The rumor in town was rife that never before were the colors of paintings so faithfully reproduced on the screen. In their own way, a slue of film reviewers lent the hypocritically shy authority of their voices to the exemplary way both art and artist have been treated in the M-G-M film. It could not possibly occur to any of them that van Gogh's unique line, the true matrix of the Expressionist School, is quite unadapted to be paralleled with photographic representationalism. Yet the movie religiously has proceeded to suggest nature in the forms painted by its hero. Manet's early Impressionism, rather than van Gogh's style, is implied by photography itself, and innocently the film rubs in this ironic homage to other artists (Manet, Monet, Seurat) by staging a very un-van Gogh *Déjeuner sur l'Herbe,* with van Gogh and Gauguin seen on the *herbe.*

True, there are no Can Can girls in *Lust for Life,* and when one comes face to face with paintings almost filling the screen, it is as though one confronted them in art gallery or museum. If it were only a question of carrying art to the masses in convenient package-size, cushioned with sympathy-getting for the artist himself, this film might be construed as a reasonable facsimile of the superlatives lavished on it. But why should it have been designed only to be thus construed? The idea that color-photography can do anything but remotely suggest the true optical import of van Gogh's oil paintings is fraudulent when based on more than simple ignorance. Various types of color-photography have their own values and prisms but as a total technique their modulations are too much fused to do even approximate justice to the notably bold analysis of van Gogh's palette. Moreover, the fixed idea of photography-panderers that nature can be landscaped, faces made up, and actual places occupied by a movie company to give a truthful report of what happened in Vincent van Gogh's life, is foolish, not to say also a bit lunatic. Outside the theatre showing the film, the spectacle of Kirk Douglas made up and posed to look like van Gogh in a self-portrait with the artist in a straw hat, Douglas' photograph being placed next to a reproduction of that painting, would be enough to make the artist cut off his other ear. The self-inquiry and self-insight revealed in van Gogh's self-portraits are so much richer than the film's whole revelation that any comparison between them is in poor taste. The allegation that they *are* comparable is propaganda for the

Hollywood mystique to which I alluded above: art as the arena of champions.

That the artist is, and has long been, universal human society's ritual sacrifice, as a version of the medicine man who specifically fails in or outlives his magic, is rather recent as a manifest doctrine but very traditional in its identification of the artist with the magician, a social phenomenon that arose in the Middle Ages and touched even such artists as Leonardo and Botticelli. Through Thomas Mann, it has come down to us in the Faust legend revamped in the artist's explicit personality. The 'point' of *Lust for Life* is dismayingly simple: van Gogh failed in everything but painting, and the fact that he even seemed, during his lifetime, to fail in that is supposed to re-initiate mortally self-satisfied audiences into the sublime irony that some champions, either in bed or with their boots on, die before their enviable prowess is recognized for what it is.

One of the more hilarious spectacles of television these days – if that sort of hilarity tempts you – is the challenge rounds in art scholarship provided by Edward G. Robinson, chief collector of modern painting in the movie colony, and Vincent Price, art-educated actor who reigns as champion in that unique corner of art history, television. For all I know, as I write these words, Price has been unhorsed by his challenger, Robinson, but they have had at least two 'draw' conflicts; the sports vernacular (by the way) is not my notion but is employed on the air and in the ads. I imagine both Price and Robinson could identify the better-known van Goghs with as much ease as they can (and did) identify the almost touching hands of God and Adam on the Sistine ceiling. After *Lust for Life*, the fans who saw the former as a Sunday painter enjoying a pseudo-van Gogh-ish end in *Scarlet Street* and the latter as a mad, quite phony, sculptor in *House of Wax*, may likewise be able to identify the better-known van Goghs. Price, indeed, was the actor who played the art teacher in the framing-story of *Pictura*, a long documentary film about great works of art; there he showed a grotesquely elementary Achilles' heel by naming one of the more illustrious ornaments of Renaissance art, Carpaccio, as 'Car-park-io.'

I don't deny it: actors can be trained to pronounce (approximately) any language. But championship in the popular arts is not based on anything, of course, so technical. There is only one real champion in Hollywood, deathless and unchallengeable, Cliché. The movie force behind *Lust for Life* – in noble repudiation of the melodramatic excesses in Irving Stone's novel – is that Cliché himself, if treated with sufficiently elaborate respect, will earn Art as well as Box Office the right to wear the Crown. Van Gogh is but the historic stand-in for Champion Kirk (Kid Cliché) Douglas. As vocally represented by Douglas, he is a delayed 'juvenile delinquent,' morally intimidated and pleading for the compassion and tolerance of adults. This calamitous index to his character is the worst, and the nastiest, aspect of the impersonation; a creepy, undignified whine is so indelibly printed in Douglas' voice by his profession's notion of 'misunderstood artist' that, no matter what he says, the false, ghastly motif is audible. Pamela Brown, as the street woman van Gogh picked up, lived with, and portrayed, is so gratuitously stagey as to provide a veritable scandal in the film's casting. Almost as unfortunate is Anthony Quinn as Paul Gauguin; his voice has been distilled in tough-guy and braggart roles so long that even the actor's obvious effort to restrain and sensibilize it does not prevent his sounding like a Hemingway good-fellow valorously making the grade as an 'artist,' rather than like the man, and gentleman, Gauguin was. (Don't forget that gentlemen, too, swear and fight on provocation.)

The films, of course, have a dreadful precedent for making out the creative temper as blusterer if not also, for good measure, drunkard and whoremaster. Because Gauguin took ship as a sailor, Hollywood felt its license to cast Quinn in the part. As usual, the original libel is in fiction itself, where in *The Moon and Sixpence* (made years ago into a film) Somerset Maugham chose Gauguin's life as an excuse to exercise his middle-class spite against those individuals who abandon a money-making profession for a starving art, who choose bohemia, degradation, and disease (anyway, that's Maugham's story) in preference to a gentleman's life. As Hollywood has always been an unofficial propaganda office for vulgarity in literature, it is odd that Maugham's archetypal libel has been perpetuated in the van Gogh film by default; perhaps, however, it is not only zeal for a simple, negotiable story-line that the artist's unsuccessful experience as art-salesman in his own family's firm, Goupil's, has been dropped from the story, making it appear that his passion to be an evangelist was no reaction from the commercial world of art but sprang virginal from the young man's breast; it may also be, in fact, because the naïve wizards of the movies believed that Vincent's evangelism seemed too much a desperate, deceived 'device' (which it was) to express his lust for life that was art. Why is a Hollywood Champion – van Gogh is now crowned as such – a Champion? Not because of his lust for life, primarily, but because of his lust for lifelikeness (i.e., 'art'). Yet the most thankless project in the world – verging, indeed, on insolence – is that of asking the films to make this same distinction clear.

The theory of representation, even for Hollywood's sublimest imaginations, is the theory of anything that can be documented by a photograph, whether it be the most outrageous romance or the most respectful treatment of a great artist's life. You may be sure a natural *entente,* Out There, has been signed in advance between the Outrageous Romance and the Respectful Treatment. Stone's novel has been consciously toned down for the film by the insistent delusion of art scholarship – already the proud avocation of Hollywood professionals – and the insistent delusion that the footstep of psychiatry, like the footstep of art, is equivalent to the footstep approaching a death-bed; not merely respectful, but positively *reverent.*

That the deeply significant sources of the artist's suffering *as artist* are what Cocteau demonstrated well in *The Blood of a Poet* and not so well in *Orpheus* should not be news to a movie audience but probably it remains news to the majority of even a select audience. The moral meaning of all such well-meant fables as *Lust for Life* is that social deviants, even artists, are 'taxed' for having unpopular professional aims and unsocial private aims. Ultimately, as accredited champions, they are

forgiven because they have created beauty 'for all' and suffered in order to create it. The compliment paid posterity is
like the compliment paid spectators by the toreador who is
fatally gored in the bullring. He has, after all, killed many
bulls for their entertainment, just as van Gogh painted many
pictures – the last, *Crows in the Wheatfield*, as it were, killing
him.

False to fact where Stone's novel is true, the film has the
artist turning away from his easel by the wheatfield and going
behind a tree to put a pistol to his head and fire. Actually, an
interval passed between the last stroke painted and van Gogh's
fatal shot. But the point is the logical continuity between painting and another personal action which the film wished to document. If the continuity had not been thus obvious, it was
feared, the crucial point might escape the audience. This
reasoning was correct because not an iota of lucidity is created
by the movie's relations between van Gogh and his works. It is
enough that the wheatfield in nature looks as much like the
wheatfield in the painting as sweating artisans could make it.
For once, the shape of the painting itself was congenial to the
extra-wide screen used throughout. Flapping crows were re-
leased upon the field so realistically that one could even sense,
back of the camera, the cage from which the restless birds
were liberated. Since all grain was known as 'corn' in Europe,
the painting is known sometimes as *Crows in the Cornfield*.
Hollywood's archeology, in the end, may be as untrustworthy
as its casual linguistics, but in its championship of 'corn' (even
behind a pseudonym) it yields to no one. My! My! Why do
some films make one feel positively bad-tempered?

14. Megalomaniascope and
The Horse's Mouth

Among the thattascopes and thissacopes of the film screen, megalomaniascope seldom gets a mention in print, but it's there, operating on all jet cylinders and at ever wider angles. It's so much there that one takes it for granted, like the false exclamation points (false teeth in a horse's mouth) that appear in the ads after excerpts from reviews. The truth is that those under the daily or weekly obligation to assess the art of the movies are extremely conscious, even self-conscious, of book and theater culture, and so, when something comes along as literate and as honest as the new portrait of a painter in *The Horse's Mouth*, adapted from Joyce Cary's novel of that name, there is an irresistible urge amid the critically disposed toward glad approbation. One of the judicious went so far as to hail the screen's first 'pure painter': the hero, Gulley Jimson, impersonated by Alec Guinness, who was so inspired as to write the script himself. Axiomatically speaking, Guinness may be said to have followed what has grown to look like a noblesse oblige of filmdom's aristocracies: more and more homage to 'literature.'

But let me add at once, in case I have not adequately pointed it up formerly, that what the aristocracy of film talent bases itself on is a respect for literature decent and empirical enough, but scarcely 'pure.' Ever since film genius was swaddled in bioscope, gyroscope and other pristine forms of mechanically reproducing visible motion, it has, both respectfully and disrespectfully, emulated anything in life or art it could lay hands on. Soon enough, this meant 'prestige films' just as, to date, the most commercial book publisher takes up 'prestige items.' But given a superficial motive the best intentions become impure and abortive. Nothing like a pure feeling for *film as such* animated Guinness either in adaptation or impersonation; nor, as the evidence shows, did his feelings for Cary's novel, however admiring, result in a chaste loyalty to the original. For some reason, to begin with, Guinness dispensed with the novel's first-person narration, although the film has long found this congenial to its techniques.

Maybe, faced by the alternative of being faithful to film or faithful to literature, the most dangerous solution of all is to try to be faithful to both; therein may lie a moral to be deeply pondered. Readers of *The Horse's Mouth* are aware – or should be – that Cary's book is an interrupted stream-of-consciousness revealing exactly how the sixty-seven-year-old painter, Gulley Jimson (whose false teeth the movie never mentions), translates his daily visual experiences into ideas for paintings. This forms an aggressive – I think too aggressive – attempt to contribute something to literature. It owes a debt to Dickens, Joyce and even to the movies. Why, then, did not the talented Guinness seize upon so obvious an opportunity of exploiting a special technical means developed by the film? For here a novel had a ready-made 'film script.' Jimson is a veritable Caligari of paintbrush and palette, regarding the world and everything sacred in it as a mere armature for the chemistry of color and the fantasy of form. What does the dialogue and script actually do? It readily shows Jimson's zany tactics in the physical world, but it only hints at his inner workings by means of his fugitive comments and casual mots. A mere spectator of the film could not know what is in Cary's novel. But it could have been translated by the movie into filmic means which have been completely mastered: the by-now well-known capacity of film to create a phantasmagoria of vision – split-second spatial shifts, meltings, montage. .... *This* was the alternative to first-person narration.

Viewers coming raw to Guinness' movie might well be delighted that some of the seamy side of genius is conveyed by it with a minimum of stale convention and with no hifalutin occasioned by awe of The Artist. Outwardly, according to Cary as followed by Guinness, Gulley Jimson, the painter whose change of style has practically ruined his career, is a bum and behaves like a cross between a confidence man and a common pilferer. But this rudimentary agreement between novel and movie operates only in a limited field, a field surprisingly circumscribed by discrepancies that have crept in as the automatic result of 'film aristocracy' processes of thought. Where it is a matter of a star vehicle (which this film is), noblesse oblige is a horse's mouth that opens up only when told to. Is Gulley Jimson, physically, a stringy old turkey with something of a goon about him? Alec Guinness isn't. Guinness is a comfortably fleshed forty-seven or thereabouts, not a hard-bitten sixty-seven, and the only decisive way he has of conveying Jimson's age is a little trot which he has had set to a tune from Prokofiev's *Lieutenant Kije* suite. This rhythmic lope, threading the action to the end, is very weak tea in a man to whom mental drives are as strong drink. The fires of his plastic passion, among other things, have burned away Jimson's flesh.

Is it funny in the novel to hear Gulley tell about hoodwinking his former or prospective rich patrons with absurd pranks? Is it funny to see him wreck the home of one lordly such pair in order to paint a mural on their wall? It is just that funny in the film. But in the novel it is a little more than funny. There it has a hint of the monstrous and the sinister; in brief: the demonic. Guinness has not only toned down the plot's bravura and the style's bravura; he has excised Jimson's capacity for being deadly earnest and rather nasty about it. (Personally, I should much have preferred to see the late W. C. Fields in the part, coached by Chaplin and with the script by Eisenstein.) When, for instance, Gulley has a physical struggle for a precious painting with his former mistress, the lady ends up dead at the bottom of the stairs; by 'accident,' it is true, but if

Cary's Jimson had been no more violent in the struggle than Guinness, she would only have konked out over the bed-end as she does in the film. Thus, when actually looking into the horse's mouth, one must opine that the true atmosphere of Jimson's life and character have nothing to do with healthy teeth and much more to do with William Blake. The actress playing Sara betrays no tithe of the basis for the original Jimson's melodramatic conception of her as the sorceress of Blake's *Mental Traveller*, who 'cuts his heart out at his side./ She lives upon his shrieks and cries,/ And she grows young as he grows old.' In the novel, Gulley recites the lines, knowing, of course, that he is as much a 'sorcerer' as she is.

One would not call John Bratby, a leader of Britain's 'Kitchen Sink School,' a sorcerer, either, though he was commissioned to do the allegoric fantasies it was inevitable to show in the film. In fact, as his first one-man show in America plainly revealed, (held at French and Co. and opening on the day the movie did), all that was necessary to prove him no sorcerer of paint was these idle, inflated canvases: *Judgement Day*, *The Raising of Lazarus*, *Adam and Eve*. His other works, done spontaneously by the kitchen sink and opposite the television set, are just as large and sprawling, but show him as a contented sort of 'angry young man' (he falls thirty-seven years short of being as old as Jimson), painting his radical-bohemian friends in various stages of dress and undress as though they were all pre-Raphaelites of the Dowdy Era. At best, Bratby – a name that would demand a novelist's genius to think up – has a talent for vigorous draftsmanship and a flair for the analytic palette. He is supposed to owe a great deal to van Gogh. This may be true: brush strokes and twisting dark outlines support it. But by every kitchen sink is a kitchen stove and on it Bratby seems to have stirred in souvenirs of a number of other dishes: Gauguin and Tchelitchew, Albright and Beckmann; exotic enough seasonings that may account for the finished dish having a surface somewhere between tapestry, woodcut and cake-frosting.

Whatever ambiguity may exist about either a factual Bratby's or a fictional Jimson's profundity and sincerity, one would hesitate before calling either a 'fraud.' I see no reason to call either a fraud. But one book reviewer, at least, accepted Cary's painter as, however glorious, just that. One wonders if perhaps the deepest insight of Guinness into the part he performs was not the 'real' margin of doubt which Jimson's antics might create, in movie-goers, about his genuine call to his profession. It is patent that for Guinness, as for Cary, Gulley is a gay old underdog. Perhaps this should be enough for any movie horse's mouth. And it may even be that the proper function of mere print is not to decide whether the genius of a hypothetic visual art (to be verified by the true optical sense) is deep or superficial. The compromising part is that in the movies, Jimson's paintings must come to immediate optical perception. Yet traditionally an aristocracy, no matter what its noblesse, is also 'cavalier.' Guinness' general impulse to be cavalier toward Cary's novel seems reflected in a large number of deletions as well as sidesteppings. Jimson's Anarchist cronies – as trampy as *he* is – have been suppressed despite the fact that Guinness must realize that Anarchism, too, has been a notable horse's mouth in our day.

According to Cary, Gulley Jimson must be catapulted from a condemned wall, on which he and his students have labored to complete a mural, before he stops painting. Hence, as Jimson is carried from the scene in an ambulance, the novel ends on a comi-tragic note of perpetual motion: the obsessed artist's non-stop painting of which, after all, Gulley's non-stop talking is the mirror image. Guinness saw fit to change this conclusion by substituting a very old movie 'tag': the monastic, frustrated genius drifting into a blank future as though it were death. The film has Jimson, following the official destruction of his mural, 'escaping' on to his wretched houseboat and drifting away on the Thames from all human contacts. Doesn't one – in fact, isn't one *meant to* – detect toward the back of the horse's mouth a famous gold tooth called Tahiti?

15. Chaplin:
Autobiographic Artist*

After Sarah Bernhardt, no artist in any medium in the last hundred years has received so much expertly qualified adulation as Charlie Chaplin, and doubtless Chaplin has been more universally appreciated than anyone. There was an element of perfectedness in his clown, of pure clean organic inspiration, which triumphed in the eyes of all spectators; intellectuals almost unfailingly enjoyed it and it struck an unstinted response from such hermetic artists and dogmatists as the Dadaists and Surrealists. Every conceivable nuance of aesthetic reaction and every verbal convention of criticism has certainly, at one time or another, in one language or another, been bestowed on Chaplin's art. Not even the cinematic genius of Griffith's early films was so absolute and invulnerable as Chaplin's first screen comedies. It was not merely that Charlie had created an authentic clown of world stature – a clown whose genius was recognizable even in flat silhouette – but that he immediately created in film a pattern perfectly adapted to it as a technical medium. As an actor, Chaplin used an art equivalent to dance-pantomime and as such, in his first series of short comedies prior to his 'feature films' (which grew longer and longer), his

* This movie letter, written for *The Kenyon Review* in 1947, was the matrix of the author's book on Chaplin.

art was actually a precursor to the mathematical precision and breathtaking pace of the animated cartoon in Walt Disney's hey-day. We should not hesitate to place Mickey Mouse and Donald Duck beside their legitimate predecessor; indeed, the miracle was that Chaplin's style was as 'correct' in the animal and mathematical senses as that of Mickey, Donald, Bugs Bunny, et al. Time and its inevitable concomitant of human experience, however, have witnessed a recession of musical completeness and brilliance in Chaplin's art. What at first seemed mere slapstick action was eventually recognized as the exact correlation of tempo, emphasis, and climax. Recession took place not because of any deterioration in the integral mechanism of the artist himself, but because of what film terms 'the scenario' – that is, plot and theme. Chaplin's art, as expression of the entire work, has gradually lost *animal* integrity as it has striven to gain *intellectual* integrity; it has lost human integrity in one field, *the aesthetic,* as it has striven to gain it in another, *the moral.*

The history of this process would form a profound chapter in the annals of modern art. Of course I can give only a sketch of it here. It may be news to those who do not follow the theatrical pages in newspapers that in *Monsieur Verdoux,* his newest movie, Charles Chaplin (as the screen reveals his name) has abandoned his traditional tramp-clown and become a sort of middle-class dandy; in brief, a version of Landru, the notorious French Bluebeard. Certain mannerisms of style remain; the image, both inert and animate, has considerably changed. The New York press, since the movie opened several months ago, has given it consistently rather sour reviews, only the aesthetically 'educated' among the reviewers praising the film for its content and for its skilful scenes and acting. That anything like a 'problem', personal or general, artistic or moral, was being historically situated by Chaplin – this, none essayed to proclaim. John Mason Brown, for example, complained that Chaplin had committed the error of becoming highbrow. Certain Red-baiting newspapers accused Chaplin of being a Communist. In a radio interview, he was mercilessly badgered by members of the press representing journals from *PM* to

The Christian Science Monitor, who took him to task for not having become an American citizen, for not having entertained troops during the war, for not having conspicuously aided the United States' war effort with monetary means. Chaplin was obviously embarrassed by this radio barrage and he was reported to be depressed over the widely unfavorable reaction to his picture. The general implication is that a genius has disserved his art by a self-conscious preachment and one certainly not to be taken as 'patriotic.' The vagueness of film criticism here plunged into the abyss below its thin intellectual ice. No artist is so great or so remote that he may be presumed in detachment from his art; art is not a costume that can be hung up or taken down at will; it is part and parcel of the human being as he develops in time. Ironically, no one has been orientated to observe that *precisely because* Chaplin wished to prove the interdependence between man and artist, he has failed as an artist if not necessarily also as an ethically inspired man. Of course, the 'correctness' of Chaplin's social criticism is a separate matter, inasmuch as the traditional weight of his art (spasmodically sustained here) does not, per se, determine his reasoning as a social thinker.

Let me hasten to say that Chaplin's 'social criticism' is far from being novel or complex. One might, from the broad view, even call it paltry. In certain radical circles, not necessarily politically denominated, 'war' as 'a business,' which is Chaplin's chief indictment of modern society in *Monsieur Verdoux*, is a hoary platitude and in itself not heating to the blood. But patently it is a considerable novelty on the movie screen, where it is stated verbally by Chaplin in the bluntest possible terms and with a bitterness of intonation carrying with it, astonishingly enough, a grain or two of smugness. Monsieur Verdoux's death-cell justification is to assert that his crimes of having murdered some fifteen innocently bigamous wives for their money has been only a small private enterprise compared with the wholesale murder of wars. A certain naïveté, naturally, appears amid the coarse integument of the comic murderer's too serious 'last words.' He is impersonal, rational, and calm, and if Chaplin does not actually seem to step out of character, as he deliberately did in the last moments of *The Great Dictator* in order to speak in behalf of persecuted peoples, it is largely because *Monsieur Verdoux* is less of a definite role, less the traditional clown 'Charlie,' than was the Little Barber in the *Dictator* film.

But we should notice an important distinction here. It is precisely *not* that a schism appears in *Monsieur Verdoux* between man and artist (each theoretically remaining intact) but that, as the change of costume and modification of personality show, man and artist have been drawn closer together. Mr Chaplin said some time ago: 'The tramp is dead.' It is true and it meant, *the art of the tramp is dead*; it has not merely been shelved for something 'highbrow.' The very fact that no obsequies are being celebrated for the artist Chaplin proves that most spectators, including his most sentimental supporters, either 'cannot see for Charlie' (are blind to the present) or are deluded into accepting the person of 'Monsieur Verdoux' as a worthy substitute for the sovereign clown. But it is not meaningless that Monsieur Verdoux is a murderer and expires at the end of the film (which has opened with a shot of his gravestone). He is a separate character, a 'role' for Charlie, in a sense in which even the 'Hitler' of *The Great Dictator* was not; for the latter was merely – as shown by the film's plot of mistaken identity – the tramp's own nightmarish charade of his social enemy, the dictator. Monsieur Verdoux is a sort of phoenix born from the ashes of Charlie, but one fears that Verdoux's ashes are without the same galvanic power: Landru was too much a mere mask for Chaplin.

From the very beginning up to *The Great Dictator,* Chaplin was always *Charlie*, a character who combined Don Quixote with Sancho Panza, the knight with the fool; it is to be noticed that Charlie always had the sexual romanticism of the Don and the practical predicament, the glum recognition of reality, belonging to the Don's servant. The gymnastic guile and terpsichorean charm displayed by Charlie in, respectively, escaping the clutches of a large wicked hoodlum and shyly wooing the embraces of a pretty girl are to be compared, as I have hinted, with the pyrotechnic rhythms of the Disney company in analogous situations. The basic thing about Charlie, socially and economically speaking, was the *underdog*, the 'mouse.' And what is the mythic definition of a 'mouse'? Nothing but a man degraded by his inferior strength and pink heart, nothing but the underdog without visible means of aggression. The inferior in strength and courage are either saved by social laws ('humanity') or must resort to strategy in preference to being passively exterminated. The drama of David and Goliath, indeed, is part of Charlie's and Mickey's myths but it is their essentially *symbolic* part, that wherein the real individual has least correspondence to the myth-character. They played 'David' only as the last alternative. It is also important that, as the Depression ex-murderer who has lost the wife and child for whose sake he conducted his murder business, Monsieur Verdoux goes more or less voluntarily to what he terms 'destiny'; i.e., arrest, trial, conviction, and execution. Is this not the mythical underdog 'realistically' confessing that the odds are too much against him, that the 'Goliath' of society will be triumphant? In the beginning, Monsieur Verdoux is only a little bank clerk thrown out of his job by the Depression that followed the First World War; one of the many 'social victims' who happens in this case to determine on a lone-wolf sort of economic reprisal. It is 'David's' own last alternative and it fails.

Not only is the history of this failure written by *Monsieur Verdoux*, but also by *City Lights*, *Modern Times*, and *The Great Dictator,* done consecutively over the last fifteen years. After all, there is no reason to quibble. The tramp, Charlie, was never quite honest until his modern period, in which he worked and tried to 'go straight.' This moral waywardness was a principal reason for his attractiveness: he *was,* and so obviously, an underdog sometimes cornered like a rat and ever ready to bite in the clinches. It was Charlie's ingenuity, his unfailing dance-grace triumphing at once over tatterdemalion clothes, homeliness, and lack of education and training (both signs of wealth), that universally delighted the spectator. And, just as though he were dancing or performing legerdemain, he finally would subdue the burly, repulsive villain. Through a combination of skill and fate, sheer effort and luck, Charlie emerged essentially unscathed. If sometimes he was as frustrated as Don Quixote himself, he obviously was still experiencing the fleshly desire of Sancho Panza; if sexually inexperienced (indeed, virtually pubescent), he was far from being sexually innocent. Here of course was another assurance of Charlie's 'universal' validity. He always had the same problem: winning a girl and avoiding starvation. So the material on which the great artist worked was the most basic known to man and orientated, moreover, to the normal being's minimum requirements: sex and bread (here so closely allied) plus something that, in the long perspective of Chaplin's life as man and artist, has an almost metaphysical status, *aesthetic idealism*, of which woman is the heart and symbol; indeed, the Don's own personal characteristic again. Yet, as Charlie had the realism of the normal male of modern times, he was invariably a fall-guy for a pretty face and shapely legs.

In *City Lights*, the romantic-sex theme took second place to Charlie's duel with the burly villain, who was no other, here, than a dipsomaniac financier afflicted with schizophrenia; when in his cups, the capitalist opens his arms and his home to the little tramp; when sober, he rejects him as a miscreant. 'Goliath,' in the Little Man Versus the Big Man drama, is obviously being socially orientated to the paunchy, Nero-like capitalist as 'the man behind' Charlie's arch-enemies of old: the huge hoodlum and the huge policeman. In *Modern Times*, the emphasis shifts to romantic sex combined with 'slave' labor; the factory sequences conspicuously bring some of the animated-cartoon machines and machine-like precision to the fore. Charlie gets occupational hallucinations which compete with his hallucination of the Ideal Cottage for Two. In *The Great Dictator* it was likewise, with the important discrepancy that the tramp has been economically stabilized; he is a barber until organized political banditry puts him (as a Jew) out of business. A curious contretemps had taken place in *Modern Times*. As Charlie was being pursued he accidentally came in the path of a strikers' protest parade. This occurrence might appear symbolic of a tide of events that overwhelmed the little tramp and made him socially conscious. The 'tide of events' took a disastrous form in *The Great Dictator*, only the coincidence of Charlie's close resemblance to the Dictator providing the irony of their exchange of places and the little barber's escape through an 'accidental' sort of destiny.

I once wrote* that Chaplin, in giving himself the dual role in *The Great Dictator*, performed a feat symbolic of his artistic and moral development. In this movie he seemed aware that the clown he had placed on the heights was a form of moral paradox since he was, in the extra dimension of professional reality, a virtual dictator over his own art; i.e., Chaplin as artist had formed a dictatorship over Chaplin the Little Tramp, and the latter was overrich with perfection in the one dimension as much as he was indigent of food in the other. Moreover, the Dictator is portrayed as a man who despairs of being loved, whereas the Little Barber looks forward to romantic happiness as well as good business. So as the Tramp became conventionalized and part of the economic structure, the lonely self on the other hand, the despondent Don, was metamorphosed into the mad political tyrant. With sound reason. This evolution revealed something in Chaplin's personal dilemma as a man; his marriages were never quite successful and he had become known as an ardent lover in pursuit of the 'right woman,' a quest which his artistic role has always echoed. His great professional standing obviously aided him in this pursuit. It was natural, therefore, that as the Great Dictator the artist Chaplin might conceive himself as someone with the power to kill (an inversion of the power to love) but lacking the power to *make himself loved*. As soon as the Little Tramp's chimerical dream of happiness in *Modern Times* temporarily becomes socially plausible in *The Great Dictator*, it reaches sudden disaster (the Nazi persecution).

In this perspective, we may sight the schizophrenic capitalist in *City Lights* as the first projection of Chaplin's own alter ego: the big money-maker. In one sense Chaplin might love his personal creation, love the wistful charm and pathetic,

* *The Hollywood Hallucination*, pp. 121–6.

gloriously comic grace of his Tramp, and consider the poetry of this symbolic hero an aesthetic ultimate: a universal symbol great enough to be permanent and to swallow his personality as a man. But his own inner development decreed otherwise. He could not bear to conceive this creature – a fantastically carnal sort of Ariel – as at one with the great professional, the all-powerful money-maker. Yes: this was a paradox of another, the realistic, dimension of life opposed to that of art. There was a profound urge to escape the ego-projection of the demon-capitalist, a Sancho Panza grown successful. This story of escape was in *Modern Times*: the Tramp imagines himself an honest worker with every worker's dream: a little cottage for two. But the haunting myth of slave labor was too much an omnipresent thing for Chaplin, as one who had known poverty early in life, to ignore even in his art. In the end, the reformed tramp is foiled; he has to hit the road with his girl and a knapsack. We leave them there but they both return in the small tradesman and his bride in *The Great Dictator*. The alter ego has revived in Hitler, a *pro*jection like a *re*jection: symbol of Chaplin the Dictator of Comedy. This man is hateful because his power is arbitrary, humanly futile. Here Chaplin encompasses the Pagliacci legend: the man whose supreme art cannot control his love life. Indeed, the Canio motif is the element producing Monsieur Verdoux, for Chaplin wished to abandon the sterile symbol of the Great Comedian, with an art powerless to win happiness, and to imagine himself as a *victim* of the economic system rather than as one who should triumph over it in vain. The 'dead' Tramp haunted and possessed his creator.

There are remarkable bits and sequences in *Monsieur Verdoux*. The best are the most sustained, those most reminiscent of sequences in Chaplin's previous films. But this is only to criticize the film's *art*. As the odyssey of a man, *Monsieur Verdoux* is Chaplin coalesced into a naturalistic paradigm of himself; the actor goes through his routines somewhat as he might in rehearsal – in dapper clothes and sleek gray hair. He is happy in a faithful wife and a child, whom he keeps in comfort through his murder business. Chaplin has determined to

consider the myth of the Ideal Cottage, full of 'romantic' satis-
factions, as a *logically given* reality. True, he is hardly ever
home, but this factor of absence only conforms with the ideal
or symbolic quality of this element: it exists primarily *as an
idea*. Meanwhile, what is happening? Verdoux is marrying
women with complete cynicism and wilfully murdering them.
I fail to see the subtlety, of which a few critics have been conscious, in regard to this 'satire' on war. If it is subtle, I hazard,
it is because these murdered ladies are symbols of the frustrated affairs in Chaplin's own life: for which Chaplin has
transformed himself to become the cruel, heartless tyrant,
mocking the nature of love. Charlie 'Verdoux' still chases
women, but with the opposite of his former moral intent. Well,
one might say, marriage itself *is* a sort of business, the orthodox business of society in self-perpetuation, and no doubt
somewhat 'vulgar' to the soul of the medieval Quixote. Marry-
ing for money becomes the supreme cynicism and murder
merely a perversion of the tender aggression of sex.

As a Bluebeard, Monsieur Verdoux must be considered, despite Chaplin's own conception, as a disguised psychopath. It
seems odd that spectators should take Chaplin's conscious
motive (the 'satire' on the 'business of war') so much for
granted; very odd, in a psychoanalytical era, to leave un-
touched the implicit proposition that extremist forms of finan-
cial as well as political dictatorships are but compensatory
superstructures of sexual failure – especially, one might add, in
the symbolic realm of art. Is Mr Chaplain perhaps unaware of
the relation of money and money-symbols to the sex life? – not
to mention that sexual pathology is one of the statistically
sound motives for murder? How carefully Chaplin has loaded
his own guns in making Verdoux secretly 'virtuous': a 'good'
husband and father. Of course, this is part of the satire on the
bourgeois who loves at home and by proxy kills abroad. My
complaint is that, whatever the obscure causes of the Love Dictator Verdoux's triumph of will, he has devoured the Little
Tramp to the serious damage of Chaplin's comic art. In this
way Chaplin has, pessimistically and bitterly, conceded the
universally symbolic triumph of Hitler's spirit in having de-

stroyed the heart and soul of the little Tramp, symbol of the common man and his naïve ideals. Chaplin's comic epic no longer contains the alter ego. But it lacks just as obviously the artistic integrity of the great clown.

Part 4
Film Aesthetics
Pro and Con

16. New Images

Dom: a film by Walerian Borowczyk and Jan Lenica
Loving: a film by Stan Brakhage
L'Opéra Mouffe : a film by Agnès Varda

What have we here? Three nominally experimental films that
are of three distinct categories of experimentalism. All three
were entered at the Experimental Film Festival, Brussels, 1958,
in good faith, I am sure, as both avant-garde and experimental,
yet in substance and approach, as well as method, they are so
diverse that at once it is evident that at least one of them over-
laps on the documentary area. All three, moreover, were distinguished by an award – the most fortunate being *Dom,* which
took the Grand Prix (about $10,000). In addition, alert critics
might be expected to determine what each one means to the
art of the film.

As one who did not attend the Festival itself, I find it natural
(as others must) to wonder how just and plausible were the
awards given these entries. Since statistics regarding the jury
and the types of film considered have been announced elsewhere, including the program notes of Cinema 16 (which held
screenings of the prize-winners in New York), I shall not give

them here. In any case, the point that engrosses me is the status of the three above-named films as avant-garde art.

The truth about avant-garde film is that it is *the* art of the film, existing as it were under concentration camp conditions, and not just the vanguard of a body of long-recognized and mature art. The 'art of the film' is, alas! not, as many imagine, a given quantity. Having no implicit existence such as other arts have won, it has to be defined and demonstrated. This is so simply because – to state it in the fewest possible words – commerce has far too strong a grip on film standards to have permitted a competent school of criticism to eliminate from consideration as art all the more or less elegant claptrap touted by critics themselves as art. Here I can merely define, not argue, this premise as such.

Let us directly regard the film art in the light cast diversely by *Dom, Loving,* and *L'Opéra Mouffe.* Putting it this way, one may classify as follows: *Dom* adheres with a truly classic purity to the postulates and precedents of the Dada-Surrealist school of Buñuel, Dali, Man Ray (incidentally one of the judges), and Marcel Duchamp; undoubtedly, this is the true avant-garde school which has been internationalized, and which Cocteau and his followers in the U.S. have systematically expanded and rationalized. It has one vital, governing premise: the mechanical recording of natural movement and the photographic surface of nature (as well as nature's colors) are 'out'; movement in film is to be as varied and arbitrary as movement in music while the image itself can be transformed or distorted in any way suiting the purposes of the film artist.

One is always aware, looking at *Dom,* that its movement is governed by 'danced' rhythm; actually, the movement is usually equivalent to the earliest cinematographic attempts to record nature, but here paced variously at will. By *Dom*'s courtesy, therefore, we can discern the same sort of movement *as aesthetic value* because (as when we are shown an antique film print of two men fighting and fencing) it is manipulated rhythmically and spatially in whatever way desired; the film's modernist music score italicizes this point. Using film, art and scientific prints, as well as direct photography of nature, *Dom* provides a consistent feeling of artifice that nowadays may strike us as 'puritanical': it is pre-eminently a *laboratory* film, the true creative work being concentrated in the ways that already created drawings and photographs are re-used; no laboratory device is actually original (I believe) and yet the ensemble, since a highly conscious idea animates it, is beautifully presented and holds together.

Dom uses a basic symbolist method, and, of course, symbolist ideas in art still mystify even a specialized art public, just as poetry itself still mystifies those who went through Shakespeare courses in school. The symbolist idea in *Dom*, however, could hardly be simpler or stricter. 'Dom' means *house* or else *master*. A woman waits for her husband or lover, whose footsteps she hears on the street outside (the fighting sequence indicates he may be away having a duel); he comes in, places his hat on an old-fashioned hatrack and appears to her as a handsome clothes-dummy's head, which she caresses only to see it soon disintegrate under her eyes (perhaps signifying the wound he has suffered in the fight).

The above, naturally, is only the synopsis. The film's central idea has been communicated, I imagine, by a sequence dealing with a primitive graphic concept of the brain's mechanical structure: man's true 'home' is his brain, which forms all his notions of the outside world. This theme has been presented in terms of an old house front, old prints, and old-fashioned props, including a very lovely 'vamp type' lady; as still images, many shots are close to the Dada collages of Max Ernst and Francis Picabia's paintings. The strictly controlled rhythms and repeated image-sequences build up suspense and tension. Someone is coming; someone waits; what will happen? A green wig is animated as though it were a spider or an octopus; it moves in minimal jumps the way the women's head is made to move as she opens her eyes on hearing the man's footsteps. Time is cyclic because – as psychology has long known – the anxiety of waiting, in the mind of the one who waits, anticipates and re-anticipates an event over and over before it really happens.

All this is simple enough and certainly familiar enough.

The distinction of *Dom* lies in an asset which a great majority of the films seen at the Festival, for one or another reason, may have seriously neglected, and whose presence in *Dom* may account for its gaining the Grand Prix. This is a careful, sensuously beautiful surface: a continuously designed and appealing area of vision whose clean, dramatic composition is never allowed to lapse. If any fault at all were to be found with it technically, one could observe that it is sometimes a little on the smart magazine 'layout' side and resembles the advertising décor influenced by the Bauhaus as well as by surrealism ... all the more surprising, then, its true inspiration. Its clean technical edges, both aural and visual, may have decided the experts in its favor. One has merely to place it next to *L'Opéra Mouffe* and a film similar to the latter, *Life Is Beautiful,* also entered at the Festival and shown at Cinema 16, to see just how 'pure' *Dom* is as an avant-garde experimental and how 'impure' the other two are.

We should notice, so far as method is concerned, that *L'Opéra Mouffe* and *Life Is Beautiful* parallel *Dom* to a certain extent. This overlap lies in the rudimentary concept of *montage* as defined by Eisenstein. *Dom* uses artificially colored clips from dated movies, photographs, and prints; *Life Is Beautiful* exclusively uses film clips from studio storerooms (jazz dancing, parades, concentration camps, atomic explosions, and a studio-made allegoric sequence as climax). All black and white, *L'Opéra Mouffe* probably photographed its sequences from scratch, but they *could* have been film clips so far as their material and approach go; strangely enough, this film too uses symbolic sequences of the animate still-life kind; a dove trapped in a glass globe, one suspects, is a coy version of Peace artificially confined in Space.

Only, in one perspective, what it pretends to be, *L'Opéra Mouffe* (a pun on 'L'Opéra Bouffe' and a poor Paris neighborhood nicknamed La Mouffe) is a sensitive documentary, and, as such, 'experimental' to the extent that it introduces imaginative moods into the documentary. We see lyrically, unaffectedly nude lovers; we see children playing monsters in masks; we see the pitifully old, the morally and physically misshapen. But is the method of showing these things imaginative *enough?* For one thing, it is uneven. At times, it is pretentious, arty, and banal (as in the young girl running slow-motion through a field, and in the trapped dove) and at other times it simply 'drifts' by adding one image statistically, rather than meaningfully, to another (as in the sequences of drunks and the people wiping their noses); in such cases, the *montage*-idea becomes very diluted. Image added to image without development or impetus is not true *montage* but picture-magazine journalism ... here 'exotic' to Americans because it depicts Paris, tritely famous sink of iniquity. Technically, *L'Opéra Mouffe* is a 'suite', a series of facets, but these facets possess no unifying principle either intellectual or sensuous. Supposedly, one thinks: 'How human! how pitiful! how sweet! how strange! ... in brief: how lifelike!' Yet, however interesting and well-photographed in the conventional sense, the 'anthology' attitude that life is an endless network of strange contradictions can never get, in terms of meaning, beyond the stage of clever reporting; it can never reach the stage of meaning that is art *as an efficient form*; it falls apart into the scattered materials of *potential* art.

Yet when, as presumably here, reporting *pretends* to be art, how undependable the reporting, as such, emerges! *L'Opéra Mouffe,* with its air of a jaunty café ballad, is deceptively 'chic' and highly irresponsible in every way. The best reason for talking about it is that it represents a decided trend in ways of contemporary thinking, insofar as these ways have a significant moral meaning. This too involves the technical procedure of *montage*. The 'trick' of placing lyric, exuberant, and happy images side by side with dreary, pathetic, and horrible ones is that we live in an age of special fear and tension, fed intimately by two world wars within half a century and the prospect of a third, ominously fatal, one. Like *L'Opéra Mouffe, Life Is Beautiful* is geared to this moral psychology. Its *montage* is sometimes audio-visual, as when we suddenly hear Louis Armstrong's familiarly funny 'life is beautiful' theme rasped out while images of a great social disaster unreel before us; in strictly visual *montage*, nightclub whoopee serves as an immediate introduction to inmates of concentration camps in all their misery. This 'allegorical space' of social protest and criticism is pure *montage* according to a basic definition.

But what are we supposed to *feel,* and what are we supposed to *conclude,* in the presence of this same allegorical space? Viewing the ape who places a wreath upon a tombstone surmounted by a marble cherub, and reading the inscription, 'Homo Sapiens', what can we feel and think but 'How ironic, how pitifully ironic! ... man is still only a thinking beast!' Actually, it is a rather stale joke, put in this way, and we occasionally laugh or groan in neurotic desperation; the filmic invention, as such, is minimal, and so is the imagination. Therefore *Life Is Beautiful,* and *L'Opéra Mouffe* too, are simply documentary treatments of a moral psychology, and 'experimental' only insofar as they play on it in terms of *montage* imagery. One may call them radical-liberal, even 'avant-garde,' journalism, but not *art.* They are 'stunts' and once their points are absorbed, they appear empty – like editorials.

One point naïvely overlooked by this 'sophisticated' school of film journalism is that the festival of the clown, part of the ancient rites of mourning death, implies the human truth which Dante epitomized in the title of his *Divine Comedy:* death is not merely death, it is also resurrection. Thus, in the two-faced masks worn by children in *L'Opéra Mouffe,* life is but the other side of the coin of death, comedy but the other side of the coin of tragedy. In human experience, it is far from being news that horror and joy, beauty and ugliness, life and death seem inextricably mixed with one another; in fact, it is the oldest truth of consequence to be discovered and honored by mankind. Modern views, those of social protest, suggest that this is perhaps because man is still imperfect, still too much of an ape, and that human cruelty, and the killing of man by man, can be eliminated from human destiny.

However laudable this viewpoint is, it has existed for many ages in many forms, and when called to our attention once more, must be highly equipped in intellectual or artistic terms to merit our praise and interest. *L'Opéra Mouffe,* substantially, is only a reporter's visual notebook about the backgrounds and conditions of significant human experience; it is inadequately processed studio material, playing a charade as an experimental film. In contrast remains *Loving*, Stan Brakhage's film, which despite its obvious subject – a couple making strenuous love in the woods – manages to be personal, spontaneous, and noteworthy because it sustains the fundamental creative attitude of *inventing* with its directly photographed nature. Not that its invention, which is rather familiar in type, goes very far, but that it fully comprehends the reaches of its given limits.

What is important is that this color film of five minutes, unassisted by sound of any kind, creates a lyric and very real mood of love-making and that, actually, it was but one of the eight films for which Brakhage received his special award. Much more valuable and interesting than *Loving*, among these eight, are *Flesh of Morning* and *Reflections on Black,* both of which I discussed in a biographic account of this young film artist in *Film Culture* for April, 1958. *Loving,* however, should stand as a blackboard example of what can be accomplished with a correct attitude, one beginning by being severe and allowing neither journalism nor artiness to spoil the result. This film is symbolic of the creative myth so intelligently recommended by Cocteau to young film-makers having very little means: take your camera out into the world and start shooting. ... No single image in the nine films shown by Cinema 16 is any more dynamically or formally beautiful than those of the atomic explosions. Until filmmakers understand the true *artistic* significance of this fact, there can be no comprehensive art of the film.

17. Ciné-Dance

The very medium of film contributes to our awareness of what a philosopher has termed the Dance of Life. Film alone, among artistic media, makes a plastic contribution to visible movement beyond what is made by dance, chiefly theatrical dance, itself. Basically, dance is the human body's movement rendered systematically and meaningfully in terms of rhythmic pattern; its expressive ends vary according to the type of dance since dance is founded on ancient ritual which may be only a grave, rhythmic pantomime or the highly active bacchanal. Dance as ballet, whether Oriental or Occidental, is an elaborate exercise derived from court ritual, and as classic ballet in the East and the West has become a complex physical technique requiring the highest skill. Modernism in ballet has simply altered the form of the old *danse d'école*. What one may call ciné-dance, or the dance of film, reduces the formal issue of dance movement to new elementals: a wholly different arc of modernism.

Film means that the question is no longer simply one of the human dancer's physical aspects but of several simultaneous types of rhythm dominated by the camera-medium. There is basic film-editing, which means portraying a photographed action in certain components, not from beginning to end from a fixed viewpoint, keeping the whole action (whether dance or not) always in view, but retaining only its significant phases. Documentary dance films strive against this same principle of editing in order to approximate what we see in the theatre. But that kind of filming has nothing to do with ciné-dance *per se*. Modern creative workers in film – such as, outstandingly, the late Maya Deren – have always understood that the camera itself is a sort of dancer and therefore, strictly speaking, a collaborator with the human dancer. Simply by arbitrarily repeating parts of a dance figure (no matter how photographed), a film modifies the dance's original form and rhythm.

In her *Study in Choreography for Camera*, Maya Deren established by direct illustration the fact that the shift from one viewpoint to another in film shots is a fundamental matter of rhythm, one might say a pulsation of space that significantly, pointedly qualifies the original dance movement. In this now famous work, done in slow motion, a solo dancer begins a figure in the woods, continues it without apparent interruption in a studio, then in a vast hall in a museum, to reach its climax on a cliff overlooking a river. The space about the dancer has also moved and in a given rhythm; this has been effected by total changes in the camera's viewpoint implying wide spatial shifts. With this method of altering environment and isolating parts of the dancer's body as he enters the new scene, a greatly condensed space gathers behind the dancer, heaps up under him, so that his dance acquires a new mysterious force (particularly in aerial suspension) while the choreographic pattern remains quite intact and he himself exerts no extra effort.

Even in documentary dance films, changes of viewpoint, while on the contrary narrow and at a minimum, are utilized precisely to avoid reproducing our experience in the dance theatre, where the action is viewed from a seat, a single unchanging point. A truly creative aim in film, however, does not simply remedy a disadvantage but rather aims at the principle of ciné-dance as a creative asset, a new form. The fertile moral of this principle is to refer us to the protean genius of film itself. What I have called basic film-editing (or montage) is an absolute rhythmic instrument which can be used to give expressive form – rhythm and harmony of meaning – to the most ordinary action having nothing to do, technically speaking, with dance. We must not overlook that changing only slightly a film camera's viewpoint, from near to far, from above to below, and always implying optical movement, refers to the film's subjective existence, not to the objects being photographed. Another American film maker, Marie Menken, using a hand-held camera, has filmed the immobile sculpture of Isamu Noguchi by swaying the camera rhythmically back and forth, making ciné-dance exclusively a matter of the medium itself. This is an elementary case but significant for that very reason.

When two commercial directors, François Truffaut and Alain Resnais, used an effective 'freeze' (or sudden arrestment of film action) for a dramatic or fantastic purpose, this common device became a big-film mannerism over the world. The obvious fact is that the 'freeze' is only a tiny fragment of what is to be termed ciné-dance. If we stop to think, the 'freeze' corresponds, in regular dance choreography, to the climactic dance pose held for a few seconds. Various filmic devices indicate the possibility of ciné-dance even without the serious, or consciously aesthetic, utilization of these devices. Slow motion in the filming of running and leaping figures has always suggested dance, whereas if the same figures were seen moving at normal tempo, they would not necessarily suggest an analogy with dance. Slow motion (as Maya Deren's films constantly reveal) is very apt also for presenting dream action and trance states, thus enabling us to gain insight into the deepest rudiment of physical movement as an expression of rhythm. Slow motion makes optically available the precise interaction of limbs and muscles, producing the kinaesthetic state: a sympathy between external body-movement and the person witnessing it.

To say that rhythm is instinctive to life, and thus inseparable from movement and ideas of movement, is not at all new. Ciné-dance, however, is a relatively recent amplification of means in what is still a relatively young art. American experimentalists have been foremost in associating the principle of ciné-dance with dance itself. A conspicuous instance of late years is the ciné-dance film made by Charles Boultenhouse, *Dionysius*, with the dancers Anna Duncan, Nicholas Magallanes and Louis Falco. The film was shot entirely in a very small studio and never shows two dancers together in the same film frame. Yet, owing to lighting effects and rhythmic montage, a truly mythic ciné-dance space is created in accordance with the mythic theme, based upon Euripides' *The Bacchae*. The dancers come into relation with each other through both plot-incident and editing. Boultenhouse uses slow motion, sharp angles and swinging camera movement (usually with marked success) to qualify and counterpoint his dancers' own rhythms.

The object of any artist is to establish a particular type of rhythm in accord with the laws of his technical medium. Ciné-dance, thus, is a formal means as distinct and available as is the voice-music of a song; ciné-dance uses a dancer and a film camera just as accompanied singing involves a voice and a musical instrument. The technique known as film animation, which may be speeded up like ordinary film, reveals how close the movement of visual forms (abstract or human) can come to musical precision; Mickey Mouse, as all of us instinctively knew, was primarily a dancer. A foreign film maker, Denys Colomb de Daunant, has made poetic documentaries on wild horses and the Spanish bullfight: *Dream of Wild Horses* and *Forbidden Bullfight*. The origin of the matador's action is, of course, lost ritual, a fact which the figures of the Spanish dance help to make plain. Daunant, however, by piling up documentary shots of whirling matadors and writhing bulls, in slow motion but very close cutting, creates the effect of true agonic dance-ritual; in other words, he reveals the rhythmic heart of the bullfight in terms of ciné-dance. Both his films convey the exciting sense of organic forms being closely knit together in a plastic action suggesting the rhythm of brush strokes in painting.

The title of one of Maya Deren's films, *Ritual in Transfigured Time*, perfectly suggests the universal limits of the possibilities of ciné-dance. Film is both a time art and a space art. Time and space in film can contract and expand, or pulsate as it were, rhythmically, as true dance partners. Their uses may be a dance action quite as much as the performance we know as theatrical dance. In D. W. Griffith's famous 'suspense' sequence at the end of *The Two Orphans*, there is, through the use of rapid editing, an effect of speed-up like the heart's when one engages in running. Physical effort and emotion go hand-in-hand with rhythmic urgency. By shifting back and forth between widely removed points in space, Griffith gave us the shape of his parallel actions as one time-space unit. Maya Deren, in the film just mentioned, isolates the same principle; besides being a dance, here film is a chase and a matter of life-and-death; by telescoping certain dance sequences, in slow motion and with 'freezes,' she produces a tension technically related to Griffith's while being much closer to actual dance. Ciné-dance is a twin plastique, participating in film and in dance as film itself participates in time and in space.

18. Film as a Force in Visual Education

After choosing the topic of this paper, I reflected that it was perhaps rash of me. The film 'as a force in visual education' assumes a lot of leeway and on due consideration seems something of a platitude while being, at the same time, controversial. For my part, I assume that the eye is to be educated in the service of both science and art; however, any power of observation which is not inspired by beauty would have little to do with the mature, experimental and imaginative aspects of the film. As soon as the science of moving photography as an expressive instrument was perfected, and this happened in the first fifty years, there remained the conquest of film as an art. While photography, at its invention, meant to imitate and rival painting, painting on the other hand, as if in reaction, became less photographic, less representational than it ever was before. Beginning with Impressionism, then Expressionism, Cubism and so forth – in brief, all that we call modernism – painting soon asserted that while form and expression were the proper plastic field of the visual arts, the field of representation could be left to photography, and, when motion pictures came in the late nineteenth century, to the film.

We find, of course, that there are contradictions involved in this over-simple dichotomy between the visual arts of painting and sculpture on one hand and the 'documentary' arts of still photography and film on the other. In passing, we can note that the quality of optical realism, or photographic exactitude, eventually reappeared in certain styles of Surrealist painting though not in the cause of naturalism or representationalism but as pure fantasy. One can put a finger on the ambiguous element in film if we consider how, in sculpture, Rodin for instance brought a feeling of movement – even to the extent of showing two stages of action in the same figure. This was an effort to transcend the temporal limits of a plastic art which technically represented only one moment of reality. Time was the crucial factor. Here was precisely what the experiments in moving photography were trying to do with the reflection of reality through the camera lens: achieve the image of an organic object in time. In the seventies and eighties, Edward Muybridge was photographing objects in motion, including a running horse.

Muybridge invented a precursor of the motion picture projector. His experiments with showing a running horse revealed the classic error of painters with their 'rocking horse' images of horses in action. During the sixties, Edgar Degas was among the painters who made this error. Yet it was also Degas, later on, who strove to put extra movement into painting by depicting horses cut off at the margin as if caught by a camera moving into or out of the picture's range of vision. It is also remarkable that in one of his family portraits, Degas showed a woman in the act of rising from her chair. Of course, many of Degas' ballet girls are shown at moments of dancing or bowing which are not climaxes of a step or a gesture but show the step or gesture in as it were the middle. All this meant the growth of cinematic sensibility.

Delacroix, by the liveliness and freedom of his brushwork no less than by his portrayal of violent action, had already gotten into painting a vivid sense of movement that was the opposite of classical repose. Actually Delacroix's brush strokes, like van Gogh's decades later, were to suggest action by their self-evident and varied directions. By breaking up the sun's rays, van Gogh conveyed a special sense of the passage of light through space, and with his pinwheel constellations seen in night skies, communicated the energy of things which, apparently, were motionless to the naked eye, but actually (as astronomy had discovered) were in movement. When we look at Rodin's *Gate of Hell,* we can see at a glance that he wished everything to seem in movement, and of course, examination of the individual figures on the Gate only confirms this: many are in the midst of falling or struggling to rise, to escape.

The development in the visual arts of a sensibility dedicated to including a sense of movement meant of course a breaking up of the firm classical contour, which although it was used at times to depict movement, as in the work of Jacques-Louis David, rested mainly on the concept of mass in a state of repose. The independent brush stroke that we see in the Impressionists' work, and that was reformulated by Seurat and the other pointillistes to create an abiding sense of molecular movement, eventually went through Cubism (which showed more than one viewpoint toward objects, that is, implied movement in the spectator if not also in the objects) and through Futurism (which showed the analyzed blur of moving objects) all the way to modern Action Painting, where, since objects are very seldom represented, the brushstroke itself portrays all the movement. The education of the eye through media has seemed, for the past one hundred years, to be an education into the pictorial possibilities of suggesting or showing movement; that is, *cinema.*

The natural question presents itself: what is the significance of the cinematic sensibility in modern art, or more properly, in terms of our topic, 'Is the film really to be considered a "force" in visual education?' Yes. It *must* be a force in visual education if it is already a force in art. It has been a force in art for an emphatic reason: the cinematic principle lies in the workings of a wonderful machine – a machine that is somewhat more than a machine. We must not forget that what the film gives us is the *illusion* of an organic object in motion, only its image, not its actual existence; and this has been obtained literally by a succession of still images, so closely spaced that when the film is re-run in a projector the movement of an object is reproduced. Organic movement has been shown in time and it has been shown in space; that is, change of form takes place simultaneously with a change of geographic environment. All this happens objectively and is transmitted to us optically. That is the point. Film tends to expand our psychic image of the world, not only as we see it in our daily lives, but as a formal visual notation, a spectacle, like an extra arm of our memory.

At this point we should proceed carefully. There is also the matter of the stage spectacle, which preceded the film by many centuries. In ancient Greek times, the orchestra circle before the skene was used as an area for the chorus to perform in, so that one was aware of certain distinct spatial dimensions. Moreover, ancient Greek theatre was in the open air and the actual time of day was a visual part of the play's action. However, in the theatre that came when the dramatic unities were abandoned, there were separate acts and scenes denoting considerable passages of time and differences of place. The modern stage of course tightened a long and complex action by various devices, such as dividing the stage space into levels and vertical sections and, particularly, through the turntable stage, which actually dates back, according to some authorities, to ancient Greece. Thus plays with many scenes could be written and performed with plausible ease. All the same, only film can knit together unlimited time and unlimited space with a perfect illusion of fluency: the fluency that we especially term *cinematic*.

Again, painting itself has manifested archaic devices to suggest the principle of space-covering and thus of time as a factor in visual art. Classical painting thought of the device of showing (even on an easel-sized work) a landscape with the various stages of a figure's progress in it. This meant the ancient function desired of a visual art *to tell a story*; that is, to depict a meaningful action with a beginning and an end. A series of pictures or a mural in sections also accomplished this. Thus we can observe the origin of the pictograph: a set of rectangles, each of which portrays some important stage of a story. A well-known example exists in sculpture in the bas reliefs which surround the altar at Chartres Cathedral and tell the story of

Jesus' life. I think it striking to consider that one late symptom of the cinematic sensibility is the use of film to portray a limited action, not through the illusion of absolute continuity, which became possible as soon as moving photography was achieved, but in terms of selecting still frames from a film reel, providing, as it were, the highlights from a continuous action: thus an edited action preserved in the form of rapidly successive still images.

In a rather spectacular way, this was done in a brief film shown a few years ago at the New York Film Festival: *La Jetée* (*The Jetty*). It was very dramatic to witness a series of frozen action postures which depicted what might be called skip-motion. It reminded me of the fact that in John Huston's filming of the romance about Toulouse-Lautrec, *Moulin Rouge*, several drawings of a music hall dancer were animated to obtain a crude cinematic illusion of her movement. Literally, film is a type of animation, but sliced so fine that there is an illusion of real action. Conventions in the arts have a way of going in cycles. When first I used to go to the neighborhood movies, they ran, besides films, illustrated popular songs, which consisted simply of a series of colored slides of still photography, usually showing love-making couples. Of course, the lovers were seen in picture-postcard poses against various natural backgrounds, resembling the more naturalistic sort of academic painting. Unquestionably, at first, the film medium pointed backward, so far as aesthetic values went; this was owing to the fact that at first photography wished merely to emulate painting; hence painters themselves began to feel (even before the movies came along) that photography had climaxed the conquest of reality as naturalism, so there was nothing left for the painter to do in that direction. Here, we encounter the reason why both painters and photographers began to look toward an illusion of movement to expand the plastic means and create new aesthetic sensations. But no new art, no new means of art, can be created simply by the wish or supposed need to be different. The fresh technical impulse in art must have its origin in a new viewpoint toward content.

What, then, was the view of content that created the cinematic sensibility in painting and sculpture as well as in the film itself? This was nothing less than the concept of spatial conquest ... and especially the rapidity of that conquest: the illusion of instantaneous passage – and in the case of image and sound, the fact of instantaneous communication. We can recall with profit the fact that Rodin's figure of Saint John the Baptist is shown walking – that is, symbolically spreading his doctrine by literally covering space. When recently I reread the whole of Proust's *Remembrance of Things Past* for the fourth time, I was struck by something that hadn't so expressly stood out for me previously. This was the fact that during the time span covered by Proust's relation of his hero's life, modern mechanical inventions such as the motor car, the telephone and electric light all came into being. Perhaps some of you recall with what romance and glamor Proust endows mere telephone operators, speaking of them as if they were goddesses – in other words, as magicians. Of course these modern inventions were later than photography if they somewhat antedated what we call true film; that is, the cinematograph.

It should be borne in mind that modern film has behind it a history of primitiveness, just as does the motor car or the phonograph. Anyone who has ever looked into a nickelodeon became aware of the rough illusion provided by the mechanism of still photographs turning on a spindle. One could stop turning the crank altogether or make the action go backwards. Such tricks of course came to be used in the movies themselves, repeatedly, for special effects. François Truffaut started a contemporary fashion when, for the end of his *Les Quatre Cents Coups* (*Four Hundred Blows*), he inserted a 'freeze' of his little hero in the act of flight from the institution where he has been detained. Here the dramatic (or if you will the melodramatic) quality of the freeze was that it left in suspense exactly the element I have singled out as the content of the cinematic sensibility – that is, spatial conquest. Not long after *The Four Hundred Blows*, *Last Year at Marienbad* came along and, with repetitions of a gesture always ending in a freeze, portrayed the hallucinated anticlimax of a lover's embrace. This effect suggests those anticlimaxes of dreams in which the dreamer seems to be making no progress though striving his utmost to reach an objective or escape a pursuer. His dream breaks off, so to speak, at the point of consummation or escape.

It is in experimental and avant-garde films that both slow and fast motion have been used seriously, for poetic effects, rather than comically, the way commercial films have ordinarily used fast motion. Through slow motion, very poetic effects were obtained in the film made of the 1936 Olympics held in Germany, while for the diving contest, some very interesting montage made this sport into an impressionistic poem of flight. In fact, slow motion prolongs the natural duration of an action by filming it at very high speed and projecting it at normal speed. The profit is in our being able to see the exact action more clearly without either psychological or physical blur. Hence, a running figure which we might see with the naked eye, or at normal speed in a film, becomes *if filmed in slow motion* like a dancer. At times, as was demonstrated in a brilliant little film by the late avant-garde film-maker, Maya Deren, *Study in Choreography for Camera*, the dancer himself provides a fresh plastic interest, shows a gain in dignity and beauty of pattern, simply by being shown in slow rather than normal motion.

To recapitulate a little: What was there about society in the nineteenth century to place so radical an emphasis on the diverse ways in which the idea of spatial conquest might be shown? The word 'conquest', after all, implies invasion and possession. Conquest has both warlike and peaceful aspects. Take for instance the conquest of far space on which science is now engaged. My purpose is not to discuss the whole ambiguous content of a word but rather to consider the meaning of human society's desire perpetually to reduce the time it takes to cover space, whether by telegraphy, telephone, television, planetary or interplanetary travel. Along with photography and the film, many mechanical inventions in the nineteenth century devoted themselves to rapid transmission of information. So we have to weigh the fact that, if photography rivalled painting, supposedly, in the art of personal portraiture, the moving photograph was also obviously a medium of information, so that one ideal function of the film (like news photos in the past) was to provide optical information in the shape of the newsreel and to provide it as swiftly as possible. Now, of course, the newsreel has been outdated by television. All this could mean only the impatient human desire for global unification in formal terms of both time and space.

Film, however, supplies a semi-permanent record. So the accumulation of an archive of informational film is something like an optical file of history in the making. And yet this is only one side of the film's dual personality: one side of its educational function. On the other side it is what primarily constitutes our topic: film as a visual art. Obviously, so far as film documentaries on art subjects are concerned, the projection of filmed images of art works in classrooms and lecture halls are advantageous, although not so easy to work with, I think, as still photographic slides. This educational aspect remains elementary and is not related to the film as a dynamic educator of the eye.

Far from being a mere machine to provide instantaneous optical information (or the historic preservation of such information), the art of film is dedicated to creating visions which are governed by all sorts of temporal rhythms; indeed, exactly like music, film should impose an optical rhythm on its material, since it exists in time; and since, like painting, it also exists in space, it should also impose a harmonious plastic design. Like a still frame (or a 'freeze') from an actual film reel, a sculpture by Rodin is a permanent arrestment of action which theoretically exists in time. Thus, action is part of the plastic design: it implies both the preceding moments and the moments following the instant it portrays. It suggests reality as a continuum: a merging of past, present and future. Hence the dominant importance of the film as candidate for being a visual art was, and is, to depict the process of change, whether it be the evolution of character and the emotional diversity found in drama, or simply locomotion from one point of space to another. Tempo is altogether incidental; what matters above all is rhythm.

It seems to me that we can draw a line of demarcation between the informational value of film, its pushbutton instantaneousness, and its aesthetic value – that is, all the plastic qualities of objects, still or moving, which the film can depict. Inevitably one of the charms of still photography was that, for the manual skill of the painter, it substituted the pushbutton ease of a sensitized plate: the instant efficacy of a machine. A parallel exists in the auditory world in the transmission of the voice by telephone or phonograph. Naturally a photographer, by taking special trouble in posing a subject, in calculating light and so forth, does much more than just snap a shutter open. For film, this 'trouble' in designing the spectacle it would record became much more complicated; not only does the film exist in time, as I say, it also exists in changing space, passing at will from one geographically distinct point to another. All this change must be under control if we are to have an art rather than a mere information agency; that is, *if* the eye is to be really educated rather than simply overwhelmed.

To return to the concept of spatial conquest. Suppose we take the historic matter of colonization of a foreign country by an imperial power. The rapidity of the conquest might or might not have been impressive. What really mattered was just what happened to the space which had been conquered. Now the same is really true of the film. A newsreel or travel documentary transports us to far places with utter ease, but what matters to the optical art of the film is not how many or just what places and persons we see, but how they are seen: how beautiful the photography is, how beautifully designed and controlled the shape of the film. At the end of the nineteenth century, facility and speed of communication, in every form aural and visual, had reached a high point of proficiency; it was simply a matter of time before the film would be perfected as a plastic instrument reproducing optical subject matter. In another fifty years – that is by 1950 – past centuries had been left far behind so far as the competence of machines was concerned in carrying visual and aural information as well as physical bodies; television too became virtually instant visual communication. One might say that some time ago the planetary globe was 'conquered' by the means of communication. What remained to be conquered was interplanetary space, and as everyone knows, this is already, by 1969, considerably advanced.

But the conquest of space by machines, I insist, has nothing whatever to do with the values of a visual or any other art, or the education in the same. In one respect this statement may seem false or arbitrary: there is the charm of fast action in the movies – the excitement of covering space and the satisfaction of doing it in the fastest time when so much may depend on speed. True, this element of competitive speeds has been a feature of many a film melodrama as it drives toward its climax. But the popularity of this sort of film is not decisive except in the realm of commercial entertainment. The fact is, the development of a slow action offers just as many opportunities for artistic vision as the development of a fast action. Hence the conquest of aesthetic space, paradoxically, has nothing to do with speed or instantaneousness, but entirely depends on the rhythmic manipulation of movement, however slow or fast, however artificial the manipulation may be. This is the importance of education by film. Take the works of the Danish film-maker, Carl Dreyer – such as *Day of Wrath* or *The Passion of Joan of Arc* – and Antonioni's *L'Avventura* and *La Notte*. They are all leisurely: everything depends on the etiquette of movement, not its rate of speed. Sometimes one may be lax enough to forget that the prose rhythms of a novel, fast or slow, should be just as well controlled as the tempi of a concerto or a symphony. Exactly the same thing is true of narratives in the film, from the simplest one-level action to the problem of portraying two or three levels, perhaps simultaneously.

Precisely what 'force,' then, did the invention of the film exert among the visual arts? It tended to introduce temporal data, or rather to re-emphasize temporal data in the arts to which it was a contribution: temporal data as the subject matter, that is to say, of *new problems in plastic manipulation*. To put it somewhat differently: it was not that the film introduced time into optional representation of the world, much less instantaneousness of communication, but that it introduced time as a new problem in optical education. We have noted how late nineteenth-century and twentieth-century styles in painting incorporated the data of motion and the existence of multiple viewpoints toward the same object. Incidentally, even the existence of *trompe-l'oeil* painting, as in Surrealist works containing multiple-image puns, was given a new impetus by film in its capacity of multiple exposure: the imposition of one field of vision on another. We find this carried to its extreme, in painting, by Pavel Tchelitchew's master work, *Hide and Seek*, at the Museum of Modern Art.

The best practitioners of film all realize, then, a basic truth: the film as an aesthetic force in itself has nothing to do with the swiftness by which space may be illusively covered. In the film, as elsewhere, aesthetic values must be separated from what is familiarly known as customer satisfaction. The universal charm of television is that simply by dial-twisting, one may bring a great variety of places and people and things, illusively, into one's own living room. At the risk of offending Marshall McLuhan, I would say that this is not education, but information, or if education, very bad education. It may have something to do with the survival of magic psychology in modern society – an interesting topic in itself – but it has nothing necessarily to do with art or the proper digestion of knowledge which we call education.

We must not think that film and the other arts are isolated in this respect. Philosophers have attacked the concept of time as meaning the shortest possible time, speed; in short, the most rapid accomplishment of any and all ends. In competitive athletics, it has meaning, but in terms of true global unification, mere rapidity is the most superficial of qualities. The same philosophers have attacked this so-called Western concept of time (to be called 'haste') in behalf of the oriental concept of a timeless sort of rest. Actually the argument hinges precisely on musical relationships. Fortunately, film experimentalists, the avant-garde film-makers, have always been healthily oriented to the possibilities of manipulating time musically; slow motion and fast motion in their films do not exist as calisthenic stunts but as vehicles of harmonic relationships, as elements which can be examined in terms of rest as well as movement, of pause in activity as well as activity.

The time of the clock, symbolized by the perpetual daily round of work, sleep and pleasure-seeking, never stops, never rests. The time of art can rest, slow down, stop and rebegin at pleasure. That whirligig of perpetual motion which is the time-image of modern men can easily be parodied in the film by ultra-fast motion: a city street at noon, for instance, can be made to seem a riot in an insane asylum; on the other hand, the same street at the same time may look like profoundly disengaged sleepwalkers. So plastic a device as the film is, so to speak, at the mercy of the artist. No law should bind him but the law of musical sensibility; without musical discipline, the cinematic sensibility would be chaos. The art of music itself demonstrates this although not in relation to vision, The film compasses both time and visually concrete space. Before the film, no other artistic medium literally did this. Classical painting and sculpture, as I say, could *suggest* it by the pictographic methods showing an action at its high points. Painting had always symbolized or suggested the actions of a story: the film came to represent them.

Did the film, then, actually replace the representational art of painting? To a large extent, it tended to do so. Yet no living art can stay chained to a mere ideal of representation. Classical painting, though it imitated the normal optical register, represented life as an idealized and romanticized reality, so that it was only partly naturalistic. Impressionism instructed us that the so-called normal optical register is itself a convention and that classical painting constitutes only a narrow range of optical modes. Exactly the same is true of the film, which can be just as fantastic and extravagant, just as eccentric, as it can be ordinary and naturalistic. Today, a number of avant-garde film-makers, surfacing from what is known as the Underground, vie with each other in speeded-up time and slowed-down time and in blurred and distorted and multiple imagery. Abstract action painting (as in the work of Norman McLaren) literally races by at high jazz tempo. On the other hand that much debated figure, Andy Warhol, was lured into experimenting with the old-fashioned stationary camera and pointing it at objects (the most radical was a sleeping man) which not only hardly moved from one spot, but exhibited a minimal and very monotonous life. Warhol's current topical importance has very little to recommend the aesthetic status of his work. His advocates argue that the smallest gestures in his films, because they mark the highest points of action to be found there, take on the character of signal events. By special courtesy and by virtue of omission, this is true. And it is also true that by compelling the optical attention on the same objects, which show only minimal and repeated changes of aspect, the eye is made to register shades of movement (and perhaps meaning) which otherwise would be lost. Technically, the argument is plausible; even, conceivably, it is educational. One might say we have a blackboard lesson about the possibility of rest and widely spaced, leisurely movements as opposed to the possibility of action, narrowly spaced and in fast tempo.

To bring the dynamic qualities of the film up to date, we have also to consider its role in so-called psychedelic consciousness: the state of perception produced in a human subject by a consciousness-expanding drug. In an essay on Warhol's films which I wrote in 1967 for *Evergreen* magazine, I tried to distinguish between what I called 'dragtime' and what I called 'drugtime' in the tempo of his films in relation to their subject matter. I think a good name for Warhol's tempo is miniaction. In some cases, he shows us persons supposed to be intoxicated by some drug or other or by alcoholic drink. But in my essay I maintained that this was not precisely the issue. I pointed out that, in the way a stationary camera eye may cling to a subject, usually a human being, for half an hour or more, while the subject simply sleeps or eats or has his hair cut, corresponds to the fascination with the simplest, most trivial sights experienced to great lengths of time by persons who take LSD, mescalin or some other drug. To a person in a normal state, we presume, it would be horribly boring to watch a man eating a mushroom for forty-five minutes. But to a person whose consciousness is 'expanded' by a drug, the same subject, for the same length of time, may be of the greatest interest. Since evidently not everybody left the theatre during one of those Warhol films, and since Warhol's cinematic methods have won him defenders – and since, too, it could not be supposed that all consenting and applauding watchers have been under the influence of a drug – one has to assume there is something hypnotic about the sheer phenomenon of forcing the eyes to concentrate on one almost changeless subject for an inordinate length of time.

Note that the tempo of Warhol's miniactions is naturalistic: the camera speed is normal; the human subjects, while they look leisurely, are neither retarding nor hurrying their behavior. Where is the catch? Well, one of the diseases of civilized life (I suppose we can agree) is boredom, and to some of us, what to others seems the liveliest entertainment, may paralyze all the faculties, so that in effect, like hypnotized subjects, we may go into senseless trances. This would be the inverse of psychedelic states: boredom *contracts* consciousness as LSD *expands* it. But suppose that, as spectators, we developed what might be called a 'drug attitude,' a mental state which had been decided arbitrarily, in advance, quite without the aid of a drug? Suppose, that is, we decided to concentrate on something very meagre and simple *as if* it were rich and complicated? Then dragtime would have been turned into drugtime by an act of will – and Warhol would have, I think, his ideal spectator. True, his later films attempt anecdotes and something like coherent dramatic situations. But these, besides being clumsily photographed as a rule, also go on for disproportionate lengths of time.

The technical nature of film supplies us with an explanation of how it is possible, without the aid of a drug, to turn the dragtime of boredom into the drugtime of interest and entertainment. For what, in the most elementary sense, does the camera eye *do*? It records what it is pointed at – and excludes everything else. That is the point: everything else is *excluded*. Of course, one can close one's eyes, one can leave one's seat. But as long as we stay put, keep our eyes open and will ourselves to follow the optical images of the film screen, we will be forced to limit the range of consciousness to what we see there. Logically, regardless of any degree of pleasure, we tend to become mesmerized, and indeed greet the slightest variation of incident – for example, if the sleeping man coughs or turns over – as an 'event.' In fact one can practise this without the aid of watching films. Simply start looking at a familiar object in your own home, purge your consciousness of all but that object, and the object will not only begin to seem new and interesting, it will induce in you a kind of daydreaminess – this may not last very long, but it will be long enough to demonstrate the principle.

Consider that the film theatre is a dark place with an oblong of light at one end and that our attention devotes itself automatically to what this oblong of light shows us. It is by *exclusion* that *expansion* is attained. Drugs tend to push into shadow that huge miscellaneous world of consciousness we perpetually carry deep inside us and allow us to concentrate almost solely on what is immediately and optically present – on what is external. As a matter of fact, is not this exactly what the films invite us to do? Also *tempt* us to do? And often succeed in making us do? I think so. But it happens that such a strategy of evading boredom is not always enough. The truth is that our eyes, like our intelligences, are too well educated to be satisfied by so crude a strategy. As mature optical organisms, we naturally crave both action and variety, so that the cult of boredom, as signified by the Drug Attitude, is definitely not enough.

Realism, at the same time, induces us to note that a part of the world's population – especially the part in its teens and early twenties – solves the problem by turning to the psychedelic dance palaces such as the Electric Circus in New York. The expanded discothèque tries to leave those who expose themselves to it no choice: it overwhelms by fortissimo sound and universally enveloping imagery. Several films are being projected all around us at once, both figurative and pure abstract. Film is not invariably relied on: a light-and-color machine may also be helping. Dancers on the floor may be tattooed with an ever-changing veil of pure color forms. In such psychedelic environments, the office of the individual will is reduced to a minimum. The subjective state we call 'being drugged' has been converted into its objective correlative: the world around us, not the world inside us, has been transformed. We merely respond obediently. All this might be called ultra-persuasion. But surely it is not education – at least it is not *visual education*; rather, it is *visual hypnosis*.

What I wished to emphasize in this talk was the element of the film as a truly educational force expressing itself in the medium of a visual art. Hence we are able to grant to psychedelic optics a certain provisional and limited status as educational. In a ballet named *Astarte*, presented by the Joffrey Ballet at City Center here in New York, several color films of two dancers are projected in various scales as an enormous background for the same two dancers who are performing for us in person much the same movements which we see magnified, distorted and fragmented from different angles in the films. Since the background or 'screen' is an unevenly curved surface, the film images are curiously distorted. The result is neither purely balletic nor purely filmic but it is surely a theatrical spectacle of a fairly exciting kind, depending on one's aesthetic temperament. One might venture to call it an experiment in visual education.

Moving color slides are also projected in *Astarte* and at first colored arclights are swept over the audience. Abstract color films (that is, simply abstract painting in motion) long pre-dated the present psychedelic era of mixed media in which the film may participate. In other words, as in *Astarte*, the role of film as theatrical spectacle transcends the mere normal window-illusion we think of as the classic film screen. Therefore we must recognize an important fact today: the film and allied optical effects have broken through this window and poured into the auditorium where we are no longer mere passive spectators but, like a chorus in a ritual, may participate by dancing or going off into some sort of trance. The upshot must be our conclusion that the film is a super-choreographic, super-musical mechanism which, by arbitrary variations of rhythm and tempo, along the gamut from utter rest to extreme activity, can create a virtually supernatural visible world, always based on nature but exercising a free will in converting that same nature.

The new optical impact, I think, is so great that we have to be careful not to be overwhelmed; we must retain an enlightened perspective and keep our values in proportion. One good way of doing this is to bear in mind the basic art of the film as such: the *classic* art of the film. Film, like painting, has always functioned as a so-called representational art. But I don't mean precisely that. As I have indicated, there is ample evidence that, while photography may remain the technical means, the optical art of film can be just as highly stylized as that of painting, and even in its classic form much expands the art of painting. This could not be so unless it were a force as well as a technical medium.

Perhaps some of you may regard this distinction between a 'force' and a 'technical medium' as rhetorical or somewhat oversubtle. But consider this; the technical media, or to speak scientifically, all technology, exists as a ready-made means to accommodate any sort of content, any grist. However, exactly this or that actual utilization of a medium will determine what 'force' the medium exerts. For example, with Pop Art, a certain section of enlightened modern taste (so called) tries to persuade us that the draughtsman's hand itself, as well as a subtle and distinguished palette, do not necessarily count any longer in painting; that is, certain printing processes, things like transformed and embellished photography, or a parody of comic-strip drawing, can communicate true plastic values, values to compete with the traditional means of hand in drawing and style and sensibility in color.

As a passing fashion, Pop Art can be taken for granted as a low ebb in taste; as a permanent addition to the art of painting, it is highly debatable. In my view, Pop Art sometimes has psychological and social interest, an amusing edge of cartoon satire, in rare cases a little pathos, but for all the plastic interest it possesses, it might as well be journalistic photography, or journalistic words, rather than a true plastic medium; in most cases it is less interesting than good journalistic photography. Thus I doubt that Pop Art is a 'plastic force' in educating the eye. Just so I would disclaim that commonplace formats in still and moving photography (while as technical media they may be intelligent and communicative) really contribute a *force* in visual education.

Film as a force is to be conceived as one highly potential, highly plastic instrument of the creative imagination. Desirably and ideally, film educates us into art by expanding and enriching the means of expression; undesirably, film might educate us out of artistic values by merely overwhelming us with display and destroying all sense of measure and relative values. I am not against talking film, against musically accompanied film, nor am I against film as an adjunct of live theatre. But film should not be prostituted to the wild, often silly extravagance of a psychedelic era, any more than should painting or music be thus prostituted. Yet, of course, the art of the film should mean far more to visual plastique and its appreciation than routine film documentaries on painting and sculpture. Insofar as the film, regardless of its subject matter, is creative and dynamic and rhythmically controlled, it is truly and valuably educational.

19. The Myth of Technique and the Myth of Reality

1.

The very first moments of *Night and the City* (an American film made in London with a London background) shows its scapegrace hero, Harry Fabian, chased by a man who wants to take a five-pound debt out of his hide. After seeing the movie, I turned to the novel by Gerald Kersh on which it is based and learned that the film-makers have retained almost nothing of it beyond the atmosphere and some rudimentary character-outlines, and that the transfer to the film medium has meant an artistic and imaginative gain. Despite its positive melodramatic level, *Night and the City* is one of the most genuine and interesting films to have come from the commercial industry in a long time. The reasons for this may not be immediately apparent to those wearily inured to the bromides of treatment and material of which this example is chock full. What is extraordinary in it is the conscious facility of execution joined to an involuntary harmony of pattern; a not unknown result of the studios' frenzied efforts to entertain.

Let us say that the original sense of this harmony is in Kersh's all too journalistic novel. Nevertheless the film-makers had to extract and flesh it forth in the assorted techniques which are the movies' peculiar property, both as intrinsic medium and stock-in-trade. Everything meets on aesthetic ground as swift and theatrical in feeling as an amusement park treadmill or chute-the-chute. As a smalltime crook crucified on his own triviality, the hero, Fabian, emerges as no mere lay figure. His kind of triviality – backed by the phenomenal presence of his impersonator, Richard Widmark – looms large today as a special aggressiveness of the man in the street. Fabian's type-dilemma is failure to fulfill that social contract signified by the currency of the realm. In his case, moreover, the dilemma is based on a fairly common mental mirage: the will to power without real gift, reason, or public good faith. Hence his shady projects are concerned aptly with the world of sports as the field of commercial rackets, and his regular insolvency is likewise the result of his inadequate sleight-of-hand at beating the game.

The film's pace, maintained at semi-hysterical level, has been adapted to the pace and temper of Fabian. The dark god of the psyche has marked out Harry's nature long ago. Cad, welcher, and cheat, he has a naïve anxiety and amateurishness, while at the same time his palpable delusion imparts to him a certain charm and pathos: he is not so much wicked as fabulous and amusing. Harry's paradox is that he possesses a very real characteristic of the film world itself: the obsession that technique – an angle, a trick, a plot – is everything and will work the wonder that tour-de-force is expected to work. It is easy for those having the successful angles to show the delusiveness of those who merely want to have them; hence, Harry's particular doom takes the form of a flash-in-the-pan success followed by ignominious disaster and death.

As in many of the mythological exhibits of the industry, while here the good people get a token showing, it is the milieu and temperament of the bad people which dominate the action; the good people involved are either intruders or simply ineffectual. Fabian is cancelled out by his own class after his finagling causes the death of a wrestling racketeer's father. The latter, an ex-champion wrestler, is the 'intruder' whose upholding of the honorable Greco-Roman game gives Fabian the idea he can corner the wrestling market and indirectly causes the catastrophe. Our hero poses to this sturdy old man (disgusted with his son's racketeering) as an enthusiast of the sport, and thereon engages his services as trainer for a new, 'honest' enterprise which he starts on a stolen shoestring. The inevitable moral proceeds to explain that honor and rackets don't mix. In an amazingly vivid and effective sequence, the old wrestler gives an impromptu lesson in the art to the vitiated current champion, finally flooring him, but dying afterward from the illegal battering he has taken. Movie methods have transcended themselves here in revealing the ultimate defeat of the genuine by the false and so doing have attained a veritable heroism. The old classical wrestler (a genial-looking monster) seems really grand in his technical or Pyrrhic victory, and this, I would observe, is exactly the way in which Hollywood and Elstree *may* seem grand whenever, regardless of the subject-matter, they exploit sound techniques and triumph through ingenuity. But note the accompanying irony. The total outcome must be the same as always, this plot being a paradigm: *genuine art* dies in reflex, having taken, in all aspects of true substance, an illegal battering from *brute craft*.

Furthermore, Harry Fabian's ineptitude is much like the ineptitude of film-making: he has true if fleeting inspiration, but lacks a valid creed. In pretending to follow what is 'classical' and sincere and honorable, he behaves even as does the theorist of the latterday fact-fiction film who pretends to honor the film's classic myth of reality while using the same shabby old formulas to exploit stories 'taken from the records' and unfabricated visual backgrounds. The error of the film-makers is as simple as Harry's error. Harry supposed that the substance of the old wrestler's Greco-Romanism was simply a *method*, a mere form which he had been taught and which sentimentally he didn't want to abandon, and not that it began by being a moral choice. He could not understand that the old man's Greco-Romanism represented a view toward life as a whole, that it fused technique with ethical substance, art with belief.

That the old wrestler's last breaths have a Promethean majesty is, as I have hinted, a minor miracle of the movies. The film industry, of course, is cannier than the Harry Fabians of the world: *it* succeeds where *they* fail. For, by one remove, Harry's is a Pyrrhic defeat. Where *he* triumphs is in the mass audience, which meekly accepts the Hollywood myth of technique as the way of truth, or more concretely, simply the way to get places by putting across the act, and ignoring accordingly the shadowy myth of substance, or the way to live organically, all at once, in the moral, intellectual, and aesthetic worlds. It is a rather sad fable, told here for the umptieth time with much more than usual point.

2.

With the apocalyptic inception of the moving photograph, film-art as the 'mirror of reality' had an origin contemporary with the high wave of naturalism in the novel. Even as the works of Zola, a railroad train arriving in a station and workers leaving a factory helped create the new myth of reality. Literary naturalism could be criticized by the great tradition of literature which it had entered, and thus it *was* criticized. Contrarily the motion picture, despite varied development and a parallel criticism, has never yielded up that first naïve niche it earned from the uncritical wonder and homage of the public. While the film's myth of reality, in respect to the advance-guard, has led to extensive exploration of pictorial plasticity as such, the great mass of film-making, impinging even on the fiction category, is still dominated by the sense of truth as a blend of quasi-scientific methods and the bare facts of life, or what might be called, aside from aesthetic preoccupations, a basic naturalism of the visible world.

So it came about that a French director, Georges Rouquier, proposing to make a cinematic record of the life of a French farming family, should proceed to organize the whole moral atmosphere of a major film project. The result was *Farrebique*, called for the farm chosen as site for this specific revelation of the myth of reality. In its cyclic pattern of the seasons and three generations of the family, this movie makes clear a naturalistic bent and what, in this perspective, is a quasi-mythical concern. Man is juxtaposed to nature as a higher animal, the animal who exploits and converts the nature around him, on which and with which he perennially lives. There is an ancient beauty about this primitive theme, and we merely have to remind ourselves of the paleolithic cave paintings to visualize the lower animals as inseparable alike from man's well-being and his vision of the world. Yet nothing could be less a serious mythical conception of man's relation to his immediate environment than this particular filmic effort to show him literally, unromantically, in harmony with it.

Not only is Rouquier's feeble myth of reality essentially non-mythical, but also, except banally and superficially, non-scientific; it lacks even that technical intensity implicit sometimes in the film as a super-microscopic or -telescopic agent. As for the animals themselves, they are far from being dramatized, idealized, or totemized; the producer's naturalistic piety fought shy of any possible accusation of artfulness in this respect. When nature is shown close at hand, it has that naïve pastoralism which Élie Faure has termed, criticizing the same trait in French painting, 'submission to environment.' Its distingushing spiritual high-note is cud-chewing contentment.

However, we do get close-ups of nature in *Farrebique* allying mammal and plant in a hint of the vegetation rite, and for this purpose the most effective device is one uniquely filmic: retarded time-photography records the twisting, waving thrusts of the plant growth. Though magically suggestive of phallic rites, this little device (by no means original) appears here as scenic and atmospheric rather than mythical. Elaborately, Spring is certainly presented to us and we even see, discreetly slighted by the framing, the bull mounting the cow. But that this last image is a weak, rhetorical sort of analogy is revealed by the surprisingly vulgar contiguous effect of a male's ground-view of a female standing on a ladder.

Rouquier motivated his film, obviously, to obtain what is known in representation of reality as *authenticity*. But just here the film myth is reduced to its nudest, its most helplessly naïve. The assumption is that the unadorned facts of the matter are to suffice. Suffice for *what*? – well, to show a truth dignifying man as nature, or at least man and nature. But on the basis of what Rouquier's camera unpretentiously shows us, exactly what is most difficult for us to do is to *connect* the human residents of the farm with the lyric *élan* of nature shown beyond its immediate premises. Throughout, Rouquier did little to induce his farmers to 'act,' but the result is hardly what he must have intended. Convincing enough in outward aspect, the farmers, old or young, whatever they do, seem hard-shelled and uncommunicative. Had they been shown in 'stills' and artfully observed, they might have had (it peeps out even so) some of the eloquence of Cézanne's or Van Gogh's rural characters. But alas, Rouquier could not judge that the human beings at Farrebique would emerge in inverse dynamic ratio to the plants and the rest of nature, so fluid and spontaneous and winning as revealed by the camera. Owing to the retarded-time-photography, we literally witness the sunlight gliding over the hills and the farm buildings, their shadows being reversed in one continuous shot; meanwhile, on the other hand, the human kinetics seem mechanical and contrastingly give the effect of being *retarded*. A faint odor of Balzac's rural provincials infuses, without dramatizing, Rouquier's farmers. They are concerned with nature only economically and as their own physical labor; primarily and ultimately, the farm is an economic investment.

After seeing these dark-garbed and undelighted farmers, hardly more eloquent than the side of a barn, it is a relief to recall the amusing if theatricalized French peasantry which seemed both humanly and nationally convincing in *La Femme du Boulanger* (*The Baker's Wife*) and *The Well-Digger's Daughter*. It would appear that an essential of screen naturalism would be lack of camera-consciousness in the human actor. Did embarrassment, after all, make these people of Rouquier's more reticent and less vital than they really are? Genuinely enough, indeed, moral apathy seems absolute monarch indoors at Farrebique. Realistically equated with the lower animals, as here, human beings can seem only enclosed, debased, and morose. Zola had a tragic sense, and when he wished to show the 'human beast,' he knew how to do so. But *Farrebique* would have to be denuded of all its pictorial flummery to seem even half-way humanly ironic. Nature, Rouquier seems to say, is neither myth nor fiction. But if this is true, the highly selective representation in *Farrebique* has imposed on us a simple-minded fraud, for it is far, far from communicating a 'whole' sense of the truth.

20. Mass Film Criticism

One of the most tangible, if dubious, myths of the century is that the movies are a mass art – i.e., as both art and commodity, 'the movies belong to everybody.' This presumed axiom is not at all limited to the ad writers, the newspaper critics and the makers themselves (who at least *want* them to belong to everybody) but compasses the sociologists, the psychiatrists and – grace permitting! – the aesthetic and technical academicians. As epidemically oppressive this idea is mainly responsible for the severe lag of film criticism as a respectable and effective entity. For serious critics, the movies function on the one hand as a set of symbolic texts for socio-psychological-mythical interpretation with aesthetic overtones, and on the other as a supposed laboratory where it is possible to show the Film has inexhaustible ways to produce what theoretically has every right to be termed 'art,' but which *is* art only because it must be in order to save 'everybody's' face.

The movies' commercialization is responsible, of course, for the hypersensitive professionalism that imbues all occupations connected with them, including supposedly disinterested 'criticism.' If the very term 'disinterested' comes into question, it is because film critics are distinguishable from, say, literary or art critics only by the fact that Shakespeare, for instance, does not need the praise or blame of literary critics to stand or fall: his plays perennially endure in theatre and library. Yet a filmic Hamlet by Laurence Olivier must be shifted critically to a fresh dimension to decide if 'the Bard' – as I think Broadway reviewers still refer to him in 1969 – has been proved screenworthy. The legitimate theatre also is a thing so much belonging to 'everybody' – to everybody, at least, in New York's five boroughs and environs – that mass-minded newspaper critics never fail to get in a dig at the supposed fact that Shakespeare's dramaturgy, especially in his comedies, distinctly 'dates.' It is easy to see why the impression should gain head that 'the Bard,' some of his comedies having been successfully rewritten as musicals, needs refurbishing for the modern stage. Shakespeare, in his relation to both the stage and the movies, provides an excellent case for deciding to what extent the process of modernization has blanket application, these days, to the arts.

If we glance at the ever-indicative realm of high fashion, we are struck by the presence of the widest (and lately the wildest) eclecticism. In recent decades designers have pilfered the centuries, period by period, for ideas on décors and women's clothes. Shakespeare, also going to the past and exotic literatures for his ideas, expected to see them appareled in contemporary dress, while Racine's neo-Classic dramas were done in place and period costumes adapted to French contemporaneity. But in their cases, one speaks strictly of *creative* convention; in the case of our contemporary theatre, it is largely a matter of *interpretive* convention. Did Anouilh, modernizing his classical subjects, center more upon theatrical interpretation or upon literary creation as the 'fashionable' cachet? It is perhaps more important to decide why the Old Vic production of *Troilus and Cressida*, seen in New York some years ago, should have conceived the play in the spirit and dress of Continental militarism during England's Edwardian era. This production seemed to lose inward dimension in ratio to its gain in outward smartness. The moral is, I think, that one should distinguish between modernity, *that which is viable at any time*, and modernization, *that which becomes viable by being brought up to date.*

The historic dialectic put in focus by the question of art's basic timeliness is change as perennially having the dynamic edge on permanence. Therefore a past which does not speak directly to a present – i.e., a past whose continuity does not flow easily, inconspicuously into a present – is one in which an urgent crisis is suspended. There are usually reasons to reject the past as there are reasons to keep it; hence, the idea of modernizing the issuing remnant, the questionable survival, makes a profuse appearance in this century. Does not the same thing seem to happen to movie stars as once happened to kings called 'Louis'? They begin to require a New Look; at least this is conceived to be all that will save them. Art museums, in service to showmanship, are constantly being given new looks, and apparently for fun, the Louvre (shades of its first residents!) illuminates certain collections on specified weekly evenings. And the Louvre is correct: light from a new direction dramatically transmutes the familiar image on which it falls even if the aesthetic gain is no more than minor.

The modernization factor is so quick within the bosom of the movies because the movies have become, all too grandly, suddenly and hollowly, a standard set of back numbers. As both industry and craft, they have blossomed and declined in an era when civilization itself has begun to have a chic 'museum' look: a look at once antique and modern, permanent and changeful, passive and aggressive. Modern poetry as an objective culture-myth in Pound's *Cantos* is essentially a research library in the survival of 'classic' virtues; now poetry is, above all, eclectic; good or bad: eclectic. But the importance of one special point has been neglected by critics. Pound happens to illustrate it in the *Pisan Cantos*, where he calls upon Paquin, early-century creator of women's fashions, to characterize his own (the poet's) pride as 'vanity': 'Pull down thy vanity, / Paquin pull down! / The green casque has outdone your elegance.'

Pound's elegant gesture does not seem so personal and isolated as it might if we consider the following passage from Rilke's *Fifth Elegy*:

> Squares, O square in Paris, unending show-place,
> where the modiste, Madame Lamort
> twists and winds the restless ways of the world,
> those endless ribbons, and out of them
> shapes new bows, ruches, flowers, cockades, artificial fruits –
> all falsely colored – for the cheap
> Winter hats of Fate

The poet has just spoken of 'this sorrowful Nowhere ... the unspeakable place ...'

> ... where the too-little
> inconceivably changes –, springs round
> into the empty too-much.
> Where the uncountable reckoning,
> numberless, vanishes.

I take it that in these two passages, Rilke meant to contrast *modernity* and *modernization*, the immanently modern and the superficially modern. The latter would be symbolized today by the phenomena of 'Sputniks' and America's 'Explorers,' etc., all of them successful experiments in bringing aviation up to date and justifiably replacing the term 'aviation' with that of 'space travel.' The first Sputnik became the fashion-plate of the Heavens. As Madame Lamort is the image of the false refurbisher of life, reviving it with furbelows, fashion at large is the image of the falsely revived hero, he who takes on an artificially new life, as with Icarus and his wax-fastened wings or the Frankenstein legend so dear to the movies. Metaphorically, Madame Lamort is a frivolous measure of the concept of death-and-resurrection as Sputnik, metaphorically, is a frivolous measure of the concept of spatial majesty, or more precisely, of 'infinity.' Aviation as *space travel* assures the expansive future of man's habitation of outer space, and however 'expensive' at first, it will become a high fashion to be yearned after and achieved even by the masses.

A perfectly good external gauge of the specious mass-look worn by the movies resides in the fashion magazines, which have a tradition older than theirs. The realm of chic, our age abundantly proclaims, includes 'everything' plus dresses – everything from Gertrude Stein and Whitehead to the latest smart novelty to arrive on the international art scene. Exquisite token of this may be found in the books of that ingenious faculty which is Cecil Beaton, the only devotee of high fashion who could safely look down on Elsa Maxwell. He deploys a wickedly elfish camera and his literary sensibility thrives on the borderland of that juicy garden of dry sophistication cultivated by the *New Yorker*. The point is that Beaton's strength is nurtured in his *mass* feeling for high fashion, which is fully as much gauged by circulation and its profits as are the currently hard-breathing movies. The latter, in losing a few million spectators to television, have long been rumored on the verge of collapse. It may not be too late for the new optical effects, hastily souped-up fiction and theatre-remodelling to save the movies' part in the universal modernization program. Little remains whereby space travel as such can help, because the movies were hardly born before they predicted (by example) trips to the moon. They also followed, decades ago as well as now, time-travel as projected by H. G. Wells' 'Time Machine.'

In the complex inner crisis of things filmic, film criticism perforce must accept a good share of the blame and ignominy. In either its low or high brackets, it has scarcely ever been aesthetically independent except where it busied itself with constructing 'working theories' on the writing desks of the craftsmen themselves. It is no accident, furthermore, that two of the most brilliant and idea-conscious technicians in film history, Sergei Eisenstein and Vladimir Pudovkin, developed their theories both of style and technique under the tutelage of the Stalinist-Marxist bureaucracy, and that the famous ABC concept of filmic composition, montage, was intellectually drawn by Eisenstein from Marx's dialectic – that is, from the adaptation of the traditional dialectic of the schools to the social ideology of revolutionary politics. The irony of such aesthetic endeavors on the part of talented craftsmen is that, even as

Pudovkin and Eisenstein became grim ideological opponents in the arena of Russian film-making, film-makers elsewhere in the world were less consciously, but just as concretely, putting the tenets of montage into wide non-ideological practice.

Obviously, the political ideology of Russian film-making was, and is, but another form of making the movies 'belong to everybody'; namely, to the Soviet Union and the 'masses' of the world. More at fault, however, than the *political* ideology of this line of filmic reasoning was, and is, its *mass* ideology. Whatever fine and valid rules of procedure the film-maker may follow, the artistic criteria for evaluating what he does must be derived from scrutiny of the product itself rather than stress on its 'working theories,' its technical postulates. Instead of pointing out and acting on this highly pivotal distinction, film critics and commentators, even outside Russia, have perennially regarded the product's value as loosely predicted on its technical postulates, *ipso facto* realized, and ignored content and widely comparative aesthetic standards as the inevitable problems of the film art. As undoubtedly brilliant a silent film achievement as is Eisenstein's *Potemkin,* its universal acclaim still reverberates chiefly because *the purity of its means is still a rarity*, rather than because *its pathetic theme attains great tragic stature*.

If English film criticism is bogged down in workaday professionalism and passive goodwill, French film criticism lifts itself only a little higher by mannered aestheticism, which actually remains parochial in its culture. The main tradition of German film criticism – individually represented in this country by Siegfried Kracauer and Rudolf Arnheim – was established by those who regarded the new art not, primarily, as one to be submitted to independent artistic judgement but as, on the one hand, a field of socio-psychological inquiry and, on the other, a field of aesthetic-technical inquiry. Kracauer's overwritten psychological case-history, *From Caligari to Hitler*, which, along with incidental aesthetic insights, views the German film wholly as the progressing agent of Nazism, is far from being the only evidence for this trend. His later book, issued in 1960, falls into the class of aesthetic-technical criticism only to renounce aesthetic values for those of 'physical reality,' clearly a strategic concession to the aims of the ambitious documentary film.

Many critics to this day – when, of course, it is a museum 'classic' – cite G. W. Pabst's pyrotechnic silent film, *Variety*, for its pure visual expressivity both as to camera-use and acting. It is not that *Variety*'s filmic virtues are actually unreal but that, since they serve a creative idea of very thin interest, they are implicitly assessed beyond their proper context. Physical 'acrobatics,' as Kracauer proves, remains the film's biggest popular strength. Dozens of striking instances of narrative technique, psychology through dialogue, and so on, could be extracted from the novel, *Gone with the Wind*, just as parallel technical triumphs are sought out in the 'classics' of film museums. But *Gone with the Wind*, either as a film or a novel, does not become thereby a better or more memorable work of art, and neither, in truth, do the classics of the film museum which are analyzed for *their* orthodox expertise.

Essentially, *Variety* represents the classical technical *fault* of filmic creation: concentration on the physical means at the expense of the aesthetic end. This, interestingly enough, is an inversion of the ethical proposition fostered by neo-Marxist rationale: the means are justified by the end. To the movies – not merely as mass art but also as mass criticism – it is, rather, the end which is justified by the means ... at least for a while. The fatal moment comes when the novelty of means seems magically dissolved. The valid filmic pioneering of D. W. Griffith in this country became inept as soon as he applied it to themes which did not strike popular sympathies in the right area; in consequence, this most distinguished American filmmaker of his time tobogganed to obscurity and enforced retirement. Much the same happened to Erich von Stroheim. Actually Griffith's mass virtues, his talent for spectacle and his respect for the film's legitimate vocabulary, had been only a *means*. For these same virtues, even in his own time, were outstanding because, primitive as they were, they were still new and startling. Ironically enough, Griffith's famous spectacles were no more artistically distinguished than second-rate historical novels and suffered from the same crudities of character-drawing and intellectual values as do such novels.

The way and degree to which famous or popular plays and novels are revised for mass presentation by the movies is notorious. Occasionally, something is made of this scandal by some newspaper critic desirous of filling a weekly column which is devoted to the more timeless problems of the object of his daily criticism. Invariably, of course, such columns exhibit the most superficial acquaintance with the true values of the familiar work in question. William K. Zinsser, the former New York *Herald-Tribune*'s critic, once found himself moved to deplore the emphasis on circumstantial details in the film version of *A Farewell to Arms*, these details covering bedroom sex and childbirth. The puniness of the cultural perspective in which such a critic thinks becomes clear on observing that the domain where the movies are guilty of so much vulgar distortion of an original is not *their degree of candor about physical processes* but their *degree of candor about moral and psychological processes*. An especially cruel irony, moreover, attaches to Mr Zinsser's complaint. Since the movies first became an industry, it has been the permanent lament of enlightened criticism that they systematically decline to acknowledge the carnal truths of sex. But now, in our 'underground' age of disillusion with sentiment, a minimal candor in such matters has won out even in Hollywood; in Europe it is growing rampant. The point is that taste in artistic affairs is bound to be the weakest factor in mass entertainments – no matter what the subject matter or the line of treatment – and taste is likewise the weakest factor in the mass phenomenon of film criticism. Taste implies intellect, morals, aesthetics but has no power over 'physical reality.'

The pale, pretentious irrelevance of aesthetic sensibility in which newspaper critics indulge is naturally to be traced to the 'mass' character of their audience and yet, of course, only a very minor proportion of all movie-goers reads the reviewing columns. Right here, in this apparent discrepancy, is my reason for isolating what *mass film criticism* really is. Film criticism, in the main, is written for the literate masses in a primary state of artistic education; thus the two main divisions of film criticism, popular/journalistic and academic/technical, find it obvious as well as convenient to assume that a movie is simply a means of translating a given artistic quality – a play, novel, or 'original script' – into a new form. The movies primarily, then, are an extension of a specifically literary culture; film criticism consequently is concerned preponderantly with the interpretive values of what is part of common education: the exposition of art classics and their principles to a 'student' public. All is clear sailing for film critic, as for film-maker, once the rule is accepted that basically film-creation is a form of higher education; in short, a novel is 'educated' into being a movie and, by the same act, 'modernized.'

Hence, the reason that no effective body of film criticism has arisen is that the profession has mechanically followed the general line – however disguised – that film-making is a science of re-creation rather than an art of creation. I must hasten to disarm those who will rush forward to say that exactly the opposite is true; that, for instance, the paperback compendium of Rudolf Arnheim's criticism, *Film as Art,* is about nothing but the uniqueness of creative filmic procedures. First, I would answer that mechanical uniqueness does not confer aesthetic or creative uniqueness; while the rules of the film camera are as essential to the movies as basic grammar is to the novel, 'grammar' is not synonymous with 'imagination'. Second, Arnheim's encyclopedic aestheticism suffers not only from a semi-barbarous language of its own but moreover leads him into naïvely drawing what *seem* simple conclusions from simple premises; these conclusions, however, are neither obvious nor inevitable and, as put, are sometimes misled and misleading. What is actually needed by film criticism, sadly enough, is a handbook in which film craft is 'translated' into literary craft so that at least a lucid linguistic system can enable one to 'read' the ABC of film craft correctly and not by semantic 'equivalents.'

It cannot be denied that, as the more scholarly writers on the movies such as Arnheim have claimed, many minor crea-

tive devices are automatically brought to birth by the mere process of re-creation or, if you like, 'cinematization.' Yet these
same writers, becoming fascinated with their own theoretic
fabric, easily allow the creative purview to slip from grasp and
begin talking as if creative film were a difficult foreign tongue
almost impossible to explain in English. As a result, even the
best-informed writers neglect the important empiric truth of
their subject: that the value of filmic devices is damaged, and
their scope fatally limited, by being subservient (as a means)
to an end which, in almost universal practice, they help not *to
create* but *only to recreate*. It follows that the technical means
assumes an undue significance and becomes a false end in
itself. Thus, film art becomes fashion: novelty, modernization,
window-dressing ... *anything but true creation*.

The 'mass quantity' so insidiously dominating film criticism
goes qualitatively from top to bottom of the aesthetic gamut
and like a chemical taint spoils even superior criticism. Does it
not seem expedient to suggest that fewer people should see and
criticize the movies as they are and more people should make
them into something different from what they are? If more
people began making them upon that premise, the chances of
creative achievement in the resulting experiments would be
much greater than they are – even today when the American
industry is desperate enough to seek the help of the more conventional Experimentalists. That the film as an art, after more
than fifty years of life, should remain virgin territory to so
large an extent is a thought which it is to official interests to
pretend is an outmoded prejudice of aesthetic snobs and old
fogies. These official interests are, of course, the museums and
the academies as well as the industry.

The 'mass' growth of art museums, inevitably, has been in
proportion to the amount, quality, and variety of their attrac-
tions. It is good – at least it is hard to argue it is bad – that the
showmanship of 'modernized' museums induces more people
to visit them regularly. Yet the thought must cross one's mind
that the Metropolitan Museum in New York, by embellishing
its types of acquisition constantly and expanding its means by

such things as the showing of film documentaries about art, is refurbishing the cultural past as forms of interior decoration both literal and figurative; the great museum becomes a study chamber of 'high fashion'. Since the movies have so varied a technical history and body of work, why should they be omitted from a program of such massive glitter?

Eclecticism, in its way, is all very fine. Surely, the Metropolitan itself has come a great distance in sixty years: a fact oddly demonstrated by a two-line reference to it in a 420-page *Historical Guide to the City of New York* published by Frederick A. Stokes and Co. in 1909, 'In the Metropolitan Museum of Art (near Eighty-first Street) may be seen a fine collection of historical relics'. 'And,' it might have been added 'some art works of historic interest,' but perhaps the distinction, now as then, is actually blurred. Since they began to be petted by departments, the movies have added a 'museum look' to their perennial 'new looks'. All a musty old 'historical relic' needs is brushing up and a showcase to look important. The point I am concerned in emphasizing is that mass-modernization is, and always has been, part of the movies' normal operation and that, more particularly, this operation has been conventionally applied to what was already a 'museum' art (literature) long before the movies touched it. This has led to an historic impasse in film criticism; conceivably film criticism might lead the movies *out* where itself was led *in*. If so, criticism would have to begin by assuming that the myth of the movies as a *mass art* is a false one and recognize it, rather, as a quite esoteric art whose latent creative powers – as distinct from 'cinemascope' window-dressing – are imperfectly understood even by the select few. The movies have actually made history itself into window-dressing, or at least into an art of the couturière, Madame Lamort. . . . Gradually, and coyly or brazenly, with the good will of most of the critical profession, the movies have induced history to return the compliment and take them into the modernized Permanent Collections. In an age of relentless mass-communication, much in the film has obtained entrance into such prestigious places with dubious and false credentials.

21. Declamation on Film

Today a formidable superstition has taken root that the eye of the film camera is not only often dedicated to the ends of illusionist realism but also, by its nature, can accomplish no other ends. How absurd! To equate photography, still or moving, with the objects which are portrayed by the artificial eye of the lens is as silly as believing that everyone sees (e.g., comprehends what he sees) just alike. Vision is a psychological as well as a mechanical process. Even the most 'objectively' made documentary is a psychologically prejudiced form of vision, automatically persuading one to see as it sees. What may seem like the most impartial reporting, as in the case of printed news-stories, is always (however obliquely) angled and thus (however consciously) attests some pre-existing attitude toward what it reports. The larger the scope of subject matter in film or newspaper, the more likely it is that a 'slanted' view of it is being taken, because so-called 'impersonality' in 'refraining from comment' erects a morally negative attitude toward all facts. This sort of negation, this poker-faced acceptance of facts, is a material influence on man's moral and emotional life.

Those who speak of 'photographic painting' as having originated in the Renaissance, when that period was inspired by the discovery of the anatomically proportioned sculpture of ancient Greece, may be unaware of how misleading their words may appear. Comprehensively speaking, the question is not one of conceiving painting in the Renaissance as having installed 'photographic' accuracy as art's classical tenet, and the flowering of all plastic education, but of ascribing to the imitation of appearances that absolute value which the *photograph* (and implicitly the *film*) has wrongly come to symbolize. It is plausible to say that what the Renaissance acquired morally and aesthetically from the Classical past was the ability to idealize the real: to create the consciously visionary; to achieve, in some sense, the 'unreal.' But André Malraux, in pointing this out in his book, *The Metamorphosis of the Gods*, nevertheless aligns Renaissance technique with photographic accuracy. To my notion, it is not to the point that the historic reputation of painting must survive this inexact juxtaposition with the formal possibilities of the photograph, but rather that the reputation of the photograph is now called upon to survive it. The confusion has been immensely promoted, of course, by the vast 'informational' tendencies of film and by so-called illusionist realism in the commercial films. But besides the illusionism of realist aims, the history of film offers a great deal of evidence for the realism of illusionist aims – a bird of a quite different feather.

To isolate from a film, for example, a single shot – that is, to take a genuine still, or a single frame, from the reel – is to verify that every compositional element which may be present in painting may also be present in film. Now, according to the care with which the mutating compositional elements of film may be controlled, they are analogous with those of legitimate painting. When it is said that film, in the main, has not progressed beyond nineteenth-century painting, the statement is itself highly prejudiced, generalized, and thus, while true in a sense, inaccurate. Many commercial films, of course, give the impression that the statement is wholly true. But the opinion, as flatly given, is critically irresponsible, and the best reason this is so is that nineteenth-century painting itself is not so much of a piece as to warrant thus referring to it. One cannot even say that what is meant is the 'academism' of illusionist realism, for

now, if one cares really to look at what has happened in painting in the last two decades, one sees that an academism of the
free abstract schools exists today, that 'wild plasticity' has become 'academically tame' since so many do it with such glib,
mediocre results. It is true that no major artist has yet essayed
the painting-in-motion of which technically the film is capable.
But this is not due to the fact that such a major achievement
is theoretically impossible.

At times, much is made by some critic of the fact that
Cézanne declared that he did not paint 'apples' but 'pictures,'
whether they happened to show apples or not. Cézanne's claim
was a timely form of art-semantics and expressed his aversion
to 'photographic' representation in painting. This did not mean,
however, that some academic painting of apples was any the
less a 'picture' insofar as no painter, however ambitious to
'imitate life,' has ever hoped to 'make' apples out of paint as
the alchemists hoped to 'make' gold out of other elements.
Ancient Greek painters, of whom legend says that their painted
fruit attracted birds to peck at it, were as much makers of
pictures, rather than *fruit,* as Cézanne was. Today, the imitation of appearances, or so-called illusionist realism, is unpopular in advanced circles; the fact remains that in this century
there exists a continuing cult of magic realism, which is
naturally affiliated with the 'imitation of life' seen in the work
of Surrealist painters such as Dali. True enough, this sort of
painting has for one aim the exact imitation of appearances but
this is used in contexts which are not naturalistic or representational at all, but fantastic and symbolic. It is well known that
the Surrealist films have carried out this principle, using photography as a medium of presenting an entirely synthetic and
imaginary, and thus quite 'unrealistic' world.

One of Malraux's formulations, in the book mentioned
above, is that painting and sculpture in ancient Egypt and
Greece aimed at 'transmuting appearances into Truth'. This is
to give art the transcendental value of religion: to place it
beyond anything to be photographically verified in this world;
or for that matter, photographically inevitable. Malraux's distinction between the 'unreality' based by the Renaissance on

appearances and the Truth based by previous ages on the transmuting of appearances is aesthetically valid but actually has nothing to do with the photograph's optional faculty of changing ordinary appearances; nothing to do with the film's or the stage's many illusions that are based on appearances but by no means identical with them. We know very well how deliberately and successfully the 'real' illusions of stage and film may be achieved. There is, therefore, a psychology by which the eccentricities of pre-Renaissance form can be placed in line with later art and which rejects as irrelevant Malraux's distinction between 'Truth' and 'appearances.' To him, Botticelli's Venus meant the visual beginnings of the Unreal – which Malraux conceives as the Untrue – but think, today, to how many people Botticelli's Venus is 'truer' than are the medieval Venuses from whom she automatically stems. The evolution of ideas of the Truth have outrun religious belief. If to Malraux and others, the Truth is still God, to some it is certainly still Beauty.

What 'truth' could Cézanne's non-photographic still lifes, or his also abstractly defined persons, be said to proclaim? That they are *not* wine bottles or wine drinkers? – that they are, rather, 'pictures'? It seems to me that Cézanne's often quoted proclamation is easily misunderstood. It was simple propaganda against the kind of painting he was repudiating. In any case, his homely, non-photographic persons seem no more or less 'true' than do the beautiful persons of Botticelli or Leonardo, painters who, according to Malraux's way of thinking, begin the line of illusionist realism that leads to our day. In fact, as beings, the persons of Cézanne's painting may be considered less eloquently human than Leonardo's intense idealizations and Botticelli's transfiguring goddesses. Specifically, the Renaissance conceived man as in the image of the gods – or vice versa as you like. What is wrong with this? Why – according to Malraux's school of thought – is the wood carving of an African ancestor 'truer' than the supernatural beings and princes whom Botticelli conceived as in one inseparable order? In every man, one might say, dwells the sacred image of his ancestors, consciously or unconsciously, whether he be a modern savage or a Renaissance prince. The manner in which he may objectify this truth, of course, would vary.

One thing which the film makes triumphantly plain is that the image, as distinct from the person or thing, is, positionally speaking, neither in front of nor behind anything, in that it is not fixed, but plastically variable; psychologically, any image, like any thing, is meshed and continuous with space, not positionally distinct and fixed in it. Although technically, most paintings imply only a moment of time, surely they also imply the ability of the spectator to take a peripatetically fluid view of the subject and the locale in which it is seen, just as a painting from a past time asserts, in fact, that the world has undergone a general change. If a painting be an 'eternalization of a moment,' it is that of a past moment which offers some contingent relationship to the present; hence, the movement of time cannot be eliminated by art. The chief function of the film camera is not to cement and exploit mere appearances, mere 'reality,' but to imply all kinds of changeability, all mutations, whether of time or space. The film camera, therefore, would imply the movement, the changing relations, between man and all sacred and divine subjects; between, in brief, man and his gods, including the direct transformation into God that is exemplified by the story of Christ. All such transformations are also subject to the mutations of spectatorship.

Is a Cézanne apple a non-apple, or is it perhaps a self-evident transformation of an apple into something merely apple-like? I cannot see that it makes any difference so long as the picture is well-painted, well-composed. Does a Cézanne still life (or one by Picasso, for that matter) belong in 'another world'? If so, then all images as such, no matter how representational, belong in 'another world.' A likeness, however mathematically accurate, can never be the thing itself. One does not eat a painted apple, any more than one kisses a woman on the screen, except of course by the process known as psychic projection, which is automatically part of the aesthetic appreciation. However, aesthetic reality is not *lessened* by the fact that a painted apple may look good enough to eat or a film actress attractive enough to kiss. The world of art, no matter how much it resembles reality, is forever physically closed to the spectator, regardless of how much he is given the illusion (as in certain stage and film devices) that he is part of the action.

In other words, illusion is not reality. A better term for illusionist realism, thus, would be realistic illusion. Compare, on this point, the very contrasting stylistic views of Vermeer and Monet toward light. Both, so to speak, 'painted light,' regardless of how immediately recognizable are the things and persons on which it falls. Each, according to his lights, was a realist of illusion. For, in the most accurate sense, the light in each painter's case intermingles with the objects shown and is inseparable from them; in the same way, no matter what the plastic style on the film screen, its chiaroscuro has claimed, as a formal element, whatever object or person has been delivered to the camera's eye. And if film chiaroscuro has not made this claim, it should have done so.

As there is a 'still' element inhering in the movies, there is a moving element inhering in painting; and not only in paintings of obvious movement, but in still lifes too. No spectator of a still life, whether by Cézanne or Chardin, can forget that the life in which he himself stands, as the ticks of time go on, is not a static thing; no matter how many technically static elements are present, he is an illusory fixedness in a realistic flux; just as he can also be, of course, the opposite, a realistic flux (peripatetic) in an apparent fixedness, such as an actual place. In this sense, man *is* a camera: a thing all eyes and capable of pointing in any direction at will. But he is not a film any more than Cézanne himself is a painting. The film and the painting are objective ways of seeing the world and should never be confused with the world either in its static or its moving aspects.

Each visual work of art, even each form of visual documentation, is a judgement of the world in terms of selectivity and the desire to inflect and transform the pulses of visual life. If a painter or a film-maker decides to ignore the mere 'mirror reflection' of the camera's artificial eye and make abstract patterns of what is visible, he both selects and transforms. Yet it must be remembered – above all with respect to film – that both these elements are form-determining, and that selectivity, even in the mode of what is called illusionist realism and allied with photography as a norm, is by no means to be equated with the rashly termed 'slice of life'. Through formal representation, one can slice life thick or fine, and even reduce plastic invention, or 'theatrical illusion', to a minimum; still, one has a formal product, not a piece of physical reality, to show for it. Necessarily the film screen, like the painting surface, is actually flat (except for certain modifications of relief in the case of painting) and thus, primarily, the third dimension is part of the aesthetic artifice.

There is the modern vogue of so-called candid photography. As recent adventurous photographers have shown, this is simply a style which aims at the transformation of the common and the given into the grotesque. Candid photography can be just as mathematically and empirically falsifying as the polite studio photography which prettifies. After all, studio photography as flattering was, and is, simply a reflection or extension of the artifices of life itself, where persons try to emphasize their best points to create an illusion of charm or beauty; candid photography simply scuttles this campaign through extravagant foreshortening and glorifying the pouch and the wrinkle. The tricks by which the film camera distorts normal or casual vision are well known and manifold; the only sorry thing about them is that often they are used for oblique or irrelevant ends, mostly 'for fun,' whereas (as the Experimental Film shows) they can be used for serious plastic purposes. *Quality* in photography has numerous devices which actually parallel the quality given a painting by brush strokes and outlines. It is simply that the commercial film, which admittedly strives to look common and undistinguished so as to conform with the eyesight of the uncultivated, does not utilize the avenues of 'quality,' of plastic form and texture.

True enough, the medium of film offers many more difficulties than the mere training of a painter's hand in wielding a brush, in forming an outline. Hence the myth of the film's true métier as the representation of physical reality, absurd as it is, is not surprising as a phenomenon. But this myth is arbitrary and uncourageous; moreover, it propagandizes for a prosaic, unimaginative and reportorial view of the world and the life with which it teems. It seems to me highly prejudicial that the chief use of the film should be a grand channel of information, like a super-journalism. As I say, as neutral as news-conveying supposedly tries to be, its very tendency is a judgement of life in terms of moral emphasis and aesthetic quality. In journalism and science, everything is implicitly on the same level of straight-faced thus-and-so, qualified only by sensationalism and coarse humor. In its sensational aspects, journalism (like science in *its* sensational aspects) merely shocks and appeals to low-grade emotional appetites; or, at the most phenomenal, anticipates a trip to the moon. Yet today, even science-fiction writers understand that a trip to the moon, though it should become as easy as a jet-plane flight to another continent, would not necessarily solve any serious human problems or provide the thrill of pleasure that is 'aesthetic.' Nowadays certain people may be weary of turning to art to achieve an ultimate satisfaction with life; this indicates the old accusation against the love of art that it is 'escapist.' On the contrary, I should say that the escapist element of the popular imagination is centred precisely in the science myth of man's trip to the moon, about which we can read so much 'news' these days. The art of the film remains 'esoteric' and 'unpopular' only because, for a variety of reasons, the masses of the people are hard to educate into the essence of *any* art. Nevertheless, art, and not physical reality, remains the film's most important métier no less than its most challenging problem.

Index